OXFORD Children's
Encyclopedia

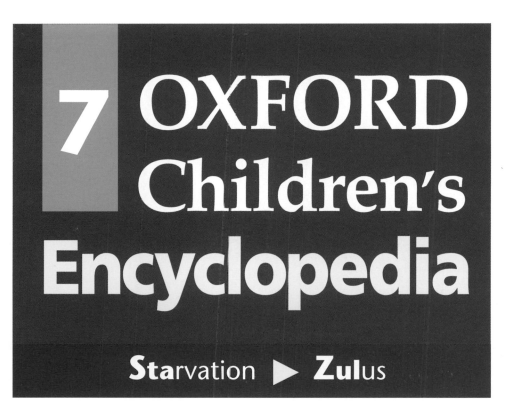

7 OXFORD Children's Encyclopedia

Starvation ▶ Zulus

Oxford University Press
1998

Oxford University Press, Great Clarendon Street, Oxford OX2 6DP

Oxford New York
Athens Auckland Bangkok Bogotá
Buenos Aires Calcutta Cape Town Chennai
Dar es Salaam Delhi Florence Hong Kong Istanbul
Karachi Kuala Lumpur Madrid Melbourne
Mexico City Mumbai Nairobi Paris São Paolo
Singapore Taipei Tokyo Toronto Warsaw

and associated companies in *Berlin Ibadan*

Oxford is a trade mark of Oxford University Press

© Oxford University Press 1991
New edition © Oxford University Press 1996

British Library Cataloguing in Publication Data
Data available

First published 1991
(ISBN 0 19 910139 6)
Reprinted 1991 (twice)

Revised 1992
(ISBN 0 19 910151 5)
Reprinted 1993, 1994, 1995

New edition published 1996
(ISBN 0 19 910173 6)

Revised 1998
ISBN 0 19 910506 5 (complete set)
Volume 7: ISBN 0 19 910513 8 (not for sale separately)

10 9 8 7 6 5 4 3 2 1

Printed in Spain by Mateu Cromo, S.A. Pinto – Madrid

How to use the
Oxford Children's Encyclopedia

There are a number of ways of finding information in the *Encyclopedia*. The best method depends on the kind of information that you want to find. After you have used the *Encyclopedia* a few times, you will become familiar with the way in which the information is arranged and will soon be able to identify the quickest route to the topic you are interested in.

2

Can ▼ Egy

Using the headings

The *Encyclopedia* has individual articles on most important topics. So if you want to find information on a general topic, the best way is usually to search through the headings of the articles in volumes 1–7, which are arranged in alphabetical order. Suppose you want to read about **Drama**. This starts with **D**, so look for the volume whose spine shows a range of letters including **D** (volume 2). Once you have found the right volume, search for the particular heading you want. Every heading is picked out in **bold** type at the top of the page on which the article appears.

Searching for people

If you are looking for information about an important person, go straight to volume 8 (Biography). The articles in the Biography volume are also arranged in alphabetical order and are usually listed under the family name (surname) as in a telephone directory: for instance, **Gandhi**, Mahatma. There is further guidance on using the Biography volume at the beginning of volume 8.

9

Index

Using the index

If you are looking for detailed information, rather than a general topic, the best way is to use the index (volume 9). For instance, you might want to find out about equinoxes. This is not a headword in volumes 1–7, but it is listed in the index. Next to it are the references **1** 180 and **2** 136. So look up page 180 of volume 1, where you will find an article called **Calendars**, and page 136 of volume 2, where there is an article called **Day and night**. Both of these include information on equinoxes.

Equator **2** 71, 72; **3** 34; **4** 137; **7** 154 — volume number
equinoxes 1 180; **2** 136 — page number
Erasmus, Desiderius **8** 85, 169

In the same way, look in the index if you need information on a person who does not have a main article in the Biography volume. The index is also the best place to look in order to find all the references to a particular topic throughout the *Encyclopedia*, even if the topic itself has its own headword. There is further guidance on using the index in volume 9.

Cross-references

Almost every article leads on to many more. Look for the **Find out more** panel in the margin of most articles. This lists other articles that have information related to the article you have been reading.

Sometimes the articles listed in the **Find out more** panel are printed in **bold** or *italic*. Articles in **bold** are very important to understanding the topic you have just read about. Articles in *italic* include a photograph or other illustration. For instance, the list on the right, which appears in the article on **Bangladesh**, tells you that the article on **Indian history** is particularly important in understanding Bangladesh, while the article on **Floods** has an illustration of Bangladesh. The other articles in the **Find out more** panel – Asia, Ganges, Monsoon and Muslims – also contain related information.

▼ Find out more
Asia
Floods
Ganges
Indian History
Monsoon
Muslims

Contents

Starvation

Food is the most basic human need, and yet at least 500 million people (one-tenth of the world's population) suffer from hunger. Most of them live in the developing countries of the Third World, and many of them are children and young people. Every year about 15 million children die of hunger and related causes, so underfed that they cannot resist disease.

Starvation occurs when a person has nothing to eat. During the first few days a starving person suffers from severe hunger pains. Gradually these pass, and the person gets progressively weaker as the body uses up its store of fat and energy. Body weight drops, the limbs decrease in size, and ultimately the person dies.

Starvation and poverty are closely linked. During the 1970s and 1980s the number of starving people in the world doubled, a situation made worse by widespread drought in Africa. Aid in the form of loans to developing countries is often seen as a solution, and many international organizations work hard to try to relieve hunger. But many people believe that mass starvation can only end if land is used more carefully to grow food and if the resources and wealth of the world are shared out more fairly. ◆

In 1991 nearly 800 million people suffered from hunger. Approximately 40 million people died of starvation.

▼ **Find out more**
Aid agencies
Developing countries
Drought
Famine
Floods
Malnutrition
Poverty
Third World
Vegetarians

Statistics

Statistics are sets of numbers, often called data, that record information about things in an organized way. Every day, people collect more and more data about the world and record it as statistics. Records are kept of the weather, price rises, examination results, population changes and so on. The word statistics is also used for the branch of mathematics that deals with this data.

Statisticians are mathematicians who invent methods to organize statistics into tables, to display them in charts and graphs, and to interpret the data with mathematical formulae, so that it is easier to draw conclusions and make predictions. For example, statisticians who study medical statistics have discovered that most people who develop lung cancer smoke cigarettes. Statisticians can compare a smoker's chances of dying from lung cancer with their chances of dying from other causes.

Organizing statistics

The table of statistics below records the marks of children taking the same examination in two different schools. The data is recorded as a frequency table which gives the number of children achieving scores in set bands. To make these numbers easier to interpret they can be plotted as a bar chart or histogram. The histogram of the scores from the two schools shows that on average the children in school A did better than those at school B, but that there is a much wider range of marks at school B. Statisticians call the range of the numbers in a set of data its distribution. They make calculations, often with the aid of computers, to find numerical values for quantities such as the average and the distribution of a set of data.

Handling and interpreting statistics

Statistics must always be handled with caution, otherwise false conclusions may be drawn. For example, it would be wrong to use the average examination marks for schools A and B to conclude that children who attend school B always do less well than those who attend school A. In fact the statistics show it was a child at school B who achieved the highest examination score. ◆

▼ **Find out more**
Averages
Computers
Graphs
Probability

Number of children		
	School A	School B
0–9	0	0
10–19	0	2
20–29	1	5
30–39	3	16
40–49	6	32
50–59	19	22
60–69	40	16
70–79	14	7
80–89	3	3
90–100	0	1

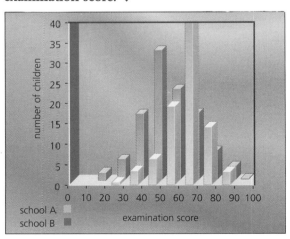

Steam engines

The first steam-powered machine was made by the Greek scientist Hero in about AD 100. It was a tiny ball-shaped boiler with nozzles sticking out of its sides. Jets of steam from the nozzles made it spin round when the water boiled.

History of the steam engine
1712 Thomas Newcomen builds an atmospheric engine. It is the first practical steam engine.
1765 James Watt repairs Newcomen's engine and improves it.
1782 Watt invents his sun-and-planet gear, a type of crank which turns up-and-down movement of a piston into rotation.
1804 Richard Trevithick builds the first steam locomotive.
1960 Britain's last steam locomotive is built.

The oldest steam engine still working is on the Kennet and Avon Canal in England. It was built by Boulton and Watt in 1812.

▶ In a steam engine, steam pressure is used to move a piston up and down inside a cylinder. The up-and-down movement is changed into round-and-round movement by a crank.

▼ **Find out more**
Agricultural revolutions
Engines
Industrial Revolution
Locomotives
Petrol and diesel engines
Railways
Turbines

BIOGRAPHY
Newcomen, Thomas
Stephenson, George
Trevithick, Richard
Watt, James

Steam engines were the first fuel-burning engines to be invented. During the 18th and 19th centuries, they were the main source of power for industry. With coal as their fuel, they drove machinery in factories and later powered ships and trains. Today, there are very few steam engines left. Other types of engine have taken over.

How they work

Most steam engines use the pressure of steam to push a piston up and down a cylinder. The steam is made by boiling water over a fire of burning coal or oil. Steam from the boiler is let into the top of the cylinder by a valve. The steam expands and pushes the piston down. When the piston reaches the bottom, the valve changes position. Now, the valve lets the first lot of steam escape and feeds fresh steam into the *bottom* of the cylinder. This pushes the piston back up. When the piston reaches the top, the valve changes position again, the piston is pushed down . . . and so on. The up-and-down movement of the piston is turned into round-and-round movement by a crank. The crank moves a heavy flywheel which keeps the engine turning smoothly. The flywheel can drive other wheels or machinery.

Steam engines work best with high-pressure steam. To withstand the pressure, the boiler, pipes and cylinders have to be very strong. In some engines, there is a condenser to collect and cool the escaping steam. The steam condenses (turns into water), goes back into the boiler and is used again. With a condenser, a steam engine can work for longer without running out of water.

FLASHBACK

The first practical steam engine was built by Thomas Newcomen in England in 1712. It produced up-and-down motion and was used to pump water from mines. In Newcomen's engine, steam trapped in a cylinder was cooled by a spray of water. This made the steam condense and created a vacuum in the cylinder. The natural pressure of the atmosphere pushed the piston into the vacuum. Newcomen's engines were sometimes called atmospheric engines because of the way they worked.

James Watt made the big breakthrough in steam-engine design. He built an engine which used steam pressure to push the piston. It also had a separate condenser for cooling the steam. Within five years, Watt had developed engines which could produce rotation and drive machinery. His engines provided much of the power for Britain's mills and factories during the Industrial Revolution.

During the 19th century, the design of steam engines improved and they became widely used. They powered the locomotives of the new railway system. They hauled coal from mines and worked the huge hammers that shaped metal. They drove the traction engines used for threshing and ploughing. And they moved ships across the sea.

By 1900, internal combustion engines and electric motors were starting to replace steam engines. They gave more power for their size and did not need huge supplies of coal and water. Today, most factory machinery is driven by electricity, and trains are diesel or electric. However, in most electric power stations, the generators are turned by huge steam turbines. ◆

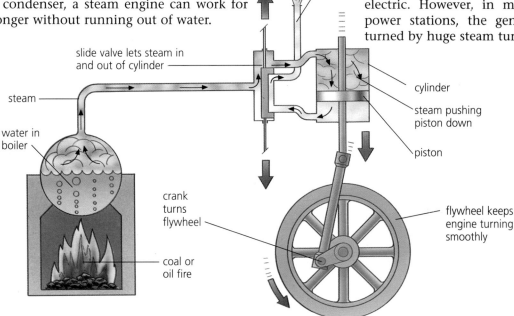

funnel

slide valve lets steam in and out of cylinder

steam

water in boiler

crank turns flywheel

coal or oil fire

cylinder

steam pushing piston down

piston

flywheel keeps engine turning smoothly

Stick insects

▲ The perfectly camouflaged stick insect will not be seen by birds or other small predators.

Distribution
Almost all warm countries, especially in south-east Asia
Size
Up to 25 cm long, the longest of all insects but very narrow
Food
Plant food, each species normally eats only one kind of plant
Phylum
Arthropoda
Class
Insecta
Order
Phasmida
Number of species
About 2000 species, most of which are stick insects, but with about 25 broad-bodied insects that look very much like leaves, and are called leaf insects.

▼ **Find out more**
Camouflage
Insects

The body of a stick insect is long and twig-like. Stick insects are usually coloured green or brown and are often covered with bumps or spines.

This makes them match the stems of their food plants so that it is almost impossible to see them. They normally sit quite still during the daytime and feed and move about at night.

In many kinds of stick insect the males are very rare, and the females lay hard-shelled, seed-like eggs without mating. This method of reproduction is called partheno-genesis. The eggs may take over a year to hatch, and when they do so, more females than males are born.

Some kinds of stick insect are kept as pets. Their cages need to be kept in a warm spot, but out of direct sunlight. They must have fresh leaves to eat. When changing the food plants, be careful not to throw away the insects. They are so well camouflaged it is easy not to see them. ◆

Stomachs

When you swallow your food, it passes down your gullet into your stomach. The stomach is a strong, muscular bag which expands as more food passes into it.

Food begins to be broken down and digested whilst in the stomach. The stomach adds acid to the food, which helps to kill bacteria in it. This provides the right acidic conditions for the working of the stomach's own digestive enzyme, called pepsin, which is secreted into the food by the stomach wall. Pepsin begins the digestion of proteins, such as meat and eggs. The muscles in the stomach wall make it contract and churn, squeezing the food up with the acid and pepsin until it forms a runny mush. This passes into the small intestine for further digestion. An adult's stomach holds about 1 litre of food. Liquids start to drain out within 10 minutes. Meat and vegetables take about an hour, but fats can take up to 30 hours. The stomach is usually empty after six hours.

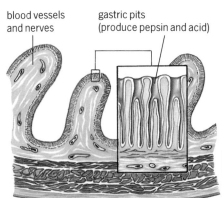

blood vessels and nerves   gastric pits (produce pepsin and acid)

folded inner surface

three layers of muscle

Ruminants

Some large plant-eating animals are ruminants which have complicated stomachs, usually made up of four parts. Plant food is stored and broken down before being returned to the mouth for chewing. It is then swallowed a second time to the next stomach. ◆

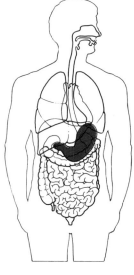

▲ The human stomach lies above the intestines and just below the lungs.

We tend to call any pain in the abdomen 'stomach ache'. Such pains are often nothing to do with the stomach at all. A true stomach ache can be caused by too much acid in the stomach, or by eating too much food.

◄ The stomach wall is folded to give it a large surface area for digestion. It is covered with holes called gastric pits, which produce acid and the digestive enzyme pepsin.

Antelopes, camels, cattle, deer, giraffes and goats are ruminants.

▼ **Find out more**
Cattle
Digestive systems
Enzymes
Human body
Muscles

Stone circles

There are more than 900 stone circles in Britain. One of the most impressive is at Callanish on the island of Lewis in the Outer Hebrides.

The great henge at Avebury, Wiltshire in southern England has three stone circles inside it. The largest in Britain, of 98 stones, is just inside the ditch.

The oldest drawing of Stonehenge is from a 14th-century manuscript. It was thought then that the stones had been transported to Salisbury Plain from Ireland by the magic of the wizard Merlin.

▼ **Find out more**
Archaeologists
Prehistoric people

▼ Castlerigg in Cumberland, one of the most impressive stone circles in the north of England.

The lives of prehistoric peoples all over the world depended on their surroundings, their environment. Hunters needed good supplies of food to kill or gather. Farming peoples and their animals relied on the weather to ensure that supplies of crops would survive.

Today we find it difficult to understand the religious beliefs of people who have left no written record to explain what they thought. Some of the first farming peoples (neolithic) built structures which must have been gathering places for the community to use for ceremonies. There were *henges*, which were enclosures surrounded by a bank on the outside and a ditch on the inside. Avebury in Wiltshire is a good example. A *cursus* was a great earth monument consisting of two parallel banks and ditches.

Stone circles were built in Europe from about 3000 BC to about 1200 BC. The circles vary in size (in fact some are not proper circles) and the stones used are of different sizes. People in the recent past have given the name 'megalithic' to the stones used, from the Greek meaning 'big stone'. Some of the stones are massive. Like the great earth monuments of the prehistoric period, building them must have required great effort involving the whole community.

There are often other types of stone structures associated with stone circles. Standing stones and stone rows can be found in many parts of western Europe. The most spectacular example is at Carnac in Brittany, France, where nearly 3000 single stones were placed in 10 to 13 rows. One massive stone weighs 345 tonnes.

What were they used for?

Because no records survive from the prehistoric period, archaeologists have to interpret the evidence they discover. Careful calculations show that most stone circles were constructed by people who knew how to measure. An engineer, Professor Alexander Thom, suggested that they were built with a standard measurement of 2.72 feet (0.829 metres), but this does not apply to all the circles that are found in Britain.

Experts believe that the circles were built as ceremonial or religious monuments. Some think that a proportion of the circles were constructed to make observations of the planets and stars. Stonehenge is a good example of this. Placing the stones very carefully, perhaps after years of observation, would give the early farmers a sort of calendar. They might watch the Sun or Moon rise over a certain stone and know exactly what time of year it was. These calculations would tell them when seasons, and the ceremonies which went with them, were approaching.

Excavations at many stone circles have revealed burials of pieces of human bone and broken pottery as if some sort of ritual had taken place. Archaeologists often find the remains of burning, too. There are a good many puzzles and problems which archaeologists have not solved. ◆

Stonehenge

The stone circles at Stonehenge in Wiltshire probably form the most famous prehistoric ceremonial site of all. The first ceremonial construction was a henge built some time between 3100 and 2100 BC. A large circle was enclosed by a bank and ditch and two stones were placed upright to mark the entrance. About 30 metres from this entrance a much larger stone, now called the Heel Stone, was put up.

About 500 years later, the first stone circle was built inside the henge. Eighty-two stones were placed in two rings, one inside the other. Amazingly, these bluestones, weighing up to 4 tonnes each, were probably dragged and carried on rafts all the way from the Prescelly Mountains in South Wales.

The circle we see today was built in about 1500 BC. Nearly 80 stones were brought about 30 kilometres to form a circle of uprights with large capping stones. These local stones, called sarsen stones, also formed five separate 'arches' we call *trilithons* (Greek for 'three stones'). The largest trilithon at Stonehenge stands 7.7 metres high.

What was it for?

Even at its earliest period archaeologists think that Stonehenge was used to observe the movements of the Sun and Moon. Just inside the henge circle were over 50 pits. Some contained pieces of flint or red clay; perhaps they were offerings. Later some of these holes were used to hold the cremated remains of people. It is clear that Stonehenge was an extremely important religious site, perhaps the most important in Britain.

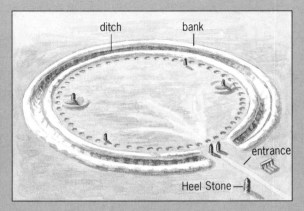
ditch   bank   entrance   Heel Stone —

◄ Stonehenge in about 2500 BC. The Heel Stone, 30 m outside the entrance, is placed so that the Sun rises over it on Midsummer Day. This stone weighs over 20 tonnes.

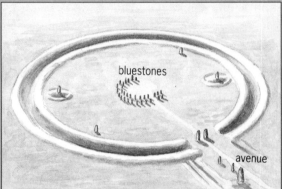
bluestones   avenue

◄ The bluestones formed two uncompleted circles in the centre of the henge. Two rows of upright stones ran from the entrance.
▼ The sarsen stones were shaped with round hammer stones. This must have taken months of work. Even after 1500 BC slight improvements were made to Stonehenge.

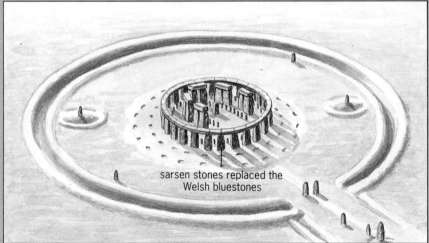
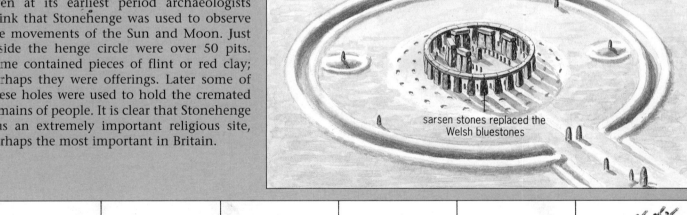
sarsen stones replaced the Welsh bluestones

1 To build the trilithons, two huge stones had to be stood firmly upright. Here, the first is rolled into its hole.

2 It was pulled upright by ropes and a movable wooden frame.

3 Once the stone was upright the hole could be filled, often with the round hammer stones.

4 To raise the capping stone, it was levered first onto timbers.

5 As it got higher, a stronger framework of timbers had to be built.

6 Once at the top of the uprights, the 7-tonne capping stone could be levered across into position.

Streams

There are many different kinds of stream. Mountain streams rush down steep valleys, foaming over rocks and waterfalls. Lowland streams wind in and out through farmland, flowing slowly between flower-lined banks. Woodland streams are clogged with fallen leaves and shaded by overhanging branches.

Streams do not contain so much water as rivers, but still they can have a powerful effect on the landscape. Rocks and pebbles roll down the mountain slopes into the fast-flowing mountain streams, bouncing along the stream bed and scouring it deeper.

Stream flow

The speed at which the water flows depends upon the gradient (slope) of the stream bed, which depends on its height above sea-level and its distance from the sea. The steeper the gradient, the faster the flow. The stream flows more slowly near its banks. In some streams the amount of water varies from one season to another. Some are fed by snow melting in the mountains in spring, and shrink or freeze over in winter, or dry up in summer.

The stream environment

Because streams are quite shallow, the water contains plenty of oxygen. It also contains nutrients (substances that provide nourishment or food) dissolved from the surrounding land. Streams have many different habitats for plants and animals. Animals that can swim live in the open water; others cling to the rocks, shelter under boulders, or hide in the mud of the stream bed. Many live among the underwater plants near the banks. Birds and mammals visit the stream to drink or to hunt for food.

Plants

The stream banks are home to many plants. Mosses and liverworts cling to the stones. Moisture-loving plants such as ferns benefit from the spray. In fast-flowing streams there are few plants living in the water, but in slower streams plants such as pondweeds and waterlilies can take root in the mud. In very slow streams, duckweed floats on the surface. Snails and other invertebrates graze on the underwater plants. The flowers on the banks attract insects, which are food for frogs, toads and newts, whose tadpoles live in the stream.

▼ The speed at which a stream flows determines the kinds of plants and animals that will live in it. More plants are able to grow in slow-flowing streams (below) than in fast-flowing streams (opposite), and in general there is a greater variety of life.

Slow-flowing stream

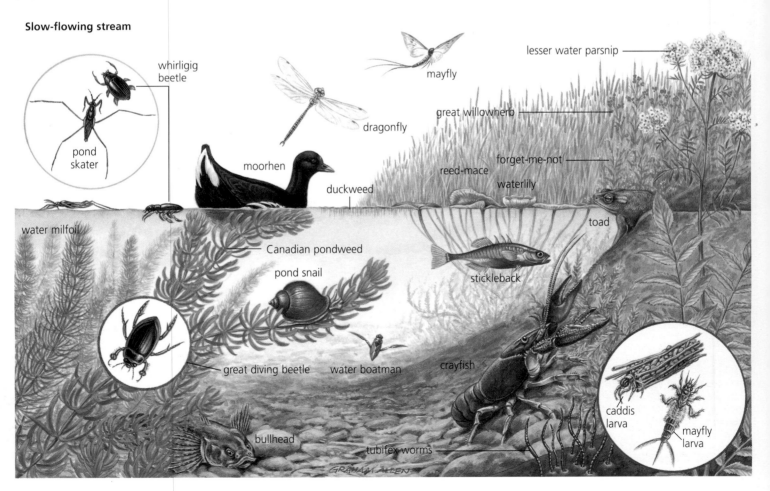

Fish

Streams are home to many small fish, including the young of larger species. The fish usually swim against the current, facing upstream, so that they are not swept away. Fish like sculpins and bullheads stay near the bottom of the stream. They have eyes near the top of their heads to spot prey in the water above. Some fish, such as loaches and lampreys, have suckers for clinging to the rocks.

In clear water, the fish have large eyes and good vision for finding their food. But in muddy waters, they have to rely on other senses. Their eyes are often smaller, and they use the lateral line system (sensory cells situated just under the skin on their sides) to sense vibrations in the water. Some use smell and taste, and may have fleshy whiskers called barbels on their chins which act rather like tongues for tasting. A few, such as the electric catfish, use weak pulses of electricity to locate, and sometimes stun, their prey.

When breeding, fish like salmon and trout lay their eggs in hollows in the gravel, then cover them with stones to prevent them being washed away. Other fish, such as sticklebacks, make nests of weed to hold their eggs.

Stream bed

Where water flows over stones, the friction of water against rock slows down the water immediately next to the rock. This layer of slow-moving water is called the boundary layer. Freshwater limpets cling to stones by suction, even in fast-flowing water. The larvae of mayflies and stoneflies have flattened bodies, so that they stay within the boundary layer. Some caddis-fly larvae build cases of tiny stones to weigh themselves down. Others spin nets to trap food.

The gravel of the stream bed is home to many different invertebrates, such as insect larvae, mites, shrimps and other tiny crustaceans. Where the stream bed is covered in soft mud, there are burrowing worms.

Fish and crayfish hide among the larger stones, waiting to ambush their prey. Some, like the bullhead, are camouflaged to match the stream bed.

Fast and slow streams

Fast-moving water can carry a greater load of sand and stones than slow-moving water. Where streams slow down, they drop their sand and gravel. Slow-flowing streams therefore have muddier beds and banks, with more pondweed and other aquatic plants. Water boatmen, pond skaters and whirligig beetles can survive here without being swept away. ◆

Fast-flowing stream

Stuart Britain 1603–1714

The next king was George I. There is an article on Georgian Britain.

In 1605, in what became known as the Gunpowder Plot, a small group of Catholics plotted to blow up the Houses of Parliament on 5 November, when King James I would open Parliament. They hid 35 barrels of gunpowder in a cellar under the House of Lords, guarded by one of the conspirators, Guy Fawkes. The plot was discovered just in time, and Guy Fawkes and the other conspirators were captured and executed. Since then, bonfires have been lit on 5 November each year to celebrate the failure of the plot.

◀ Sir Richard Saltonstall may have had this picture painted to tell the story of his family, with two scenes in one picture. The pale ghostlike lady in bed is his first wife, Elizabeth. She is dying, and stretches out her hand to her two children who are painted at the age they were when she died. Richard is 7 and still wears skirts like his 3-year-old sister Anne; he will soon be old enough to be dressed like his father. The lady with the new baby is probably his second wife, Mary, and their son Phillip, born in 1636.

The family in the picture above lived in England in the early 17th century at a time when there were so many difficulties between the king and Parliament that they led to civil war. English people fought each other; neighbours, friends and even members of the same family sometimes found themselves on opposite sides.

Sir Richard Saltonstall, the father in the picture, owned land and a big house in Chipping Warden, Northamptonshire. Many of the ordinary people who lived nearby worked for him, and rented their houses and any land they had from him, so he influenced their lives in many ways.

Many powerful landowners like Sir Richard sat as Members of Parliament (MPs). When the king summoned Parliament, they would go to Westminster to make laws, and agree to taxes. They were worried about the way the Stuart kings, James I and Charles I, were using their power. Kings still believed their power came from God, and that they should not share it with anyone. Parliament did not always agree. There were two great problems: money and religion.

James I and Charles I were often short of money. When they had it, they were extravagant. So they often asked Parliament for extra taxes. But MPs wanted to control how the king spent his money, as this would give them a lot more power. They often refused to grant taxes if they did not like what the king and his

advisers were doing. When both kings found ways of raising money without asking Parliament, there was even more trouble.

Many MPs were Puritans who wanted the Church of England to have plainer services and churches. The Puritans hated and feared Catholics. Catholics were the bogymen of Stuart England, especially since the Gunpowder Plot of 1605. In fact, this was very unfair as most English Catholics just wanted to worship freely, and get on quietly with their lives. Charles I had a Catholic wife, and liked elaborate church services. This made Parliament afraid he was going to make England Catholic. They wanted to have much more say over religion. Things became much worse when Charles I ruled without Parliament for 11 years, until rebellion in Scotland forced him to call the Long Parliament in 1640.

Civil War

The English Civil War was fought because of these problems. From 1642 to 1646, Cavaliers (for the king) fought Roundheads (for Parliament). When Parliament's New Model Army won the war, many Roundhead soldiers had very new ideas. Some of them, called Levellers, even wanted ordinary people to share in governing the country. Oliver Cromwell and the other army leaders did not agree with these ideas, but when Charles I joined forces with the Scots in 1648, and fighting started again, they decided they no longer wanted to be ruled by a king. In 1649, Charles was put on trial and executed.

For the next 11 years, England did not have a king. It was called a 'Commonwealth'. From 1653, Oliver Cromwell ruled as Lord Protector. He kept England peaceful, and made it strong abroad. The Levellers' movement was broken up by 1649, but Cromwell did allow people to worship in the way they wanted (except Catholics). However, he too found it difficult to get on with Parliament, and had to use the army to help him rule. This was unpopular. Taxes were heavy because the army cost a great deal, and landowners did not like soldiers interfering in their local area.

Restoration of a king

When Cromwell died, most people wanted the old familiar way of doing things. In 1660, Charles I's son Charles II was invited back from exile and crowned as king. This was called the Restoration. Charles II had to be careful not to offend Parliament, though there were still no rules about how much power he should have.

The Glorious Revolution

The next king, James II, was an open Catholic and tactlessly ignored laws made by Parliament. The horrified ruling classes united against him and his reign lasted only three years. In 1688 he

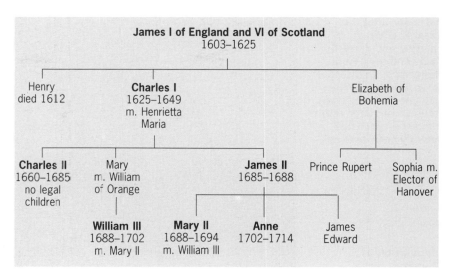

was forced to escape into exile in France. Parliament asked his Protestant son-in-law and daughter, William and Mary, to become joint king and queen. They agreed to share their power with Parliament, and this change (which was peaceful in England, though not in Scotland and Ireland) is sometimes called the Glorious Revolution.

By the time of the last Stuart, Queen Anne, rulers of England had become 'constitutional monarchs'. They could still choose their ministers, and command the army and navy, but they also had to keep rules made by Parliament, especially over money and religion.

Ireland was governed by English rulers. Most Irish were Catholics, except in Ulster where Protestant English and Scots settled. There was a Catholic rebellion in 1641. In 1649–1650 Cromwell led a harsh campaign to bring Ireland under English control again. By 1714 Irish Catholics owned only 7 per cent of the land of Ireland. English landowners had taken the rest.

Scotland had the same Stuart kings as England, but remained a separate kingdom. In 1650–1651 Cromwell defeated the Scots. Scotland was occupied. In 1707 the Act of Union united England and Scotland as part of a united kingdom. After the Glorious Revolution many Highlanders became Jacobites, who supported the exiled James II and his descendants.

Wales was ruled in the same way as England, with similar law courts and counties.

◄ The execution of Charles I, 30 January 1649. This is the only time an English king has been put on trial and publicly executed. Even many Roundheads were horrified at his death. But Oliver Cromwell and other leaders believed that the execution was the only way to bring peace to the new Commonwealth of England.

James I of England and VI of Scotland
1603–1625

Henry died 1612

Charles I 1625–1649 m. Henrietta Maria

Elizabeth of Bohemia

Charles II 1660–1685 no legal children

Mary m. William of Orange

James II 1685–1688

Prince Rupert

Sophia m. Elector of Hanover

William III 1688–1702 m. Mary II

Mary II 1688–1694 m. William III

Anne 1702–1714

James Edward

▶ London after the Great Fire. Many churches and a new St Paul's Cathedral were designed by Christopher Wren. Wealthy families had fine brick and stone houses, with large sash windows, which had recently been invented.

Famous books
King James Bible 1611
Book of Common Prayer 1662
Pilgrim's Progress 1678

Population of England
1600: about 4,100,000
1700: about 5,300,000

The Royal Society was founded in 1662 'for the improving of natural knowledge'. Its members included the great scientists of the day. Isaac Newton was a member from 1672, and president in 1703.

The rich landowners and wealthy merchants in Parliament had much more say in running the country, and became even more powerful and prosperous.

The widening world

By the end of the 17th century, great changes had taken place in Stuart Britain, but change was slow for ordinary people. They still could not vote or sit in Parliament. Times were often hard, especially when there was a bad harvest. During the Civil War, if people lived near any fighting, soldiers took their crops, animals and equipment, and often brought disease with them. By the end of the century, the country was generally more prosperous. Slightly fewer people died young, so the population continued to increase.

London

London was the biggest city in Britain, with a population of about half a million by the 1660s. Buildings spread outside the old city walls. Slums full of filthy tumbledown houses grew up to the north; the rich built grander houses to the west. There were fashionable new coffee houses, bull-baiting rings, bear-baiting pits, and theatres. When the Thames froze hard in 1685, there was a Frost Fair on the ice.

There were problems in London's crowded, busy streets. Traffic jams of carriages, carts and animals were common. The smoke from coal fires polluted the air. Disease spread easily. The Great Plague of 1665 was the last of several outbreaks of bubonic plague. Fire was a common danger; the most famous and devastating one was in 1666.

London was always full of merchants and traders from abroad, and there were other foreigners who settled there. Oliver Cromwell allowed Jews to live and work in England in 1656. Huguenots (French Protestants) came as refugees from France where they had been persecuted for their beliefs. They found work as silk-weavers, clock-makers, doctors and silversmiths. Rich people often had African servants, bought from English merchants, who profited from the slave trade.

Trade

Trade grew enormously. At the beginning of the century, England had only one important industry, the woollen cloth trade. Corn often had to be imported to feed everyone. By 1700 enough corn was grown to export some, and new goods, including tobacco, tea, coffee and chocolate, were imported. Much more sugar was coming into the country, and some of it was refined in London. Cotton, silks, fine china, dyes and jewels came from the East. Trade led to wars with Dutch and French rivals and to colonies in North America and the Caribbean. The East India Company, which brought many of the luxury goods from the East, established settlements in India too. In the next century these colonies grew into an empire. ◆

Submarines

Submarines are sea-going vessels that can travel underwater as well as on the surface. Most submarines are in countries' navies; they patrol the oceans, and can fire torpedoes or missiles. Special submarines called submersibles are used for engineering and exploration.

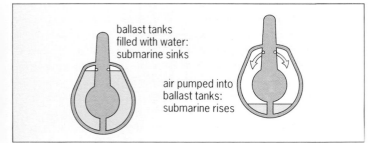

ballast tanks filled with water: submarine sinks

air pumped into ballast tanks: submarine rises

▲ A submarine can float or sink by emptying or filling its ballast tanks. Submersibles like this are used for exploration and oil-rig maintenance.

When a submarine cruises below the surface of the sea, the commander uses a periscope to see where it is going and to identify other vessels on the surface. This is a special telescope that is raised up like a hollow mast with a sloping mirror at each end and lenses inside. The upper mirror is above the surface and reflects the light downwards to the lower mirror, which reflects the image into the commander's eyes.

The world's biggest submarines are the Russian Typhoon Class. They weigh over 26,000 tonnes.

In 1960 the submersible *Trieste* reached a record depth of 11,000 metres.

▼ **Find out more**
Divers
Floating
Navies
Nuclear power
World War II

Submarines have long hollow ballast tanks, which can be filled with air or water. To dive and stay underwater, the tanks are filled with water so that the submarine can sink to a particular depth and then remain there.

As the submarine is driven forward by its propellers, fins called hydroplanes tilt to force it downwards or upwards. Then to return to the surface and float there, the water is blown out of the ballast tanks by compressed air so that the submarine becomes lighter and rises again.

Submarines cannot use diesel or petrol engines when submerged, because these fuels need oxygen, which is not available, to burn. Instead, small submarines use electric motors and batteries. Larger ones are nuclear-powered. Their nuclear reactor boils water, giving steam that powers turbines to drive the propellers. Nuclear submarines can stay submerged for many weeks.

A *submersible* has a cabin that is built of extremely thick metal to withstand the great pressure of the surrounding sea water. The crew work by operating movable arms attached to the cabin. These arms can hold tools or can be used to pick up objects.

FLASHBACK

The first vessel to travel underwater was built by the Dutch inventor Cornelius Drebbel. It was propelled by oars from Westminster to Greenwich on the River Thames in 1620. The first proper submarine was the *Turtle*, an egg-shaped wooden vessel built by the American engineer David Bushnell in 1776. It was very like a modern submersible, but was used to attack a ship during the American War of Independence.

In 1875, the Irish engineer John Holland built the first of a series of submarines in the United States. The modern naval submarine is descended from them. ◆

The first nuclear submarine, the USS *Nautilus*, was built in 1954. In 1958 it travelled under the Arctic ice and actually surfaced at the North Pole.

▼ Submersibles like this can work at much greater depths than a diver.

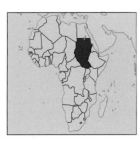

Sudan

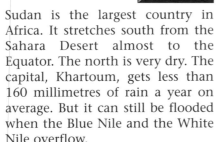

Sudan is the largest country in Africa. It stretches south from the Sahara Desert almost to the Equator. The north is very dry. The capital, Khartoum, gets less than 160 millimetres of rain a year on average. But it can still be flooded when the Blue Nile and the White Nile overflow.

Without the Nile, northern Sudan would be total desert. There is a narrow strip of farmland, about 100 metres wide, on each side of the river. Most of the people in the north are Muslims who speak Arabic. As you travel south, the land changes. More grass, with bushes and small trees, grows in the semi-desert. Then baobab trees appear. They can store water in their trunks. Further south, as the rainy season gets longer, there is taller grass and more trees. A region called the Sudd is swampy, and floating vegetation blocks the river channels. Cattle-herding is important to some tribes in this area. Near the border with Uganda and the Democratic of Congo there is tropical forest.

Area
2,505,800 sq km
Capital
Khartoum
Population
29,250,000
Language
Arabic, English, Nubian
Religion
Muslim, traditional, Christian
Government
Republic
Currency
1 Sudanese pound = 100 piastres = 1000 millièmes

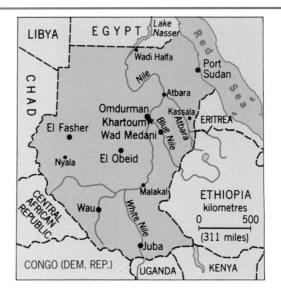

In the south many people are Christians. They speak a variety of African languages, not Arabic. Many do not like being ruled by the Arab north and have been struggling for independence since 1963.

Periodic fierce fighting, together with droughts, has brought much suffering, and many refugees have fled to camps organized by aid agencies. In addition there have been refugees from Ethiopia and Zaïre (now the Democratic Republic of Congo), at times of civil war in these countries. ◆

▼ Find out more
Africa
Drought
Nile
Refugees
Sahara

▼ Suffragettes often interrupted politicians' speeches, shouting 'Votes for Women' and waving banners and placards. They organized meetings and demonstrations, especially in London.

Suffragettes

By 1900 British women still did not have the 'suffrage', or right to vote, which men had gained in 1884. Since then Suffrage Societies had been working peacefully for 'Votes for Women', and there had been a number of unsuccessful attempts to change the law in Parliament. In 1903 Mrs Emmeline Pankhurst, believing in 'Deeds not Words', founded the Women's Social and Political Union. Many middle-class girls became suffragettes. They chained themselves to the railings of the prime minister's house at 10 Downing Street. They burned empty buildings and letter-boxes, and smashed shop windows. Emily Davison threw herself under the king's horse at the Derby, and died.

Suffragettes were very determined and, when in prison, many refused to eat. The government did not want them to die, so they were forcibly fed. This was horribly painful, and suffragette posters made sure everyone knew about it. In 1913 the 'Cat and Mouse Act' allowed suffragettes on hunger strike to leave prison, but put them back there when they were better. Neither side would give in.

In 1914 World War I changed everything. Suffragettes backed the war. Women proved they could do all kinds of work. In 1918 women over 30 got the vote, and in 1928 the age was lowered to 21, the same as for men. So did the suffragettes or the war bring 'Votes for Women'? Perhaps it was both. ◆

Suffragists
National Union of Women's Suffrage Societies (NUWSS): founded 1897
Leader Millicent Fawcett
Colours Green and white, red added later
Suffragettes
Women's Social and Political Union (WSPU): founded 1903
Leaders Emmeline, Christabel and Sylvia Pankhurst, Emily Davison
Colours
Green (Give)
White (Women)
Violet (the Vote)

▼ Find out more
Edwardian Britain
Victorian Britain
Women's movement

BIOGRAPHY
Pankhurst family

Sugar

Sugars are sweet-tasting substances produced naturally by plants and animals. They are made up of the elements carbon, hydrogen and oxygen, and so they are carbohydrates – a type of food that we use to produce energy. Sugars are the simplest of the carbohydrates in our diet. The most common sugar is sucrose, usually known simply as 'sugar'.

Sugar (sucrose) is made from both sugar cane and sugar beet. Sugar cane grows in tropical countries such as the islands of the Caribbean, Brazil and India. Sugar beet grows in temperate areas such as Britain. The process used to extract sugar is similar for both cane and beet, and the refined white sugar made from each is exactly the same. This sugar is ground to give finer products such as castor and icing sugar. It is also compressed into sugar cubes. Some refined white sugar is coloured with molasses to make soft brown sugar. Brown sugars such as muscovado, Barbados and demerara are made from unrefined raw cane sugar. They have more flavour than ordinary soft brown sugar. Molasses and black treacle are by-products of the cane-sugar refining process.

FLASHBACK

Sugar cane was cultivated in India in prehistoric times. The Indians discovered how to extract sugar crystals from it. Sugar was known in Europe during the Roman period, but it was rare and expensive. Later, the Arabs brought sugar cultivation to the

sugar cane

cane cut and crushed

sugar beet

roots sliced up and soaked

sugary liquid

molasses from sugar cane

sugary liquid boiled and condensed

sugar crystals separated from liquid

sugar

Naturally occurring sugars

Fructose found in honey and some fruit
Glucose found in most starchy foods
Lactose found in milk
Maltose found in barley malt
Sucrose found in sugar cane and beet and in maple syrup

Honey was used for sweetening before sugar became common.

◀ **Sugar cane is cut and crushed. Sugar beet is sliced up. The strips are soaked and a sugary liquid is extracted. This liquid is boiled and condensed by evaporation. Sugar crystals separate from the liquid in centrifugal machines.**

Mediterranean, and huge plantations were developed on Cyprus. Christopher Columbus took the plant with him to the West Indies in 1493. It grew so well there that huge plantations were set up by Europeans. The plantations were worked by African slaves, and the owners made so much money that sugar was known as 'white gold'. During the Napoleonic wars the supply from the Caribbean to Europe was cut, so more and more sugar beet was grown. ♦

▼ **Find out more**
Caribbean history
Chocolate
Diets
Food
Honey
Nutrition
Slave trade

Sumerians

The Sumerians lived in southern Mesopotamia, near where the rivers Tigris and Euphrates meet. They irrigated the land, making it very productive, and the farmers used oxen and ox-carts to work it.

By about 3800 BC, wealth from the farms allowed the Sumerians to build great cities such as Ur, Uruk, Eridu and Lagash. At one time there were about 50,000 people living in Uruk. Here, skilled metal-workers operated, while architects designed elaborate palaces and temples. To honour their gods they built *ziggurats*, huge pyramid-shaped temples, where their priests could study the stars.

At Ur the ziggurat was built for Nanna, the moon god. Ur was the most important Sumerian city, with mud-brick walls some

27 metres thick. It was excavated by a British archaeologist, Sir Leonard Woolley, between 1922 and 1934. He found many gold objects and jewels in the Royal Cemetery, some of which can be seen in the British Museum in London. There were also clay tablets covered with cuneiform writing. Ur was most prosperous between 2070 and 1980 BC. It then began to decline and was abandoned in the 4th century BC. ♦

▼ **Find out more**
Ancient world
Mesopotamia
Writing systems

BIOGRAPHY
Abraham

The Sumerians invented the *cuneiform* kind of writing.

◀ **This gold helmet probably belonged to a Sumerian prince called Meskalam-dug. It was buried in one of the graves in the Royal Cemetery at Ur. The helmet was hammered out from a single sheet of gold alloy. The holes around the edge were to hold the padded lining.**

Sun

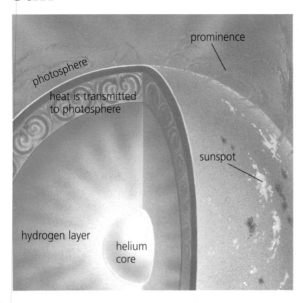

▶ A cross-section of the Sun. The helium core is about one-quarter of the radius of the whole Sun; it contains much of the Sun's mass. The energy made in the core slowly travels through the thick hydrogen layer and heats the photosphere.

photosphere

prominence

heat is transmitted to photosphere

sunspot

hydrogen layer

helium core

Distance from the Earth
149,600,000 km
Equatorial diameter
1,392,000 km
Rotation period
27¼ days
(as seen from Earth)
Mass
332,946 × Earth
Volume
1,303,946 × Earth
Surface temperature
6000 °C
Core temperature
16 million °C

The Sun gets 4000 million tonnes lighter every second as it generates nuclear energy from hydrogen. It takes light 8.3 minutes to travel from the Sun to the Earth.

The Sun is 5000 million years old.

In 5000 million years the Sun will become so bright that it will be impossible for anything to live on our planet.

▶ This special picture of the Sun was taken in 1973 from Skylab, a space station in orbit round the Earth. It shows up the 'graininess' of the Sun's surface and a giant plume of gas erupting from a solar flare.

▼ Find out more
Atoms
Aurora
Eclipses
Energy
Nuclear power
Seasons
Solar System
Stars

The Sun is an ordinary star, like the ones you can see at night, but for us and all the things that live on the Earth it is very special. Without the heat and light energy from the Sun, there would be no life. Even things we get from the ground and burn to get energy, such as coal, gas and oil, are the remains of plants and animals that grew in sunlight millions of years ago. People have always recognized how important the Sun is and they often worshipped it as a god.

Energy from the Sun

The Sun is a giant ball of hot gas, 150 million kilometres away, that could hold more than a million Earths inside its volume. Near the outside of the Sun the temperature is about 6000 °C but in the centre it is more like 16 million °C. In the Sun's hot core, enormous amounts of energy in the form of heat and light are produced by a process called nuclear fusion. This energy makes the Sun shine.

As well as heat and light, the Sun gives out X-rays and ultraviolet rays that are harmful to life. Most get soaked up in our atmosphere and do not affect us. Sunlight is very strong and no one should ever stare at the Sun or look at it through any kind of magnifier, binoculars or telescope. Your eyesight would be badly affected or you could even be blinded. Even with dark sunglasses or film it could still be dangerous to look at the Sun, so it is best not to risk it at all. Astronomers study the Sun safely by looking at it with special instruments.

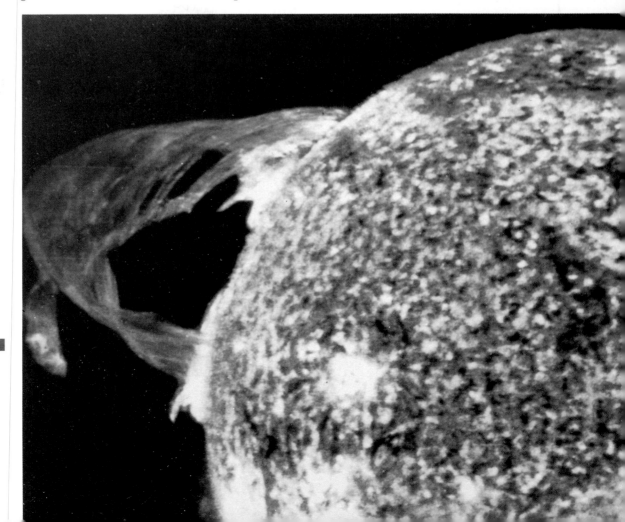

Sunspots

Close-up pictures of the Sun show that it looks like a bubbling cauldron as hot gases gush out then fall back. Some of the gas is streaming away from the Sun all the time into the space between the planets. The faint halo of glowing gas round the Sun only comes into view in a total eclipse.

Sometimes there are dark blotches on the Sun's yellow disc. These sunspots can be many thousands of kilometres across and last for several weeks. They are cooler than the gas surrounding them, and so appear darker. The average number of spots on the Sun goes up and down over about 11 years. When there are a lot of spots, the Sun is active in other ways too.

Action on the Sun

Giant tongues of hot gas leap out violently from the Sun to heights of 1 million kilometres or more. They are called *prominences*. Near to sunspots, flares like enormous lightning flashes can burst out. Particles that shoot out from the Sun take about two days to travel through space to the Earth. When they reach us, they cause the lights in the night sky called the aurora and can interfere with radio signals on the Earth. ◆

Superconductivity

When the temperature gets very cold, strange things begin to happen to materials. Superconductivity is one of them, and it could be the answer to many engineering problems.

Normally, it takes energy to push an electric current along. That is why you need a battery in a radio – it provides the energy to push electric currents around the radio's electronic circuits. The current needs to be pushed because otherwise the material will not let the current through. We say the material has *resistance*. Some metals, such as copper, have a very low resistance, which is why they are used to make electrical wire. We call these *conductors*. The energy that gets spent pushing a current along is turned into heat. That is why some electrical machines feel warm.

At extremely low temperatures, the resistance of some materials almost completely disappears. We call this superconductivity. Minus 273 °C is the coldest temperature that it is possible to reach – it is called *absolute zero*. Metals have to be cooled to within a few degrees of absolute zero before they become superconductors. Unfortunately, keeping things that cold is very difficult – and very expensive. So scientists are constantly trying to find materials which are superconductors at higher temperatures.

Using superconductors

When the problems of superconductors are solved, electrical wires will be able to carry huge currents with only a tiny loss of energy.

Microchips for computers will use far less energy, which will stop them becoming too hot. This could mean computers which work far faster than they do today.

Electromagnets made with superconductors could be small but very powerful. This means that the body scanners in hospitals will need much less electricity.

Huge amounts of electricity could be sent along thin wires instead of thick overhead cables. ◆

Superconductivity was discovered in 1911 by the Dutch physicist Heike Kamerlingh Onnes.

Superconductor scientists measure temperature in kelvins (K) as well as degrees centigrade. On the kelvin scale, absolute zero is 0 K, and 0 °C is 273 K.

▲ A magnet floats freely above a piece of superconducting material which has been cooled by liquid nitrogen.

Strangely, some of the best conductors at room temperature, such as copper, gold and silver, do not become superconductors.

Superstitions

Superstitions are ways in which people try to attract good luck or stop bad luck happening to them. Many superstitions are very old. The custom of wearing a 'lucky stone' or charm goes back to the time when people believed that these charms would prevent evil spirits or illness entering their bodies. Similarly, all over the world people place objects over their doors to stop evil spirits entering the house. Some people used to believe that bad luck would come down the chimney if they let the fire go out in the hearth.

Many superstitions are associated with birth, death, marriage and the New Year. For example, on New Year's Eve unmarried girls may pour hot, liquid lead into a glass of water in the hope of seeing it turn into the face of the man they will marry. Also, if a woman wanted to have a baby, she would place special corn dollies (made of plaited straw) in her house.

Sailors everywhere in the world are superstitious. For example, some believe that tattooing their bodies protects them from danger at sea and that a sailor who owns all or part of a caul (the skin that protects a baby before birth) will never drown.

Often superstitions begin with a real event. For example, the superstition that it is unlucky to walk under a ladder goes back to the time when condemned people had to step under one in order to reach the gallows where they were to be hanged.

It is possible for the same object to attract different superstitions in different parts of the world. In most countries black cats are considered unlucky because they were once associated with witches, but in the British Isles people say that they bring good luck. ◆

▼ **Find out more**
Ghosts
Witches

Surfing

▲ When a surfer launches from the peak of a wave and drops down its face, this is known as 'taking the drop'. The timing of this manoeuvre is vital, and it often takes considerable nerve on the part of the surfer.

Surfing is the sport of riding a surfboard towards the shore on the face of a wave. Surfboards are made of light, hard, plastic foam, covered with resin and fibreglass. Body-surfing, without boards, is also practised.

The size and shape of a wave depend largely on the land it travels over. For surfers, the 'tube' is the most exciting shape of all. This happens when a wave curls over. The surfer tries to ride into and through the tube.

The basic surfing position is with one foot in the centre of the board, the other pressing down at the back. But by changing the position of the feet and body the surfer can change speed and direction. Expert surfers are skilful and daring, with a fine sense of balance. They aim to catch an unbroken wave and then slide down its face.

The best surfing and the biggest waves are found off the beaches of Hawaii in the Pacific Ocean and along the coasts of Australia and California. But good surf can be found in many other places, including African and South American beaches, and beaches in France and Japan. Surfing professionals tour the world, and a dozen or more competitions offer over 100,000 dollars in prize money. Judges on the beach mark surfers for grace, timing and style, and the difficulty of the waves selected. Points may be awarded for reaching the best part of a wave first, length of ride, tube riding, turns and other routines and manoeuvres.

FLASHBACK

British sailors saw Hawaiian Islanders surfing more than 200 years ago. In modern times surfing developed as a competitive sporting activity in the 1950s.

Amateur world championships were first held in 1964, for both men and women, and annual professional world championships began in 1970 (1977 for women). ◆

Surgeons

A surgeon is a doctor who deals with conditions where an operation is needed. Surgeons are trained to carry out operations. If an illness cannot be treated by medicine, a surgeon will operate using special surgical instruments. A surgical operation is usually carried out in a hospital under anaesthetic.

Surgeons usually specialize in particular operations. A *general surgeon* operates on almost all parts of the body. A *neurosurgeon* carries out surgery on the brain, spinal cord and nerves. An *orthopaedic surgeon* operates on bones and joints. This includes setting broken bones and also joint-replacement surgery. A *cardiovascular surgeon* specializes in heart surgery and diseases of the blood. A *plastic surgeon* rebuilds or replaces damaged parts of the body ('plastic' here means reshaping). *Ophthalmic surgery* is concerned with the eyes, and *ENT surgery* with the ears, nose and throat.

In *transplant surgery* ('spare-part' surgery), surgeons replace or repair parts of the body with parts from other people. *Microsurgery* is a modern method of surgery used for some operations such as those on the eye, the inner ear, the brain and the spinal cord. The part of the body being treated is greatly magnified by a special operating microscope. The surgeon can then use very tiny instruments to work in those parts of the body difficult to reach by ordinary methods. Sometimes computer-controlled robot hands are used to handle these tiny instruments. Surgeons are able to use microsurgery to sew on limbs that have been accidentally cut off.

Keyhole surgery is the popular name for a method of operating called 'minimally invasive surgery'. The surgeon uses a flexible telescope called an *endoscope*. Endoscopes are passed through three or four very small incisions (cuts) in the skin. The surgeon examines the patient using the endoscope and performs certain operations without having to make a large incision. A television monitor shows the surgeon what is happening inside the patient. Removal of the gall bladder is often carried out in this way.

Lasers are now used for a variety of operations. A laser is a special kind of very narrow light beam that can cut without causing bleeding. Its surgical uses include the destruction of small growths, the treatment of some eye conditions, and the removal of unwanted tattoos from the skin. In *cryosurgery*, extreme cold is used to remove unwanted tissue, such as cataracts or cancerous growths.

FLASHBACK

During the Middle Ages, surgery was dirty, painful and dangerous. Hardly anything was known about how the body worked. Simple operations, such as pulling teeth and blood-letting, were often carried out by barbers, who had little or no training. During the 16th century, medical training began to include anatomy – the scientific study of the human body by dissection (cutting up dead bodies). This was largely due to the work of a Belgian doctor, Andreas Vesalius (1514–1564). A French surgeon, Ambroise Paré (1510–1590), is often called the 'Father of Modern Surgery'. He started as a barber-surgeon and studied the works of Vesalius. He did much to improve surgical methods. ◆

The first recorded surgical operation done under anaesthetic was to remove a cyst from a man's neck. This took place in Jefferson, Georgia, USA, in 1842. The surgeon, Crawford Long, used ether as the anaesthetic.

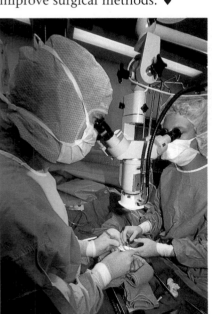

◄ Surgeons carrying out microsurgery on a patient's hand. The surgeons and their assistant need to use binocular microscopes to see what they are doing during the operation.

Suriname

Suriname is a small country on the north-east coast of South America. Most of the people live on the coastal plains, while inland the Guiana Highlands rise from savannah grasslands and dense jungles. The climate is tropical with temperatures on the coast averaging 26–27 °C all year round. Suriname's economy relies heavily on bauxite (aluminium ore), by far the most important export; its oil and timber resources have not been exploited. Suriname was a Dutch colony for 161 years until independence in 1975. Many of the inhabitants are descended from people from the Dutch East Indies (now Indonesia), transported to work in the sugar plantations. ◆

Area
163,265 sq km
Capital Paramaribo
Population 415,000
Language Dutch, English, Hindi, Javanese, others
Religion Christian, Hindu, Muslim
Government Republic
Currency 1 Suriname guilder (florin) = 100 cents

▼ **Find out more**
South America

Surveying

Before a map can be made, the positions of all the main features, such as hills, roads and churches, must be found. This is called surveying. To produce the map, the measurements must be scaled down. For example, 1 kilometre on the ground might be shown as 1 centimetre on the map.

Many hills have a concrete post called a triangulation pillar at the top. It was originally put there to help surveyors. With a special type of instrument called a theodolite, the surveyor could measure the directions and levels of other pillars and landmarks. By moving from one pillar to another, the whole country could be surveyed.

Today, surveying has been made much easier by the Global Positioning System (GPS). Signals from satellites are picked up by a small receiver, which then works out its position on the Earth's surface to within a few metres.

Theodolites, which date back to the 16th century, are still used for small surveys, such as the site of a new building. ◆

An instrument called an electronic total station is the modern version of the theodolite. It sends infrared pulses towards a target, measures the time taken for the pulses to reflect back, then calculates the distance and direction of the target.

▼ **Find out more**
Architecture
Maps
Roads
Satellites

Swaziland

Sandwiched between South Africa and Mozambique is the small but beautiful kingdom of Swaziland. Its king is called the *Ngwenyama*, which means 'lion'. Swaziland contains high plains, called the high veld, in the west, with lower plains in the centre. The Lebombo plateau, an upland region, runs along the eastern border.

The Swazis speak a language called siSwati. They are mostly farmers, who grow maize and rear cattle to feed themselves, and may also grow tobacco and cotton to sell. The main crops are sugar cane and citrus fruits. The cultivation of these is controlled by large commercial companies. Timber and asbestos are also exported. On special occasions, such as royal ceremonies, the Swazis wear traditional clothes, made of animal skins and brightly coloured cloth. On these occasions spectacular dances are performed.

Swazis began to settle in what is now Swaziland nearly 200 years ago, founding the kingdom which survives to this day. Swaziland was a protectorate controlled by Britain from 1902 until 1968, when it became an independent monarchy. ◆

Area
17,400 sq km
Capital
Mbabane
Population
835,000
Language
English, siSwati
Religion
Christian, Traditional
Government
Monarchy
Currency
1 lilangeni = 100 cents

▼ **Find out more**
Africa

▼ **Baskets, mats and other local products at market in Mbabane, Swaziland's administrative capital in the north-west of the country.**

Sweden

Sweden is the fourth largest country in Europe. Over half its land surface is covered with dense forest, mostly pines, and it has over 95,000 lakes. Most of the country is fairly flat, but there is a long chain of mountains in the northwest where Sweden borders Norway. There are thousands of islands off the coast.

Sweden is a large country with a great many natural resources, including timber and valuable mineral deposits, especially iron ore. However, it has a population smaller than that of greater London. There are very few large cities and there are long distances between them. In parts of central and northern Sweden you could drive for a whole day and pass only a handful of other vehicles. Because of this, Sweden is rich in wildlife. Elk live in most parts of the country. Wild bears can be found in the forests of central Sweden.

The average winter temperature in Kiruna in Swedish Lapland is –15 °C (+5 °F), where the winter snow can stay for up to 200 days. At midwinter in Kiruna there is no daylight at all. But in the summer, temperatures rise to over 15 °C (60 °F), and in June and July the Sun never sets completely. This is why Sweden is one of the countries known as 'The Land of the Midnight Sun'.

Because of the resources Sweden possesses, its people have a very high standard of living. Their homes are usually well designed and built to keep out the winter cold. Almost all Swedish families have a car and most Swedes still prefer to buy a Swedish-made car – either a Saab or a Volvo.

Sports

Skating and skiing are popular pastimes in Sweden and the national sport is ice hockey. Swedes also enjoy visiting the countryside. Berry and mushroom picking are very popular during the late summer and early autumn months. Most Swedes live within 10 kilometres of a lake, so it is not surprising that water sports and pastimes are very popular, especially sailing and fishing.

FLASHBACK

In the 17th century the Swedish kings ruled an empire which included Finland and parts of Denmark, Germany and Poland. During the 18th century the country produced some of the most famous European scientists, such as Linnaeus and Celsius, whose name is used for the temperature system.

In the 19th century Sweden became a developed industrialized nation. Norway, which had been part of it since 1815, became independent in 1905. Sweden did not take part in either of the World Wars and has remained a neutral country. After a referendum it joined the European Union in 1995. ◆

Area
449,964 sq km
Capital
Stockholm
Population
8,700,000
Language
Swedish, Finnish, Lappish
Religion
Christian
Government
Parliamentary monarchy
Currency
1 Swedish krona = 100 öre

▼ **Find out more**
Europe
European Union
Midnight Sun

BIOGRAPHY
Borg, Bjorn
Linnaeus, Carolus
Nobel, Alfred Bernhard

▼ The city of Stockholm is situated on 20 islands and peninsulas beside the Baltic Sea.

Swimming

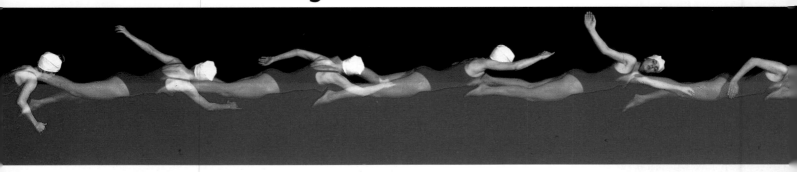

▲ The front crawl is the fastest stroke. It was developed early in the 20th century by the US swimmer Johnny Weissmuller, who won several Olympic titles before starring in *Tarzan* movies.

The fastest human swimmers average more than 8 km/h over a straight 50 m swim.

The fastest time for swimming the English Channel is 7 hours 17 minutes, set by Chad Hundeby (USA) in 1994. Some swimmers have made double and even triple crossings. The records for each, 16 hours 10 minutes and 28 hours 21 minutes, were set in the same swim by Philip Rush (New Zealand) in 1987.

There is more on swimming as a sport under Water sports.

Record-holders in the animal world
sailfish 109 km/h
killer whale 55 km/h
leatherback turtle 35 km/h
gentoo penguin 27 km/h

▼ **Find out more**
Dolphins
Fishes
Porpoises
Sport
Water sports
Whales

Swimming is the way in which an animal pushes itself through water. A wide variety of animals can swim, including hedgehogs, cows and even moles. Fishes, whales, dolphins, seals, penguins and millions of aquatic insects and microscopic animals spend much of their lives in the water and have to swim in order to hunt for food. Animals such as antelopes and reindeer swim across rivers as they migrate, or when escaping from predators.

The basic principles

In order to swim, an animal must push the water back (to move forward) and down (to stay afloat). Simple wave-like movements of the body can achieve these thrusts, but often fins or paddles are used as well. Many animals, such as frogs, turtles and water beetles, keep their bodies stiff and use their legs to provide the thrust.

Often an animal's feet, or sometimes the whole of its legs or arms, are shaped like paddles to provide a greater surface area to push against the water. Turtles and seals have flippers; dolphins and whales use their large tail flukes. Fishes have fins, and ducks, seagulls and otters have webbed feet. Many small shrimps and water insects have fringes of stiff bristles on their legs which have the same effect.

In order to offer little resistance to the water, the bodies of swimming animals tend to be streamlined – that is, they are more or less torpedo-shaped. The water can flow smoothly round them. This is why many marine animals have very small ears or no external ears at all. Fishes are covered in slime to help them slip through the water.

Different techniques

When swimming, an animal needs to thrust against the water while maintaining a good streamlined shape. Like rowing a boat, the 'paddles' are spread out against the water when pushing, but folded close to the body when gliding forward. Human swimmers have several different ways of doing this, and four of these 'strokes' are used in competitive sport.

Swimming for sport and exercise

In *breast-stroke* the feet provide most of the thrust. They are brought together in a scissors motion, producing a rather jerky movement. In a good breast-stroke, the head is level with the water on the forward stroke. This brings the face into the water but improves streamlining.

In the *front crawl*, the body lies flat on the surface of the water, and both arms and feet provide thrust. As one arm pushes against the water, the other is brought close to the body to improve streamlining. The legs kick up and down. This is a very fast stroke, popular in competitions. It is also used for long-distance swimming.

In *backstroke*, swimmers lie on their backs. Their arms reach alternately above their heads, and enter the water level with the shoulders. This is a relaxing stroke but is also used in competitions.

The *butterfly stroke* is used only for competitions. It resembles the up-and-down motion of dolphins. The arms are brought forward above the water, and the legs kick up and down.

The most famous long-distance swim is the English Channel, a difficult challenge across the sea separating England and France. At its shortest, the swim is 34 kilometres. This in itself is not difficult, but the tricky tides on the way can make it twice as far. Thousands of swimmers from all over the world have tackled it, but only a small proportion has been successful.

Swimming is a good form of exercise, especially for the elderly and the disabled because the body is partly supported by the water. It puts minimal strain on the limbs, yet offers a chance to practise bending them, and at the same time exercises the heart and lungs. ◆

Switzerland

Area
41,293 sq km
Capital
Bern
Population
7,000,000
Language
German, Swiss German, French, Italian, Romansch
Religion
Christian
Government
Federal parliamentary republic
Currency
1 Swiss franc = 100 rappen or centimes

High mountains make up more than half of this small inland European country. They are the Swiss Alps, which attract many tourists, in winter for skiing and in summer for mountaineering and sightseeing. Cattle are taken up to the high Alpine pastures in spring and summer while grass in the valleys is cut for hay. Their milk is used to make famous cheeses such as Gruyère and Emmental. The milk is also used in the Swiss chocolate industry.

Engineering in the Alps

The Alps are the site of many fine engineering projects. Fast-flowing mountain rivers have been dammed to generate hydroelectric power. This energy for towns and factories all over Switzerland is very important because the country has no coal or oil. Major road and rail routes linking northern and southern Europe cross the Alps.

Fast and efficient electric railways use long tunnels and amazing loops and bridges. Swiss engineers invented the rack railway to take trains up steep slopes, and these mountain railways are very popular with tourists.

Industry and wealth

Near the French border is a lower range of mountains called the Jura. The Swiss clock and watch industry is centred on Neuchâtel at the foot of the Jura. For centuries, skilled people have made valuable products such as watches, but Switzerland has to import nearly all the raw materials that are used.

Large towns and cities with factories and offices are in the lower land between the Jura and the Alps. Machinery, locomotives, tools, textiles, and many items for the optician's and the chemist's shop are made here.

A peaceful country

Switzerland has been a neutral country since 1815. This means it remained peaceful when the rest of Europe was at war. It is a federation of 26 states called cantons and has four national languages. The headquarters of some United Nations and many other international organizations are in Bern and Geneva. The International Red Cross was founded here and its badge is the Swiss flag with the colours reversed. ◆

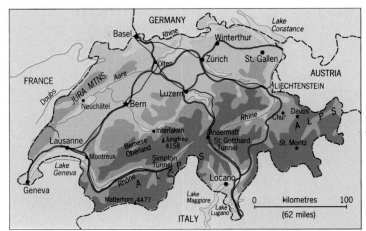

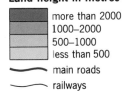

Land height in metres
more than 2000
1000–2000
500–1000
less than 500
— main roads
— railways

▶ Summer in the Bernese Oberland. Cattle can be seen grazing on the meadows to the right of the photograph.

▼ **Find out more**
Alps
Dams
Europe
Railways

Symbols

Have you ever wondered why we throw confetti over a bride and groom at their wedding? Some people throw grains of rice instead. They are using a symbol that is thousands of years old. Grain is important. It will grow into next year's plants that feed us. By throwing grain over the couple we show that we wish them to have plenty of everything. A symbol is something that represents something else. Quite ordinary objects, pictures, clothes, colours, and actions may be symbolic.

Flower language
Red rose symbol of love
Lily symbol of purity
Laurel symbol of victory
Rosemary symbol of remembrance
Peony symbol of marriage
Lotus symbol of wisdom

▶ In ancient Egypt cats were considered special and were often commemorated in works of art.

Some famous symbols
Cat On the continent of Europe and in the USA, a black cat is considered unlucky. In Britain it stands for good luck.
Tiger stands for speed and power.
Oil used to anoint a king or queen at a coronation symbolizes the giving of wisdom through the grace of God.
Swastika a prehistoric, universal symbol of creative force; in Sanskrit it means 'so be it'. It was also used as a symbol by the Nazis in Germany.
Wheel in Buddhism, represents the unending cycle of birth, life and death.

▶ The rainbow symbolizes hope.

Objects

The same object can be either ordinary or symbolic. For instance, a cat can be a symbol for magic, since European people used to believe that witches turned into cats. In ancient Egypt the cat was considered so special that if you killed one, you yourself could be sentenced to death. This was because the cat symbolized Isis, the Mother goddess, and people needed her protection against evil.

For Jews, Christians and Muslims the rainbow in the sky is the reminder that God created it after the great flood, as a symbol of the everlasting bond between himself and all life on Earth.

Pictures

The yin and yang symbol, which is Chinese, says a very great deal. It tells us that there are two forces in the Universe, the female and the male. The female symbolizes the night, the Earth, and is called yin. Yang symbolizes the mountains, the sky and light itself. Each has in it a small part of the other. Together they form the indivisible force of life.

Actions

At the last supper before Christ died, he washed the feet of his apostles. By this symbolic act he showed that he loved and served them, and that they in turn should love and serve others. The cross, which for the Romans was a symbol of shame, became the symbol of all Christians.

▲ The fish was an early, secret symbol for Jesus.

▶ The dove is a symbol of peace.

Colours

Any colour can be used as a symbol. The colour white may symbolize purity, and is worn by brides in Christian countries; but a white bird may symbolize the soul of a dead person or, in the case of the dove, the spirit of life and of peace. In ancient Rome a white mark on a boy's foot was a sign that he was for sale as a slave. ◆

▲ The Chinese symbol of yin and yang.

Symbolic colours
Red danger, passion
Green hope
Blue harmony, coolness
Purple royalty

▼ **Find out more**
Flags
Graphic design
Icons
Maps

Symmetry

◀ Compare the two halves of this butterfly on either side of the line of symmetry.

▼ The dome of this church in Malta is an example of rotational symmetry. If you were to rotate the central dome by an eighth of a circle (or two-eighths, or three-eighths) it would still look the same. Such symmetry is a feature of the classical style of architecture in Europe.

A butterfly is a beautiful example of symmetry in nature. Draw a dividing line down the middle, and each part and pattern on one side has the same shape, size and position as on the other side. This is known as *bilateral* ('two-sided') symmetry. The dividing line is called the line of symmetry.

We are almost symmetrical about a line down the middle of us, though there are very slight differences between our two sides. We may have a mole on one cheek or one arm may be very slightly longer than the other.

Some things have more than one line of symmetry. For example, the capital letter H has two. Its left side is symmetrical with its right, and its top half is symmetrical with its bottom.

Some things have *rotational symmetry*. This means that they look the same if you rotate them. For instance, the letter S looks the same if you rotate it by half a turn.

Shapes can have more than one type of symmetry. For example, the capital letter H has rotational symmetry as well as its two lines of bilateral symmetry. ◆

How to test for symmetry

Are faces exactly symmetrical? To find out, stand a mirror on a photograph of someone's face. Place the mirror so that half the face and its reflection make up a whole face. Does the person look any different?

Try the test on some words to find out if they are symmetrical. Here is one to start you off: MUM.

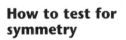

▼ **Find out more**
Kaleidoscopes
Patterns
Shapes

Symphonies

Symphonies are pieces of classical music for orchestra. Most symphonies are divided into 'movements': individual sections which follow one another to make the complete symphony. Usually there are four movements. The outside movements balance each other, so that the symphony usually begins and ends with movements that are quite complex. The inside movements make a contrast. One is usually slow, and the other is lively, often in a dance rhythm, like a scherzo or minuet. Some composers write symphonies where the order of movements is altered, or they leave some movements out, run movements together, or even write one-movement symphonies. But the symphony is always a major item in any concert. A symphony may take between 15 minutes and an hour to play, and there are some that last longer than an hour. ◆

Joseph Haydn wrote at least 104 symphonies: he is known as 'the father of the symphony'.

Symphonies are usually known by a number (Beethoven's Symphony No. 7), but some symphonies have names: Mozart's 'Prague' and 'Jupiter' symphonies; Beethoven's 'Eroica', 'Pastoral' and 'Choral' symphonies; and Prokofiev's 'Classical' Symphony.

▼ **Find out more**
Classical music
Orchestras
BIOGRAPHY
Beethoven, Ludwig van
Brahms, Johannes
Dvorak, Antonin
Elgar, Edward
Haydn, Joseph
Mendelssohn, Felix
Mozart, Wolfgang
  Amadeus
Prokofiev, Sergei
Schubert, Franz Peter
Tchaikovsky, Pyotr

Synagogues

The place where Jews gather together for study and prayer is called a synagogue. Another name for it is the school or house of meeting. Jews think that it is important to study and discuss religion as well as to worship. Study includes learning Hebrew, the language of the Jewish Bible.

The focus of a synagogue is the scrolls of Torah (teaching or law). These are placed in beautifully decorated covers in a cupboard or alcove which is called the Holy Ark. The ark is at the end of the synagogue, which faces Jerusalem. A light usually burns in front of the ark as a symbol of the presence of God. The first ark was a portable chest for the Ten Commandments given to Moses.

Another important part of a synagogue is the *bimah* (reading desk), which is usually in the centre. At the main point in a service, everyone stands while a scroll is carried from the ark to the reading desk and a member of the congregation reads the portion of scripture for that week. Synagogues can be decorated with abstract patterns or symbols but Jews do not make statues or paintings of God or their great prophets.

The main services are on Friday night and Saturday (the Jewish Sabbath), and at festivals. They are led by a rabbi (teacher) or any learned person appointed by the community. In Orthodox (traditional) synagogues women sit separately and the rabbis are always men.

FLASHBACK

Synagogues probably began during the exile of the Jews in Babylon in the 6th century BC when Jews could not visit Jerusalem and the first Temple in Jerusalem had been destroyed. When the second Temple was finally destroyed by the Romans in AD 70, synagogues and homes became the main centres of Jewish worship. ◆

The word 'synagogue' comes from a Greek word meaning 'gathering'. Greek-speaking Jews 2000 years ago were already using it to mean synagogue.

The first five books of the Old Testament of the Bible are a translation of the Hebrew Torah. To Jews it is much the most sacred part of the Bible, given by God directly to Moses. The whole Torah is read aloud in every synagogue in the course of the year, one portion on each Sabbath. After this there is another scriptural reading called *haphtarah*, from the Prophets.

▼ **Find out more**
Bible
Festivals
Jews
Temples

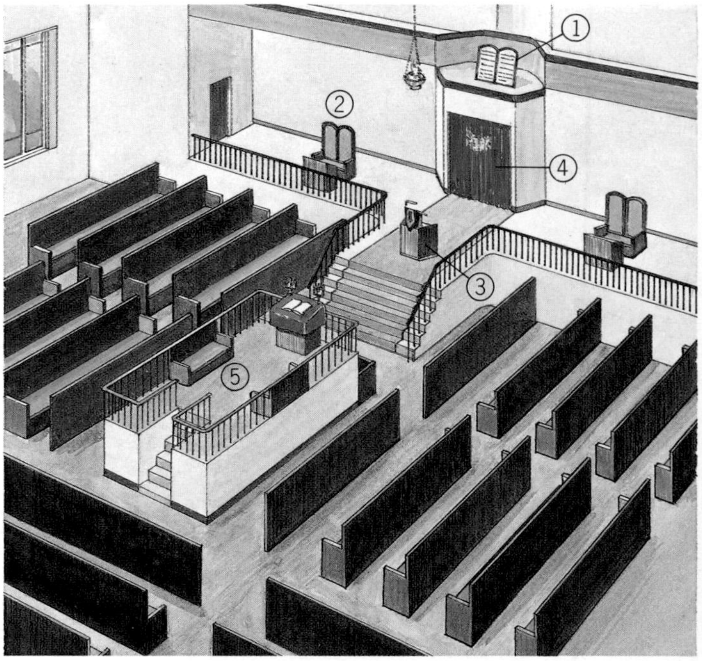

▼ This illustration shows the interior of a modern synagogue.
1 Ten Commandments
2 rabbi's seat
3 pulpit
4 Holy Ark
5 bimah (reading desk)

Synthetic fibres

If you look at the labels on your clothes, you will probably see that some of them are made of polyester, nylon or acrylics. These are synthetic fibres. Your clothes may also be made of cotton or wool, which are natural fibres.

Fibres are long, thin, hair-like filaments and they are twisted together to make thread or yarn from which fabrics are woven or knitted. Fibres are used to make sheets, blankets, carpets, curtains and furniture covers, as well as clothes. Synthetic fibres are often used instead of natural fibres. They may be stronger and resist wear, damage and flames better than natural fibres; they may not crease or be stretchy; or they may look different, perhaps shiny.

Making fibres

Natural fibres – cotton, wool and silk – are obtained directly from cotton plants, fleece and silkworm cocoons. Synthetic fibres are made in factories. Nylon, polyester and acrylics are in fact plastics, which are made of chemicals that come mostly from oil. The plastic is hot and liquid when it is made. It is then forced through a device called a spinneret, which contains fine holes. Long fibres emerge from the holes. They either cool and set solid, or the fibres enter a solution that causes them to solidify.

Some synthetic fibres are made of cellulose instead of plastic. Cellulose is a natural substance present in plants, and the fibres are made by dissolving wood pulp in chemicals and then forcing this solution through a spinneret to form fibres of cellulose. Rayon and Tricel are synthetic cellulose fibres.

FLASHBACK

The first synthetic fibre was a cellulose fibre made by the French chemist Hilaire Chardonnet in 1884. He used the fibre to produce artificial silk. Nylon was the first plastic fibre, invented by the American chemist Wallace Carothers in 1935. Polyester and acrylics soon followed, being first developed in the 1940s. ◆

The first electric light bulbs contained carbon filaments made by heating synthetic cellulose fibres. Today, carbon fibres made in the same basic way are incorporated into plastics to produce materials that are light and extremely strong. These carbon-reinforced plastics are used to make skis, tennis rackets, racing bicycles and aircraft parts.

Acrylic fibres feel soft like wool, and they are used to make blankets and winter clothes.

▼ **Find out more**
Asbestos
Fibres
Oil
Plastics
Wood

Syria

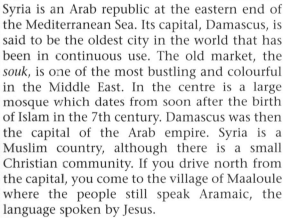

Syria is an Arab republic at the eastern end of the Mediterranean Sea. Its capital, Damascus, is said to be the oldest city in the world that has been in continuous use. The old market, the *souk*, is one of the most bustling and colourful in the Middle East. In the centre is a large mosque which dates from soon after the birth of Islam in the 7th century. Damascus was then the capital of the Arab empire. Syria is a Muslim country, although there is a small Christian community. If you drive north from the capital, you come to the village of Maaloule where the people still speak Aramaic, the language spoken by Jesus.

Syria's south-western neighbour is Israel, with whom Syria has fought two wars. In 1967 Israel captured the Golan Heights in southern Syria which command the road north to Damascus. Huge sums of money have gone into buying weapons in preparation for another possible war.

Syrians work in a variety of jobs, but the largest number work in farming. They grow cereals, vegetables and many kinds of fruit. An oil industry is being developed. In country areas you will still see young and old people alike wearing simple, loose robes. In the cities it is more common to see European-style clothes.

FLASHBACK

Syria has seen many armies march over its land. In the Middle Ages Crusaders passed through on their way to Jerusalem. From the 16th century Syria was ruled by the Ottoman Turks. In 1918, after World War I, it came under French control. It became independent in 1946. There were many turbulent changes of leadership in the years that followed until President Assad took power in 1971. ◆

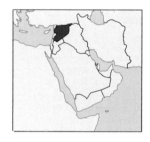

Area 185,180 sq km
Capital Damascus
Population 13,500,000
Language
Arabic, French, Kurdish, Armenian, others
Religion
Muslim, Christian
Government Republic
Currency
1 Syrian pound = 100 piastres

◀ Rich carpets cover the floor of the magnificent Umayyad Mosque in Old Damascus.

▼ **Find out more**
Arabs
Crusades
Israel
Middle East
Muslims
Ottoman empire

Table tennis

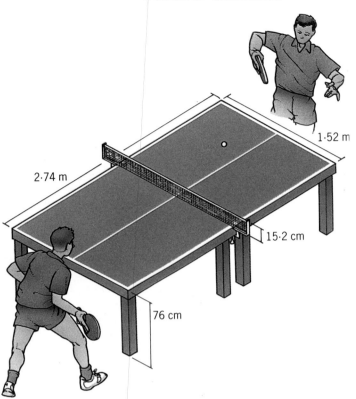

2·74 m

1·52 m

15·2 cm

76 cm

The game was invented in England at the beginning of the 20th century as an after-dinner game. The company that made the equipment called it 'ping-pong'. The name 'table tennis' took over in the 1920s as the game became more widespread and more athletic.

Table tennis is an indoor game played by hitting a small, light plastic ball to and fro across a table. The ball has to be hit so as to clear the net but bounce on the table beyond it. Volleying is not allowed, and the ball must bounce just once. The service must bounce on each side of the net. Players score points by hitting shots that their opponents are unable to return. The game can be played with one player a side (singles) or two a side (doubles).

The bat is made of wood covered with rubber. The rubber can be fairly thick so that it grips the ball to put spin on it.

The ball can just be tapped to and fro, but the secret of good fast play is to be able to hit hard, controlling the ball by putting spin on it with the bat. Because the ball is very light, spin greatly affects both its flight through the air and its bounce on the table. The receiving player has to judge the spin which is on the ball and respond by hitting it correctly. ◆

▼ **Find out more**
Tennis

Taiwan

Taiwan is an island in the Pacific Ocean about 120 kilometres from the south-east coast of China. It is a mountainous island, with the highest peak, Yu Shan, rising to 3997 metres. Taiwan lies on the Tropic of Cancer and has a warm, humid climate for most of the year. Rice is the most important food crop, but tea, sugar cane and bananas also grow well in the high temperatures, good rainfall and fertile soil.

Taiwan's industry and economy have been growing very fast since the 1960s. Electronic goods, clothing and footwear from Taiwan are exported all over the world and the hard-working Taiwanese have a high standard of living.

FLASHBACK

Taiwan, which used to be called Formosa, was at one time part of China. It was occupied by the Japanese from 1895 to 1945. When Chiang Kai-shek (Jiang Jieshi) fled from China in 1949, two million Chinese followed and Chiang set up an independent government on the island. ◆

Area
36,174 sq km
Capital
Taipei
Population
21,000,000
Language
Mandarin Chinese, Hokkien, Hakka, others
Religion
Buddhist, Confucian, Taoist, Christian
Government
Republic
Currency
1 new Taiwan dollar = 100 cents

▼ **Find out more**
China

BIOGRAPHY
Chiang Kai-shek

▼ **The New Year dragon dance in Taipei.**

Tajikistan

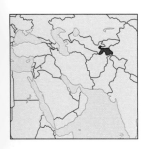

Tajikistan is a country in central Asia, where the snow-capped Pamir mountains form part of the country's border, with Afghanistan to the south and China to the east. The highest peak rises to 7495 metres, and more than half the country is over 3000 metres above sea-level. Mulberry trees are grown to the west in the fertile valley of the river Amu Darya. Silkworms reared on the trees provide silk for the spinning mills which are run by hydroelectric power. Cotton, fruit, wheat and vegetables are also grown on irrigated fields. Tajikistan is rich in minerals such as coal, oil, gas, zinc and lead, and mining is an important industry.

The country was invaded by the Persians in the 6th century BC and briefly ruled by Alexander the Great. It was invaded by the Mongols in the 15th century, then taken over by Russia late in the 19th century and became part of the Soviet Union in 1924. In 1991 Tajikistan became independent, but for a while after that there was unrest because the people were not happy about the way they were governed. ♦

Area
143,100 sq km
Capital Dushanbe
Population 5,700,000
Language
Tajik (Persian)
Religion Muslim
Government
Parliamentary republic
Currency
1 rouble = 100 copecks

▼ **Find out more**
Asia
Commonwealth of
  Independent States
Russian Federation
Russia's history
Soviet Union

Tanks

The first tank ever built was No. 1 Lincoln, which first ran in 1915.

The fastest tank is the Scorpion, a British reconnaisance vehicle that can travel at 75 km/h.

More than 50,000 Soviet T-54/55 tanks were built between 1954 and 1980.

A tank is like a moving castle. It runs on tracks so that it can travel across rough and soft ground. There are two types of tank: large, heavy battle tanks and smaller, faster reconnaisance tanks used for scouting.

Tanks can travel across ditches and rivers. Some can even travel short distances under water. Others are used to clear paths through minefields. A tank has one main gun that can turn right round, so it can fire in any direction. A tank's steel plate armour can be more than 12 centimetres thick at the front, but even thick armour can be pierced by modern shells. The Russian T-12 anti-tank gun fires shells which can go through armour 41 centimetres thick.

FLASHBACK

The first tanks were used in 1916 in World War I. They were slow and unreliable but were very useful for moving across muddy, uneven ground and bursting through barbed wire and over trenches. The tank was developed in Britain and France from the idea of the new tracked farm tractors. Tanks helped the Allies to win the campaign of autumn 1918. ♦

The British Mark V tank, which was brought out in 1916, weighed 29.5 tonnes and had a maximum speed of 7 km/h.

Most modern tanks weigh at least 50 tonnes. With their powerful diesel engines, they can travel at speeds of 64 km/h or more.

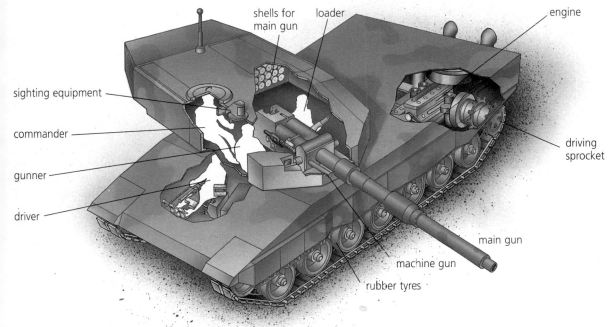

shells for main gun
loader
engine
sighting equipment
commander
gunner
driver
machine gun
rubber tyres
main gun
driving sprocket

◄ **Layout of a modern tank. The driver sits at the front. The weapons are mounted in a rotating turret which also houses the rest of the crew. The engine is at the rear of the tank.**

▼ **Find out more**
Guns
Weapons

Tanzania

The name Tanzania was made up in 1964 when the large country of *Tan*ganyika, on the mainland of East Africa, united with the small island state of *Zan*zibar, which also includes the island of Pemba. Tanzania is a beautiful country. Many wild animals, including antelopes, buffaloes, elephants, giraffes and zebras, roam freely across its national parks.

Landscape and climate

Tanzania contains Kilimanjaro (5895 metres), Africa's highest mountain. This mountain is near the Equator, but it is always capped by snow and ice. Tanzania also contains part of Lake Victoria, Africa's largest lake, and part of Lake Tanganyika. But most of Tanzania, apart from the offshore islands and the narrow coastal lowlands, consists of high plains covered by grass and woodland. Tanzania has a tropical climate. Near the coast, it is very hot throughout the year. The dry high plains are cooler. The rainiest places are in the north and in the mountains.

▶ A herd of wildebeest grazes in the foreground of Kilimanjaro.

Area
945,050 sq km
Capital
Dodoma
Population
28,200,000
Language
Kiswahili, English, others
Religion
Christian, Muslim
Government
Republic
Currency
1 shilling = 100 cents

▼ **Find out more**
Africa
Evolution of people

BIOGRAPHY
Leakey family
Nyerere, Julius

▶ These villagers are 'winnowing' millet. They beat the millet to separate the chaff (husks) from the grain.

The people and how they live

About 120 languages are spoken, and so to be widely understood Tanzanians use a second common language, known as Kiswahili. Many Tanzanians also speak English. Most Tanzanians are farmers. The chief food crop is maize, but some farmers grow coffee, cotton, sisal (used to make rope) and cashew nuts. Tanzania produces some diamonds. The main industrial city is the port of Dar es Salaam.

FLASHBACK

Olduvai Gorge in northern Tanzania is of scientific interest. Here, in the 1960s, Louis and Mary Leakey dug up fossils of creatures that lived 2 million years ago. These remains are probably those of the ancestors of modern people.

In the late 18th century many slaves were sold in a market on Zanzibar until it was closed in 1873. Germany ruled Tanganyika from 1891 until World War I, when British troops invaded the country. British rule continued until the country's independence in 1961, when Julius Nyerere became its first president. ◆

Taoists

Tao (dao) is a Chinese word which means 'the way'. It is used both for the way to live your life and to express religious belief in the Truth (God). Taoists base their ideas and practices on the teaching of Lao Zi, who lived in the 5th century BC. His ideas were written down in the book called the *Dao De Jing*.

▼ **Find out more**
China's history
Confucians
Symbols

Taoism, like Confucianism, has influenced most Chinese people, whether or not they call themselves Taoists. It teaches harmony and balance between all opposites; these are called the yin and yang forces. Yin is female and watery; yang is male and solid. Taoists believe that by observing and learning from nature, people can find a way of always going gently, without using force. ◆

Tapestries

The so-called *Bayeux Tapestry* is really an embroidered picture. It is not woven as is a true tapestry. It can still be seen today at Bayeux in northern France.

Arras in Flanders was famous for tapestries in the late Middle Ages. In England tapestry was called arras.

Tapestries are woven pictures or patterns often used as wall hangings. They are made on a loom, and the pattern is woven into the textile by the weft threads. A high warp loom has the warp threads, which are neutral in colour, hanging vertically. The weft threads, in various colours, are woven backwards and forwards across parts of the warp to make the pattern.

Some tapestries made in the Middle Ages are quite like larger versions of miniature paintings from illuminated manuscripts. Later, artists such as Raphael painted 'cartoons' as designs for tapestry weavers to follow.

The finest tapestries were made in workshops in France and Flanders. In 1662 Louis XIV, King of France, developed the Gobelins workshop in Paris into a factory for making tapestries. ◆

▼ Find out more
Bayeux Tapestry
Weaving

BIOGRAPHY
Raphael

▲ This tapestry named 'Sight' is one of a set of six, called the Lady and the Unicorn, woven in the late 15th century. It would have brightened a castle room. Tapestries with thousands of flowers in the background are known as 'mille fleurs'.

Distribution
Throughout the world
Smallest species
Echinococcus granulosus, about 8 mm long, is one of the smallest species.
Largest species
Diphyllobothrium latum, which infects humans, may be 20 m long. Whales have even larger tapeworms.
Number of eggs
Very large in all species. The rat tapeworm may produce about 100 million eggs in its lifetime.
Phylum
Platyhelminthes (flatworms)
Class
Cestoda
Number of species
About 2500

Tapeworms are hermaphrodites; they have both male and female sex organs.

▼ Find out more
Invertebrates
Parasites
Worms

Tapeworms

Tapeworms are so-called because they are long and flat, like a tape measure. Adult tapeworms cannot see, smell or hear. They have no way of escaping from enemies, or of catching food. They are parasites and live protected inside the intestines of their final vertebrate hosts. Here they are surrounded by digested food, which is taken in through the body wall.

Adult tapeworms are made up of many body sections produced at the front end of the worm. The mature sections at the end of the worm are full of eggs. These are passed out in the faeces of the host animal. When the eggs are ingested (eaten) by an animal they hatch into larvae which develop a sac around themselves in the muscle. If the muscle (meat) is eaten by humans and other vertebrates the adult worms may develop. Cooking meat kills the larvae. ◆

Tasmania

Tasmania is an island off south-eastern mainland Australia. The climate is cool and wet. It has many mountains, forests, lakes and orchards and a small population. It is famous for its apples.

Once, Tasmania was joined to mainland Australia, but about 12,000 years ago the level of the seas rose and it eventually became an island. Wallabies, possums, penguins, Tasmanian devils, seals, and many species of snakes are some of the animals native to Tasmania. Its first inhabitants were Tasmanian Aborigines, a slightly different people from mainland Aborigines. Tasmania was named after the Dutchman Tasman who was the first European to visit it in 1642. In 1803 the first settlers arrived, mostly convicts transported from Britain. European numbers increased and they eventually destroyed the Aborigines. ◆

Area
68,330 sq km
Capital
Hobart
Population
472,200
Government
Part of the Federal government of Australia
Language
English
Currency
1 Australian dollar = 100 cents

The Tasmanian devil is a flesh-eating marsupial. It has strong teeth, a big head and a bushy tail. Extinct in Australia, it survives only in the remotest parts of Tasmania.

▼ Find out more
Aborigines
Australia

BIOGRAPHY
Tasman, Abel Janszoon

Taxes

The governments of countries need money to spend on things which benefit the whole country. Such things might include defence (the army, navy and air force), health services, education and roads. To get the money it needs, a government passes laws saying how much money individual people and businesses have to pay to the government.

One of the main kinds of tax is *income tax*. People have to pay a certain percentage of their income to the government. The amount of income tax people have to pay varies. Those who earn more money pay a higher percentage of their income in taxes. Companies may have to pay tax on a proportion of their profits. These are examples of *direct taxes* on individuals and businesses. Inherited wealth may also be directly taxed.

Other taxes are added on to the price of goods and services. In Europe the main tax of this sort is called Value Added Tax (VAT) and in the United States it is called a sales tax. These taxes are charged on what people spend, rather than on what they earn. They are called *indirect taxes*. Indirect taxes can be used to change people's behaviour. If a government wants drivers to use unleaded petrol in order to reduce pollution, it may put higher taxes on leaded petrol. If it wants to discourage people from smoking, it might put a high tax on cigarettes.

Governments draw up budgets every year, outlining how much they plan to spend and how much they are likely to raise from taxes. In Britain, for example, the Chancellor of the Exchequer (finance minister) makes a budget speech in November, and members of the public listen carefully to hear how much they will have to pay in taxes the following year. ♦

▼ **Find out more**
Economics
Government

Tea

Tea is made from the dried young leaves of a small bush that grows mainly in the subtropical areas of south-east Asia. It is a hardy evergreen plant which will grow at an altitude of up to 2000 metres. It likes an even rainfall and ground that is easily drained. Tea grows less quickly in the higher areas and this produces the best quality. India, China and Sri Lanka are the best-known tea-growing areas, but tea is also grown in Taiwan, Bangladesh and parts of Africa.

Tea is drunk by half of the people in the world. It was first introduced into England in 1657, and is the most popular drink sold in the UK.

Growing teas

Tea bushes are grown together in plantations. The bushes must be 3 years old before they can be plucked. They are pruned from 2 years on, to make sure that they produce plenty of leaves and that they grow to the right shape for easy plucking. Tea picking is a highly skilled job done mainly by women.

Types of tea

There are two main types of tea. One of them is green tea, which is picked and quickly and fully dried. It has a mild flavour and is very popular in China and Japan.

Black tea is darker in colour and stronger in flavour. This is the favourite type of tea in Europe. The leaves are only partly dried. They are then put into rolling machines which break up the leaf cells. This releases the natural juices which give tea its special taste. After rolling, the leaves are spread out in a damp atmosphere and left to ferment to a bright coppery colour. Then they are dried and graded according to size. Very often the names of types of tea describe their size and appearance. Examples are Orange Pekoe, Broken Pekoe, and Pekoe Fannings. The final stages are tasting and blending. ♦

▼ **Find out more**
Farming

Some teas like Assam, Darjeeling and Ceylon or Sri Lankan are sold on their own. Others are blended. English breakfast tea is a blend of Assam and Ceylon tea. Earl Grey is a blend of black China and Darjeeling tea flavoured with bergamot, a delicate citrus oil.

▶ Tea leaves on the bush. Tea is picked by hand: just one bud and the first two or three leaves are taken from each young shoot.

Teachers

In Britain every new teacher has to have a university degree. In some countries only the teachers of older pupils need a degree qualification. Teachers of infants and juniors may have a different type of training in a special college.

Teachers are people who help children and adults to learn. Most teachers work in schools, colleges and universities, but some work in other places. Children who cannot go to school may have home tutors. Some teachers help to train workers in their place of employment.

The first teachers

There have been teachers since ancient times. Teachers in the past were often priests who taught their own particular religious practices to their pupils. Jews, for instance, learned from their rabbis (religious teachers) in the synagogue. Even in the earliest days, though, some teachers thought about how children should be taught as well as what they were to be taught. The Roman writer Quintilian, who lived in the 1st century AD, said that study should be made interesting and that children should be encouraged by praise rather be told off for getting things wrong.

Teaching methods

The first schools were usually reserved for the children of rich families. Teaching for all children did not happen until the 19th and 20th centuries. Teachers then taught pupils what they would need to know to become useful workers later in life. Few students learnt more than the basics of reading, writing and arithmetic. The teacher would stand at the front of the class and get them to recite their multiplication tables from memory.

Some teachers, though, thought that children should be given the chance to develop their own interests and abilities, regardless of the career they would later follow. This led to the development of 'child-centred' teaching methods, where the teacher would encourage each child to develop their own interests and skills. Teachers nowadays are likely to use a mix of both these approaches. ◆

▼ **Find out more**
Schools

Technology

Cars, concrete and batteries are all examples of technology. So are bricks, bridges and computers. Technology is about making things which can do useful jobs. Sometimes scientific discoveries lead to new technology. For example, when X-rays were discovered, people soon realized that they could be used to take see-through photographs of bones. At other times, scientists do research so that new technology can be developed. Before the Space Shuttle could be built, scientists had to find materials to withstand the heat of the Earth's atmosphere.

Technologists

People who produce new technology are called technologists. *Materials technologists* develop new plastics, fabrics, metals and building materials. *Food technologists* find new ways to prepare, store and pack food. *Information technologists* deal with computers and their uses. Engineers are technologists. They produce vehicles, roads, bridges, chemical factories and machinery.

Alternative technology

Modern technology uses lots of energy. Metals are melted, bricks are baked, and engines and power stations need fuel. Many people think that we waste too much energy: we could use bicycles rather than cars; wind could turn our generators; and we could build with local stone instead of transporting bricks over huge distances. These ideas are called alternative technology.

FLASHBACK

Prehistoric people were the first technologists, making simple stone tools over a million years ago. But the age of modern technology began in the 18th century, with the first steam engines. By 1900 power stations were being built. These led to the world of electricity and electronics we know today. ◆

Technological 'firsts'

1290 Mechanical clock (the Chinese had water clocks in the 7th century)
1712 Steam engine
1790 Wrist-watch
1804 Railway locomotive
1826 Photograph
1839 Pedal bicycle
1876 Telephone
1879 Electric light bulb
1885 Petrol-driven car
1894 Radio signals
1903 Aircraft
1926 Television
1946 Electronic computer
1957 Space satellite
1959 Hovercraft
1971 Pocket calculator, Digital watch
1975 Home computer
1982 Compact-disc player, Synthetic vaccine
1984 Cellphone
1985 Genetic fingerprinting
1992 Interactive CD

Nanotechnology is the building of microscopic devices. Scientists can now move individual atoms on the surface of a material, using a special type of microscope. They can also make the parts for devices such as an electric motor that would fit on the end of a pin.

▼ **Find out more**
Biotechnology
Energy
Engineers
Industrial Revolution
Industry
Information technology
Materials

Teeth

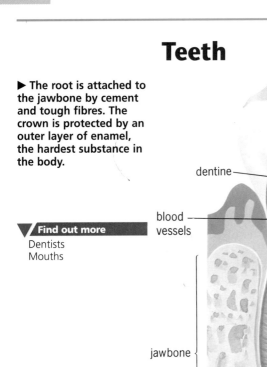

crown

dentine

blood vessels

jawbone

gum

root

nerve

▶ The root is attached to the jawbone by cement and tough fibres. The crown is protected by an outer layer of enamel, the hardest substance in the body.

▼ **Find out more**
Dentists
Mouths

▼ Teeth develop inside the jawbones before birth and first appear at about 5 months of age. By about 6 years children have 24 teeth. Twenty of these are milk teeth, and these fall out between 7 and 11 years. They are replaced by larger permanent teeth.

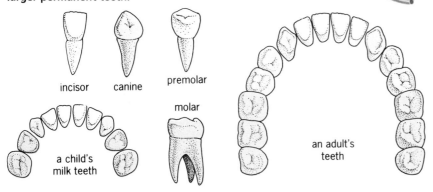

incisor   canine   premolar

molar

a child's milk teeth

an adult's teeth

Most vertebrates (animals with backbones) have teeth. They are used for holding, cutting and chewing food, so they have to be very strong. The part of a tooth that you can see is called the *crown*. Below the crown, hidden in the gums, is the tooth's root. This fixes the tooth firmly into the jawbone.

Most of the tooth is made of hard material called *dentine*. The crown is coated with an even harder material called *enamel*. Inside the tooth is a cavity filled with pulp. The pulp consists of blood vessels and nerve fibres.

A baby is born with no teeth showing. Hidden in the gums are tiny growing tooth buds. The baby has two sets of buds. The most rapidly growing set are the first, or milk, teeth. These appear during the first five years. Then they fall out and are replaced by the second, or permanent teeth. These should last all your life.

Special teeth

In most animals teeth are specialized for different jobs. Our upper and lower front four teeth have straight chisel-shaped ends. They are called *incisors* and are used for slicing mouth-sized pieces from food. On each side of the incisors is a single pointed tooth. This is a *canine* tooth. The canines are more developed in meat-eating animals and are used for puncturing the skin of their prey. Our back teeth, behind the canines, are broad-topped and bumpy. These are called *molars*. When you chew, you rub the upper and lower molars together, grinding up food into small pieces for swallowing.

In plant-eating animals the molars are large and have many ridges to enable them to grind up large amounts of tough grass and leaf material. Meat-eating animals also have special molars for chewing meat with the sides of their jaws. The edges of these teeth slide past each other like the blades of shears.

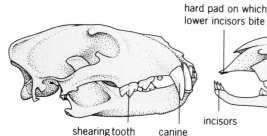

▲ **Lion (carnivore)**
Carnivores have long canines to kill prey and hold onto them. Massive shearing teeth crack bones and cut flesh.

shearing tooth   canine

▲ **Sheep (herbivore)**
Herbivores cut grass by moving their chisel-edged lower incisors sideways across a thick pad on the upper jaw.

hard pad on which lower incisors bite

incisors   molars

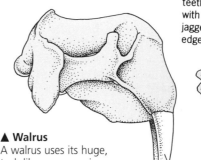

▲ **Walrus**
A walrus uses its huge, tusk-like upper canines like ice picks as it hauls itself out onto rocks or ice by the edge of the sea.

tusk

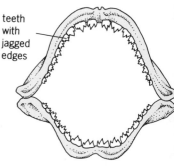

teeth with jagged edges

▲ **Shark**
The jagged teeth cut through flesh like a chainsaw and hold prey firmly in the mouth.

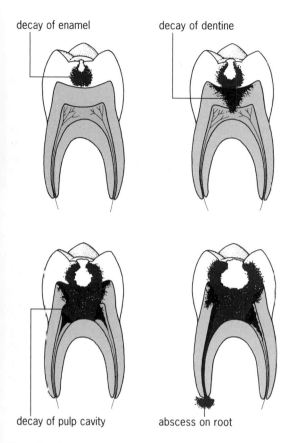

decay of enamel   decay of dentine

decay of pulp cavity   abscess on root

Tooth decay

If you eat too much sugar and do not clean your teeth regularly, you will get tooth decay.

Tooth decay occurs when small pieces of food, trapped in the teeth, are broken down by bacteria that live in the mouth. This produces acid which slowly damages the hard enamel coating the crown. Then it attacks the softer dentine, causing a hole or cavity. This results in toothache.

Apart from avoiding too much sugar, the best way to prevent tooth decay is by carefully brushing your teeth after every meal and before you go to bed. ◆

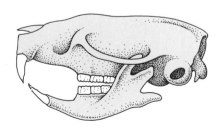

▲ Rat (rodent)
Rodents have long incisors with sharp edges, like chisels, for gnawing.

Telephones

A telephone lets you talk to other people almost anywhere on Earth, simply by pressing a few buttons. There are hundreds of millions of telephones in the world. A complicated network links all of these telephones. The network is really a telecommunications network. It carries fax messages, television and radio signals, and computer data as well as telephone calls.

Speaking and listening

You speak into, listen to, and dial numbers on a telephone receiver. When you speak, sound waves of your voice go into the mouthpiece. A microphone there changes the vibrations into patterns on a tiny electric current. These are called signals. These signals travel from the receiver into the telephone network. When people telephone you, signals come from the network to the earpiece of your receiver. There is a thin metal diaphragm inside the earpiece. This diaphragm vibrates and produces sound waves that enter your ear.

Getting connected

When you press the number buttons on your telephone, the receiver sends signals to your local telephone exchange. The exchange uses the numbers to route your call through the telephone network – to another local telephone, to another telephone exchange, or to the telephone network of another country.

The very first words spoken over a telephone were 'Mr Watson, come here, I want to see you'. They were by Alexander Graham Bell to his assistant, who was in the next room.

A thin optical-fibre cable can carry 40,000 digitized telephone calls at the same time.

The new models of portable phones will be able to communicate directly with satellites. They will work in even the most remote parts of the world.

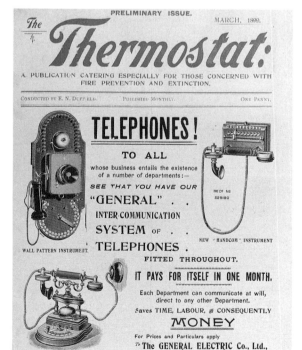

◀ An advertisement for telephones at the end of the 19th century.

▼ The routes of three different telephone calls from a caller in Oxford, UK. The local call goes only through the local exchange. The 0171 code sends the second call from the local exchange to one in Central London. The third call goes through four exchanges, two in the UK and two in the USA, before reaching its destination.

Forms of signal

The signals from your telephone go to the exchange as a changing electric current along a copper cable. From there, they can take many different forms before they get to the other telephone. Optical-fibre cables link most telephone exchanges together. Signals travel along optical fibres as pulses of laser light. Microwave beams, sent between dishes on tall towers, link some signals. Some international calls go along undersea optical-fibre cables, and some go via satellites high above the Earth.

The exchange digitizes most signals before they go through the telephone network. This means that the changing electric current is measured and changed into patterns of just the digits 0 and 1. It is easy to send these as pulses of electricity or light microwaves. The digital signals turn back to normal signals before the exchange sends them to your telephone.

Mobile telephones

Mobile telephones are a cross between a normal telephone receiver and a walkie-talkie radio.

Their signals go by radio to a radio mast. From the mast, the signals link into the normal telephone network. They only work while they are close to one of the special masts.

FLASHBACK

The Scottish-American inventor Alexander Graham Bell invented the telephone almost by accident. He was experimenting with a telegraph machine in 1875 when he realized it was transmitting sounds. He soon built the first telephone receiver. The first telephone exchange, which connected 21 people, was opened in 1878. By 1887 there were 150,000 telephones in the United States, 26,000 in Britain, 9000 in France and 7000 in Russia. Although the first automatic exchange was built in the 1890s, operators still worked most telephone exchanges until the 1920s. Electronic exchanges were developed in the 1970s. A transatlantic telephone cable was laid in 1956, and the first communications satellite, Telstar, was launched in 1962. Development of optical fibres carrying digital signals took place in the 1960s. ◆

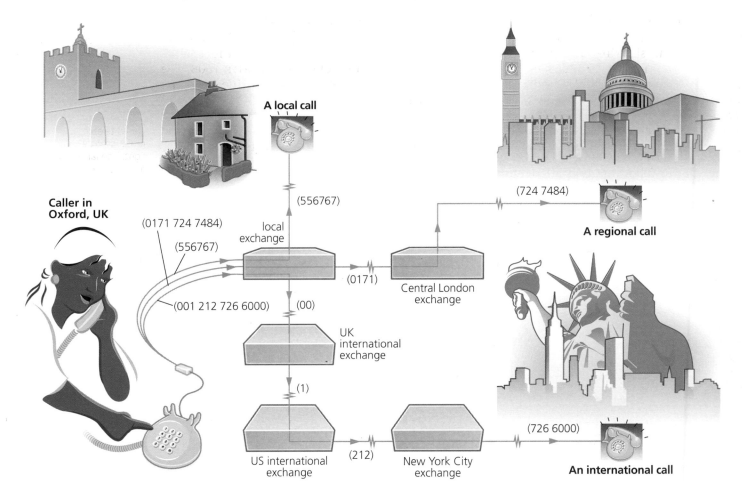

A local call

Caller in Oxford, UK

(0171 724 7484)

(556767)

(556767)

(001 212 726 6000)

local exchange

(00)

(0171)

Central London exchange

(724 7484)

A regional call

UK international exchange

(1)

US international exchange

(212)

New York City exchange

(726 6000)

An international call

Telescopes

When you look through a telescope, distant things seem nearer and bigger. A telescope collects light and funnels it into your eye, allowing you to see things that are too faint to be seen by eye alone. A telescope also lets you see more detail than your eye alone can see.

Telescopes with lenses and mirrors

The simplest telescope is a tube with a lens at each end. This kind is called a *refracting telescope*. The lens at the front collects light and brings light rays together to form an image of a distant object. The lens that you look through is called the *eyepiece*. It magnifies the image of what you are looking at. A *reflecting telescope*, or reflector, uses a concave (dish-shaped) mirror to collect light. The main mirror concentrates the light onto a smaller mirror which then reflects it into an eyepiece. Many telescopes are made so that the eyepiece can be changed. A stronger one gives more magnifying power.

The bigger a telescope's main mirror or lens, the more light it collects, and the fainter the things it can see. Larger telescopes also show more details than small ones. The blurring effects of the atmosphere often prevent telescopes from showing as much as they should. Astronomers try to overcome this by building telescopes on high mountains or putting them in orbit above the Earth.

Really big telescopes are always reflectors because they have many advantages over refractors. Astronomers seldom look through

large telescopes. Instead, they use them to take photographs or to focus light onto electronic instruments.

FLASHBACK

No one knows for sure who invented the telescope. Hans Lippershey, a Dutch spectacle-maker, is usually said to have been the first. He made a telescope out of two lenses in 1608. The next year, news of the invention reached the Italian astronomer Galileo Galilei, who built one for himself and turned it on the sky. In 1671, Sir Isaac Newton announced that he had made the first reflecting telescope. ◆

▲ A large reflecting telescope. The Anglo-Australian Telescope in New South Wales, Australia, has a main mirror 3.9 m across.

distant planet

Radio telescopes collect radio waves instead of light. The largest, built in a natural hollow in the ground in Puerto Rico in the Caribbean, is 300 m across.

The Hubble Space Telescope (HST) was launched into Earth orbit in April 1990. Shuttle astronauts had to correct the shape of its 2.4-m main mirror in December 1993. Orbiting clear of the atmosphere, HST can see far more clearly than telescopes on the ground.

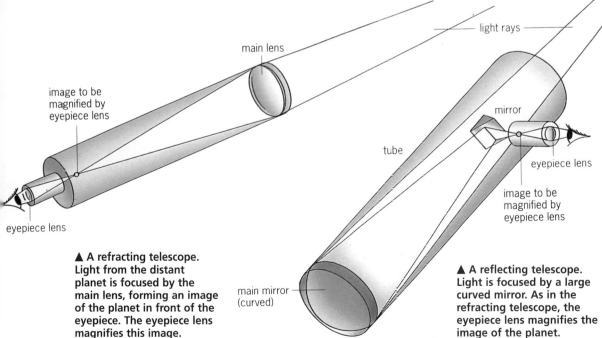

light rays

main lens

image to be magnified by eyepiece lens

eyepiece lens

tube

mirror

eyepiece lens

image to be magnified by eyepiece lens

main mirror (curved)

▲ A refracting telescope. Light from the distant planet is focused by the main lens, forming an image of the planet in front of the eyepiece. The eyepiece lens magnifies this image.

▲ A reflecting telescope. Light is focused by a large curved mirror. As in the refracting telescope, the eyepiece lens magnifies the image of the planet.

▼ **Find out more**
Astronomers
Lenses
Observatories

BIOGRAPHY
Galilei, Galileo
Huygens, Christian
Newton, Isaac

Television

Television (TV for short) is a way of sending moving pictures from one place to another. A television camera turns moving pictures into an electrical signal. The signals are sent to your television set by radio waves, via satellites, or through cables under the ground. A television set turns the signals back into a moving picture.

In developed countries, almost every home has a television set, and television has a huge effect on our lives. For most people, television is the main way of getting news and entertainment. We see events from around the world as they happen – sporting spectacles, wars and natural disasters. We laugh at comedy shows, become hooked on soap operas, learn about wildlife or science, and listen to people discuss current affairs.

In western countries most people watch a few hours of television each day. If they have the right receiving equipment, they can choose from dozens of channels. Unfortunately, some people become addicted to watching. Advertisers pay huge sums of money to have their products shown during the commercial breaks in television programmes, especially the programmes they know millions of people will be watching.

What is a TV picture?

Moving pictures are made by showing still pictures one after another very quickly. Each still picture, called a *frame*, is slightly different from the one before. Our eyes cannot react quickly enough to see one picture change to the next, and our brains are fooled into seeing a moving picture.

A television shows 25 or 30 frames a second. In the UK and most of Europe, television pictures are made up of 625 lines, and 25 frames are shown every second. The system is called PAL. In the United States and Japan, pictures have 525 lines and 30 frames are shown every second. This system is called NTSC. Each frame is made up of hundreds of thin horizontal lines. Each line is made up of hundreds of coloured dots. You do not see the lines or dots because they all merge together to make up the complete picture.

Television cameras

The job of a television camera is to turn the moving scene it sees into an electrical signal which can be sent to a television set. A lens collects light from the scene, just like an ordinary camera. Inside the camera is a light-sensitive device which scans the pattern of

The largest TV screen in the world was built by Sony for an international exhibition in Tokyo. It measured 45 m by 24 m.

The smallest TV screen is on a Seiko TV-wrist watch. It is black and white, and measures just 30 mm across.

In high-definition television (HDTV), pictures are made up of thousands of lines instead of hundreds. This makes pictures far more detailed.

In digital television, television signals are made up of a list of numbers. This gives clearer pictures. In the future, all television will be digital. It will also be in widescreen format, just like movie pictures.

In closed-circuit television, the signals from the camera are sent straight to a television. Security cameras in banks and shops are closed-circuit systems.

Video cameras record pictures which can be shown on television later. They use a light-sensitive microchip called a CCD to change the picture into an electrical signal. CCDs can also be used to make tiny TV cameras.

▶ **Signals from the aerial are separated into signals for brightness, colour and sound. The phosphor coating on the screen is made up of a huge number of coloured stripes. These stripes are lit up by the beams which are fired rapidly across and down the screen by the electron guns. The shadow mask makes sure that the beams only hit stripes of the right colour.**

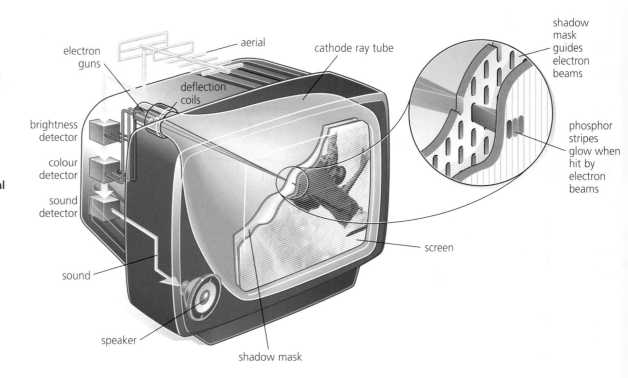

electron guns

aerial

cathode ray tube

shadow mask guides electron beams

deflection coils

brightness detector

colour detector

sound detector

phosphor stripes glow when hit by electron beams

sound

screen

speaker

shadow mask

light, line by line, dot by dot. It works out how much green, red and blue light there is in each dot, and codes this information in an electrical signal. When it has scanned one frame, it starts on the next. In this way, the moving scene is turned into an electrical signal. Sound is added to the signal later.

How a television set works

The job of a television set is to make a moving picture on its screen and to make sound through its speaker, using the signals it receives.

Signals from many different television stations arrive at your television set. The first thing it does is pick out the signal from the station you want. This is called *tuning*. Next, it takes the signal apart to make signals for red, green and blue, and for sound. It uses these signals to re-create the picture on its screen and to make sound.

Behind a television screen there are three 'guns' which shoot streams of tiny particles called electrons at the back of the screen. The red, green and blue signals control the output of one gun each. The beams of electrons are not themselves coloured, but they make red, green and blue light when they hit the screen. The sound signal is sent to an amplifier and speaker.

Flat-screen televisions work in a different way. The colour signals control the colour of thousands of tiny squares in a liquid-crystal display (the same sort of display that a calculator has). Researchers are also developing large, flat-screen televisions which you could hang on the wall like a picture.

Sending television pictures

There are several ways of getting the signals from a television camera to your television set.

In *terrestrial* (Earth-based) television, the signals are sent from a transmitter as radio waves and are picked up by a normal television aerial.

In *satellite* television, the signals are sent by microwaves to a satellite orbiting the Earth. The satellite sends them down again, scattered over a wide area. To collect them, you need a small satellite dish.

In *cable* television, the signals travel through electrical cables under the ground, straight to your television.

FLASHBACK

John Logie Baird gave the first public demonstration of television in England in 1926. However, he used a cumbersome mechanical camera with a huge spinning disc.

The pictures were shaky and blurred. By the time television broadcasting started in the 1930s in the UK and Germany, electronic cameras and television sets had been developed. The first programmes were news reports, song and dance shows, and films. The shows were live because pictures could not be recorded. All pictures were in black and white until 1953, when the first successful colour pictures were broadcast in the USA. ◆

▲ A television studio during the recording of a chat show. The host, panel and audience are closely surrounded by cameras recording their movements, and microphones recording what they say. The powerful lights above often make the studio very hot.

◀ A family in the 1950s watching one of the early colour television sets.

▼ Find out more

Cables
Cameras
Colour
Drama
Electronics
Films
Information technology
Radio
Satellites
Video

BIOGRAPHY
Baird, John Logie
Zworykin, Vladimir

Temperature

Temperature in °C

centre of Sun	15,000,000
surface of Sun	6000
bulb filament	2500
gas flame	2000
molten iron	1500
boiling water	100
Death Valley, USA	50
human body	37
warm room	25
melting ice	0
food in freezer	–18
Vostok, Antarctica	–80
liquid oxygen	–180
absolute zero	–273

▲ **Typical temperatures on the Celsius scale. On this scale, ice melts at 0 °C and water boils at 100 °C under normal conditions.**

Absolute zero is the lowest possible temperature that can exist. The Kelvin scale measures temperatures using absolute zero as its starting point. On this scale absolute zero is 0 K and water freezes at 273 K.

The lowest temperature yet reached was 0.00000003 (3 hundred-millionths of a degree) above absolute zero.

▼ **Find out more**
Atoms
Cold
Heat
Molecules
Thermometers

The temperature of an object tells us how hot it is, but this is not the same as the amount of heat the object contains. A red-hot spark from a fire is much hotter than a cup of tea, but the cup of tea is larger and has more heat in it.

We use thermometers to measure temperature. They are marked with a scale showing the degree of hotness. Most countries use the *Celsius* scale (sometimes called *centigrade*). On this scale, the numbers were chosen so that water freezes at 0 degrees and boils at 100 degrees. Sometimes, weather forecasts and cooking temperatures are given in degrees *Fahrenheit*. On this scale, water freezes at 32 degrees and boils at 212 degrees. On a warm day the temperature will be about 20 °C.

All materials are made up of tiny particles called atoms or molecules. These particles are constantly on the move. In solids and liquids, they vibrate; in gases, they shoot about at high speeds. If the temperature of something rises, this means that its particles are moving faster. Similarly, if its temperature falls, its particles are slowing down. But particles cannot slow down forever. There comes a point at which they can lose no more speed. This point is called *absolute zero*. It is the same for all substances, and is at a temperature of −273 °C (−460 °F). The *Kelvin* scale measures temperatures using absolute zero as its starting point. On this scale absolute zero is 0 K and water freezes at 273 K.

At one time, scientists thought that atoms and molecules would stop moving altogether at absolute zero. But from the laws of atomic physics, they now know that there must always be some movement. Absolute zero is the temperature at which atoms and molecules move as slowly as they ever can. ◆

Temperature tricks

Try this experiment to trick the temperature detectors in your skin. Get three bowls of water: one with cold, one with warm, and one with hot water (as hot as you would use for washing up). Put one hand in the hot water and the other in the cold. Now put them both in the warm water. What does it feel like?

Temples

▲ **The Parthenon, a temple dedicated to Athene, the goddess of wisdom. The Parthenon was built in the Doric style in the 5th century BC. Inside the temple was a statue of Athene made of gold and ivory.**

A temple is a particular type of religious building. Sometimes people believe that the god they worship actually lives in the temple, and sometimes the temple contains holy relics (remains). Christian, Jewish and Muslim places of worship are not now usually called temples.

The oldest temples in the world include prehistoric structures on the island of Malta dating from about 2000 BC, and there are many very impressive remains of Egyptian temples dating from a few centuries later.

The ancient Greeks built many beautiful temples, and several of them still survive in fairly good condition. The most famous is the Parthenon in Athens. However, we have to use our imaginations to visualize how wonderful they must have looked when they were new, brightly coloured and adorned with superb marble sculpture. Inside they sometimes had a huge statue of the god made of gold and ivory. The statue of Zeus in his temple at Olympia was so magnificent that it became one of the Seven Wonders of the World. Temples built by the Romans were often very similar to those of the Greeks, with a stately row of columns running round the exterior. However, the greatest of all Roman temples is very different. This is the Pantheon in Rome, erected in honour of all the gods. It is a vast circular building with a dome on top, and it still survives in amazingly good condition.

Some Hindu temples are small shrines, housing an image of God, but others are enormous, with towers built to look like the Himalaya mountains, the home of the gods. There is often a series of courtyards and halls, but the most important part is the shrine room for the image of God. Images help Hindus to feel a close relationship with God as they can bring their offerings and say their prayers in front of them.

Buddhists place statues of the Buddha in their temples. Sometimes the statue contains relics of the Buddha. These help people to feel close to him. They bring offerings of flowers and sometimes fruit to the temple and try to follow the example of the Buddha by looking at the peacefulness of his image and meditating in front of it.

FLASHBACK

The Temple of Solomon is often mentioned in the Bible. It was originally built by Solomon, king of the Hebrews, in about 950 BC and then destroyed by King Nebuchadnezzar II of Babylon in 587 BC. A second temple was begun about 60 years later, and this was enlarged to enormous size by King Herod from about 20 BC. It was destroyed by the Romans when they captured Jerusalem in AD 70. The Western (or Wailing) Wall in Jerusalem is the only surviving part of the Temple of Solomon. There is a picture of it in the article on Jews. ♦

▲ A Hindu temple in southern India. Here we can see an elaborately carved tower and images of the gods high on the walls.

▼ **Find out more**
Buddhists
Greek ancient history
Hindus
Jews
Seven Wonders of the World

Tennis

Tennis is a racket-and-ball game played indoors or outdoors on a grass, clay, wood or synthetic surface. Games can be played between two opponents (singles) or between two pairs of players (doubles).

The ball is put into play by *serving*. This is making a shot from behind the baseline which must bounce in the opponent's service court before being returned. The server throws the ball in the air and hits it, without allowing it to bounce, over the net and into the diagonally opposite service court. Players are allowed a second service if their first is a *fault*. Faults usually occur when the ball does not land in the service court or if the server steps over the baseline. If both services are faults, the opponent wins the point. Players serve from the right-hand side for the first point in a game, and then from alternate sides.

When a service is 'good', play continues until one player fails to return the ball fairly into the opponent's court and so loses the point. A player must hit the ball after it bounces once or, except when returning serve, on the volley.

In order to win a game, one player or pair must score four points and lead by at least two points. The first point is called 15; the second, 30; the third, 40; and the fourth, *game point*. A score of zero is called *love*. If the score becomes 40–40, it is called *deuce* and the game continues as if the score were 30–30. The next player or pair to win a point is said to have the *advantage*, and if they win the next point, they win the

▲ Bjorn Borg (Sweden) set a modern record by winning five successive Wimbledon men's singles (1976–1980).

▲ A modern tennis racket and ball. Racket frames were traditionally wooden, but in recent years aluminium and carbon-graphite rackets have become very popular.

The oldest tennis trophy is the Davis Cup, a men's international knockout competition first held in 1900. A similar competition for women, the Federation Cup, has been played since 1963.

Tennis balls are made of rubber and covered with wool or manufactured fibres. In major tournaments the balls are replaced at the end of the first seven games and then after every nine games. This is because they change shape and pressure slightly when hit, and are likely to bounce differently.

A ball that hits one of the lines bounding the playing area (singles or doubles court) is called 'in', as is a service that hits a line bounding the service court. A ball that lands in court after hitting the net cord is 'in'. A service hitting the net cord and then landing in the correct service court is called a let, and that service, whether first or second, is replayed.

Women champions have enjoyed longer reigns than men in tennis. Margaret Court (Australia) won a record 24 grand slam titles (11 Australian, five French, three Wimbledon, five US), twice as many as the leading man, Roy Emerson (Australia).

The first Wimbledon tournament was held by the All-England Croquet Club to raise money to repair their pony-roller. A profit of £10 was made. In 1996, the total prize money at the Wimbledon championships was over £6.4 million.

▼ **Find out more**
Sport
BIOGRAPHY
Borg, Bjorn
Navratilova, Martina

game. Otherwise, the game will continue until one side gets a two-point lead. Service changes to the other player or pair after each game.

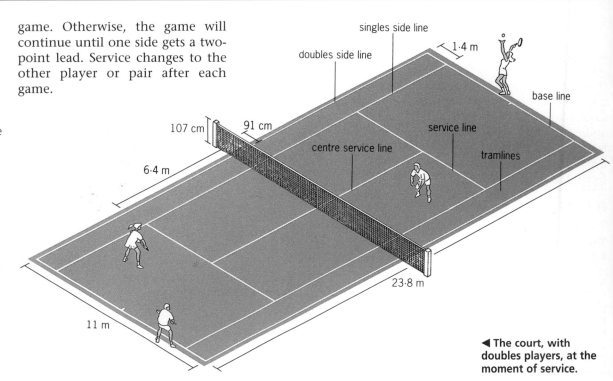

◄ **The court, with doubles players, at the moment of service.**

Six games are needed to win a set, provided that there is at least a two-game lead. If not, a *tie-break* game may be played when the game score is 6–6. The first side to win two sets, or three in some tournaments, wins the match.

Players change ends after the first game of a set, and then after every two games. In doubles, partners take it in turns to serve their service games, but either player may serve first in a new set. The players receiving service must do so from the same side throughout a set. After return of service, either partner may play the ball.

Competitions

Tennis tournaments are played all over the world, sometimes as part of 'grand prix' series, with big prizes for the winners. The US, French, Australian and Wimbledon Opens make up the 'grand slam'. Both men and women are ranked or 'seeded' from 1 to 200 by computer, according to their performances over the year.

FLASHBACK

'Real tennis' began as a game played inside French monasteries in the Middle Ages. It was called 'real' (royal) because kings played it. In Britain in the 1860s some people took tennis outdoors and invented 'lawn tennis'. Rules for the game as we know it were drawn up for the first tournament at Wimbledon, in 1877.

Until 1968, tennis was played chiefly by amateurs, with only a small band of professionals touring the world and playing in special tournaments.

Since 1968 all the major tournaments have been 'open' to both amateurs and professionals; today, all the top players are professional. ◆

The tie-break was introduced to most tournaments in the 1970s after some amazingly long matches. The most famous took place at Wimbledon in 1969, when Pancho Gonzales (USA) beat Charlie Pasarell (USA) 22–24, 1–6, 16–14, 6–3, 11–9. Nowadays when the game score reaches 6–6, players have a tie-break game. They swap service every two points and the first to win seven points takes the game and set, as long as there is a two-point lead. If not, the tie-break continues until a two-point lead is established.

▼ **The exciting, balletic Suzanne Lenglen (France) took Wimbledon by storm in 1919, when she won her first singles title, starting the cult of the personality in tennis. She went on to win six Wimbledon and six French Open singles titles and an Olympic singles before turning professional in 1926.**

Termites

The biggest termite queens are very large. The largest, when swollen with eggs, may measure 10 cm in length. For part of the year she may produce thousands of eggs a day, but she cannot do this all the time. She is unable to move her huge body, but is cared for by her worker children. Termite queens are very long-lived. Most survive for 15 to 20 years, and some may live to be 50.

▼ **Find out more**
Ants
Bees
Grasslands
Insects

▼ **An Australian termite mound. Some termite mounds are huge. They contain food stores and fungus gardens, cells for eggs and young, and the cell in which the queen and her mate live.**

Termites are sometimes called 'white ants', for most of them are about the same size as ants and, like ants, they live in huge family colonies. Many are paler than ants, and, unlike ants, termites live only in the warmer parts of the world. At a certain time each year, huge numbers of winged termites emerge. Hosts of birds and other creatures look forward to this, because termites are valuable food for them. But plenty survive, and after a brief mating flight they shed their wings and found a new colony.

The termite nest includes a queen, who is the mother of all the insects in the nest, and a king, who is their father. Much of the work of the nest is done by young termites, which hatch out not as grubs but as small replicas of their parents; in some species, however, there are true workers, as with ants. Soldiers form another group. These may be very large and have such big jaws that they have to be fed by the workers. Soldiers of some species employ chemical warfare. They have pointed heads from which they squirt a sticky stuff that entangles any invaders.

Termites eat only plant food, and because of their numbers they may be pests, damaging crops or the timbers of buildings. Where they do not conflict with humans, they are very important recyclers of dead material. ◆

Terrorists

People who use violence or threaten to kill people to achieve some political aim are called terrorists. They try to create terror either to gain publicity from the world media for their cause or to pressurize governments into agreeing with their demands.

Terrorist methods include bombing, shooting, taking hostages and hijacking (taking over by violence) vehicles, ships or aeroplanes. Hostage-taking and hijacking are often done in order to pressurize governments to release captured terrorists or to gain ransom money, which can be used to buy arms or explosives. Many victims of terrorism are innocent civilians.

Some governments sometimes use methods that are similar to those of terrorists in order to intimidate groups that oppose them, either in their own or another country; but these actions are not usually called terrorist.

After World War II, the state of Israel came into being after many years of conflict between armies occupying Palestine and opposing groups of Jewish and Arab terrorists. Terrorism continued in the Middle East as Palestinian groups used it to try to get their lands back from Israel. One notorious action was when a small group of Palestinians entered the Olympic village at the Munich Olympic Games in 1972 and murdered Israeli athletes.

Bombing campaigns were used by the Irish Republican Army to further its aim of uniting Northern Ireland and the Republic of Ireland. Some terrorists use acts of violence against their own government. In 1995 a car bomb blew up a US government building in Oklahoma City, killing 168 people.

Some governments have been accused of supporting terrorists, giving them arms, money and a safe place to live while they plan violence against other countries. ◆

Airports have been terrorist targets in many countries. Security is one way of combating this, particularly by searching people's luggage for weapons and explosives. Ways of searching include X-ray machines, metal-detection equipment, and dogs which can sniff out explosives.

▼ **Find out more**
Airports
Explosives
Ireland's history
Israel
Palestine

Textiles

In 1801, the Frenchman Joseph Marie Jacquard (1752–1834) invented an automatic loom that could weave patterns in cloth. The weaving mechanism was controlled by cards punched with holes that were fed into the loom. Different sequences of holes produced different patterns. Fearing that the Jacquard loom would put them out of work, French weavers at Lyon tried, unsuccessfully, to drown its inventor in the River Rhône.

▶ Producing a batik design in Java, Indonesia. Batik is a method of decorating textiles with dye. First, a design is drawn on a piece of fabric. Those parts which are not to be dyed are covered with wax. The fabric is then dipped into the dye. The wax-coated areas do not absorb the dye and the wax is then removed by boiling the cloth. This process can be repeated to obtain different shades or to apply new colours.

Textiles are all around you: they form the clothes you wear during the day, and the bedding that you sleep in at night. You wash with textiles, using a flannel and a towel made of fluffy textiles that soak up water easily. In your home and school, more kinds of textile make up the carpets, curtains and furniture covers. Cars contain textiles on the seats, inside tyres and in filters used in the engine. And textiles are used to make many other useful products, including belts, parachutes, tents, sails, nets and bandages.

Making textiles

A textile is a cloth or fabric, and it is made from fibres. These include cotton, silk, flax and wool, which are natural fibres that come from plants and animals. Synthetic fibres are made in factories and include nylon, polyester and acrylics. Many textiles contain a mixture of natural and synthetic fibres.

The first step in producing most textiles is to twist the fibres together to form a yarn or thread, like the cotton on a reel or the wool in a ball of wool. Yarn is made by spinning machines. The yarn may then be dyed a particular colour before being made into a cloth

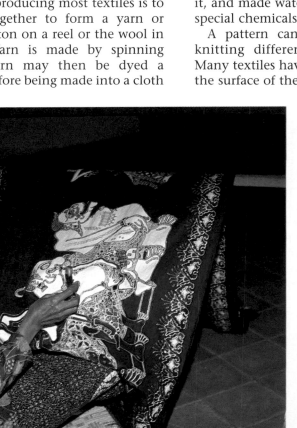

or fabric. This is mainly done by *weaving*, in which two lengths of yarn are woven together on a loom, and by *knitting*, in which the yarn is linked in loops. *Felting* is a third method of textile manufacture, in which the fibres are stuck together.

The textile may next need various kinds of treatment. It may be washed or cleaned to remove dirt and impurities, bleached to whiten it, and made waterproof or fireproof by adding special chemicals.

A pattern can be formed by weaving or knitting different coloured yarns together. Many textiles have patterns that are printed on the surface of the fabric by large rollers bearing the pattern of coloured dyes, in the same way that pictures are printed on paper using coloured inks.

Other kinds of textile

Brocade is a fabric with a raised pattern that is woven into it. Chiffon is a light woven textile. Corduroy is a fabric with ridges running lengthways. Damask is a fabric with a woven pattern on both sides. Denim is a strong woven cotton cloth often used for jeans and other tough garments. Lace is an open fabric containing small holes and elaborate patterns made by stitching or by knotting the yarn. Linen is a fabric made from flax. Muslin is a very light and plain open woven fabric. Satin is a fabric woven with a smooth surface so that it appears shiny. Tweed is a heavy woollen cloth with a rough surface. ◆

Area
514,820 sq km
Capital
Bangkok
Population
58,300,000
Language
Thai
Religion
Buddhist
Government
Parliamentary monarchy
Currency
1 baht = 100 satang

Thailand

Thailand is a country in South-east Asia. It is a tropical country of rice plains, mountains and rainforests. Much of the rainforest has been cut down in recent years. The central area is a flat, damp plain criss-crossed with irrigation canals and ideal for growing rice, which is the staple food. Thailand is the world's leading exporter of rice. The climate is hot and sticky most of the year round. During the rainiest season, between May and October, more than 1500 millimetres of rain may fall. A 'cool' season lasts from November to February, but even then average temperatures are about 26 °C.

Bangkok, the capital of Thailand, is a busy city of nearly 6 million people. This is where the king and queen of Thailand have their Grand Palace. Although Bangkok's streets are full of cars and modern buildings, the city's 300 Buddhist temples, many with curved roofs in orange and green tiles, give Bangkok a distinct atmosphere. Most Thais are Buddhists, and a majority of the men spend some part of their lives as monks learning about their religion in one of the country's 27,000 *wat* (temples). Monks in orange robes can be seen walking the streets in Bangkok, as they do all over Thailand.

The economy is expanding rapidly, notably through new industries such as electronics. As well as rice and the new industrial products, Thailand exports textiles, rubber, tin and gems (rubies and sapphires).

FLASHBACK

Civilization is very old in Thailand: items manufactured in bronze have been found dating back 6000 years. Thailand (called Siam until 1939) has been a country for over 700 years, and remains of more ancient cities date back to at least AD 500. The Thai country has been invaded by the Burmese and others, but it is the only country in South-east Asia which has never been a European colony. The name Thailand means 'land of the free'.

Thailand was occupied by Japan in World War II. Since then, the army has played a leading role in the country's affairs (it owns two of the six television channels). Army generals have ruled the country for much of the time. Student demonstrations led to the fall of military governments in 1973 and 1992. ◆

▼ **Find out more**
Asia
Buddhists
Kings and queens
Palaces
Rice
Vietnam War

▼ Wat Phra Keo, one of many Buddhist temples in Bangkok, is an example of classic Thai architecture, with its pointed, many-tiered roofs. The shrines, some covered with gold leaf, often house religious relics.

Theatres

Theatres are buildings put up especially for plays, ballet or operas to be performed in. They have to do several things. They must be big enough to hold a lot of people, and let them see and hear clearly. They must allow actors to get on and off the stage easily. And there must be room to store all the things like scenery and costumes which are needed when you put a play on. If they look splendid and have comfortable seats, so much the better.

Theatres today

Theatres today are built in all shapes and sizes. Some of them have the audiences sitting all round the actors, like a circus. This is called theatre-in-the-round. Some of them have a 'picture-frame' for the action to take place in; and some of them have the audience sitting in curved rows rising up around the stage. Some theatres, like the Swan Theatre in Stratford-upon-Avon, have been built to look like theatres of the past. The Swan Theatre has a stage very like the ones Shakespeare's plays were first seen on, but it is a modern theatre none the less.

Japanese theatre

In Japan, people developed a particular kind of theatre for staging the ancient drama called the *No*. The masked actors entered the plain, square stage across a structure like a little bridge from the Mask Room. There was no scenery, but sometimes simple objects like a bell or a tree were brought on to indicate where the action was taking place.

Most theatres have what is called the Green Room. This is a room in which the actors wait before they go on stage. Originally it is said that the room was painted green because green is a soothing colour. Green, it was believed, would calm the nerves of the actors before they performed. In theatres nowadays the room is not always green, but it is still called the Green Room.

▼ An artist's reconstruction of a scene from *A Midsummer Night's Dream* at the Globe Theatre, London, in Shakespeare's lifetime. A new Globe Theatre has recently been built in London, following this earlier design.

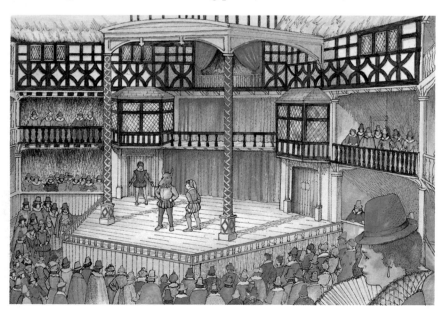

▲ The famous theatre at Epidaurus in Greece. This theatre was built around 200 BC and seats more than 12,000 people. It has a neutral 'backdrop' of beautiful mountains. You can still sit here in the open air to watch a play, just as audiences used to do in the days of ancient Greece.

Greek theatres

The first theatres in Europe were built in Greece about 2500 years ago. They were open to the sky, and often built against a hillside, with rows of stone seats rising up around a circular space for acting. This space was called the *orchestra*, which originally meant dancing-floor. Behind the orchestra was a building called the *skene*, from which our word scene comes. Sometimes the skene contained a crane for lifting an actor who needed to 'fly' in order to play a god or goddess.

Shakespeare's theatre

Another famous theatre was also open to the sky, the Globe Theatre in London. This was the theatre that William Shakespeare wrote his early plays for, in the reign of Queen Elizabeth I. It was built in the shape of a circle surrounding the stage. In one of his plays, Shakespeare calls it a 'wooden O'.

The stage was bare, but there was a balcony above it where actors could play scenes on the battlements of a castle or in the upper window of a house. The building behind the stage was called the 'tiring house'. The actors would use it as a dressing room.

The audience would stand on the ground around the stage. They were sometimes called groundlings. Richer people could pay more money and sit in the galleries going all the way round the theatre. It burnt down in 1613, when a cannonball fired from the stage set it alight, but was rebuilt the following year.

The theatre goes indoors

If people wanted to put on a play with scenery, they had to have a different sort of building. In the early years of the 17th century a kind of play called a masque was popular. This had a lot of spectacular scene-changes, with clouds floating to and fro across the stage and gods flying past in chariots. Masques were often set to music as well. A play like that would be ruined by bad weather, so this sort of play was performed in great halls with roofs, including Whitehall in London.

The stage was differently shaped from that of Shakespeare's time. Very often the designer who painted and arranged the scenery wanted the audience to look at it as if it were a picture, from the front and not from the side. So they built a frame around the stage and sat the audience in front of it, all looking the same way. This frame was called a proscenium.

In the limelight

To put on a play indoors you need lights. At first people used candles, but they were not very bright, and sometimes theatres caught fire.

Gas lighting was used in Britain in the reign of Queen Victoria. This provided the footlights and also limelight, a bright light used for the spotlights. We still use the expression 'in the limelight' when we are talking about someone being the centre of attention. But there was still a fire risk. Covent Garden, London, was twice gutted by fire in the early 19th century. Once electric light started to be fitted after 1887, theatres became safer.

The scenery used in Victorian theatres was very complicated. Some theatres even managed to have horses racing on rollers. But it took so long to set up the stage for such plays that audiences got tired of them.

Whatever theatres are like in the future, they will still have to do what theatres have always done: provide a setting in which people have an opportunity to watch and hear (and sometimes join in with) actors performing live drama. Often, the people who work in and visit the theatre prefer a simple, direct way of staging things, and so are leaving special effects to the cinema and to television. ◆

Many actors believe it is bad luck ever to mention the title of Shakespeare's play *Macbeth*. They always refer to it as 'the Scottish play' or some other form of words that does not mention the title.

▼ A theatre does not have to be a permanent building. These performers in Covent Garden, London, have set up a temporary street theatre to entertain their open-air audience.

Thermometers

A digital thermometer displays its readings using numbers.

A maximum and minimum thermometer records the highest and lowest temperatures reached over a period of time.

The first thermometer was invented by Galileo Galilei in 1592. Known as a thermoscope, it used the expansion of water to measure temperature.

▲ An electrical thermometer, with digital display, for taking body temperature.

▶ Some thermometers are just a row of squares printed on a strip of paper. The squares are treated with special chemicals so that they change colour at different temperatures. The green rectangle indicates a body temperature of 36 °C, which is just below normal (37 °C).

Thermometers are instruments that measure temperature (hotness). Some depend on the fact that liquid mercury or alcohol expands when heated. The more the temperature rises, the more the liquid in the bulb in the end of the thermometer expands and moves up the narrow tube. The position of the liquid gives the temperature on the scale. Other thermometers are electrical. They have a tiny probe connected by wires to a measuring unit. When the temperature changes, the flow of current from the probe changes. Electrical thermometers are widely used in industry. One of their big advantages is that the measuring unit can be far away from the probe. Often, the reading appears as a number, like the numbers displayed on a calculator. ◆

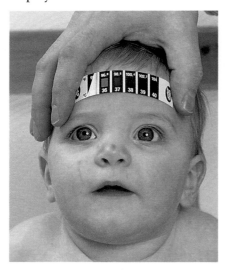

▼ **Find out more**
Cold	**BIOGRAPHY**
Heat	Galilei,
Temperature	Galileo
Thermostats	

Thermostats

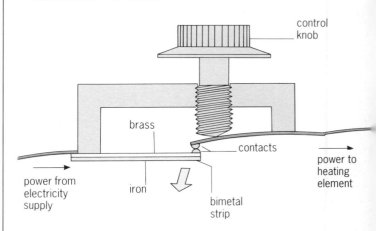

Most irons, ovens and refrigerators have a thermostat in them. Its job is to keep the temperature steady by automatically switching the power on and off. For example, when an iron is just hot enough, the thermostat cuts the power. It brings the power back on again when the iron cools. You can see the light going on and off as the thermostat does its job.

Many thermostats have a tiny bimetal strip in them. In fact, this is two strips of different metals stuck together. When the bimetal strip warms up, one metal expands more than the other. This makes the bimetal strip bend. The contacts move apart and the power is cut. When the temperature falls, the bimetal strip straightens and the contacts touch again.

Not all thermostats are electrical. Some gas ovens have a thermostat that controls the flow of gas. ◆

▲ A bimetal thermostat. When the temperature rises, the bimetal strip bends. This separates the contacts and cuts the power. Turning the control knob and pushing the contacts together means that a higher temperature will be required before the bimetal strip bends enough to separate the contacts and cut the power.

Part of the brain acts as a thermostat, helping to control body temperature.

The first thermostat was patented by Andrew Ure in Scotland in 1830. Bimetal thermostats were first used on electric irons in 1924.

▼ **Find out more**
Central	Metals
heating	Refrigerators
Electricity	Temperature
Heat	Thermometers

Third World

The term 'Third World' began to be used in the 1950s during the Cold War to mean those countries which did not belong either to the western powers or to the communist bloc. The rich nations of western Europe, North America and Australasia made up the 'First World'. The USSR and Eastern Europe used to be known as the 'Second World'.

Most Third World countries are poorer countries trying to develop their economies to catch up with the richer countries of the world. These days such countries are more likely to be called developing countries or less developed countries (LDCs). Most are in the southern hemisphere, so people talk about the divide between countries of 'the North' and 'the South'. ◆

▼ **Find out more**
Cold war
Developing countries

Thunderstorms

Thunderstorms come from the biggest clouds in the sky. The clouds are called cumulonimbus and have a wide flat top and a narrower bottom. They bring heavy rain and often there is thunder and lightning.

Thunderstorm clouds have electrical charges. At the top the charge is positive, while at the bottom the charge is negative. The ground below a thunderstorm is also positive. When all these charges build up, there is a lightning flash which very briefly lights up the sky. Thunder is the noise we hear when the air in front of a stroke of lightning is rapidly expanded because of the great heat. Thunderstorms have bigger raindrops than other clouds. This is because the raindrops move up and down inside the cloud again and again, and each time they do another circuit inside the cloud they collect more water. When the drops are very big, they are too heavy to stay in the cloud. Sometimes the air in the cloud is cold enough for the raindrops to freeze, and then they fall as hailstones. ◆

▼ Find out more

Clouds
Hailstones
Monsoon
Rain

BIOGRAPHY
Franklin,
 Benjamin

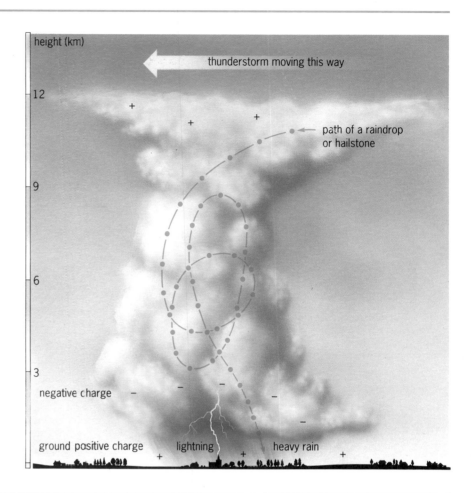

Tibet

Tibet lies to the north of the Himalaya mountains in central Asia. Much of the region is a plateau which is over 4000 metres above sea-level, the largest and highest plateau in the world. The landscape is barren, very dry and very cold. Much of it is uninhabited. About half of the small population herd yaks, sheep and cattle. In many parts of Tibet the yak is the only pastoral animal that can live in the harsh conditions. It is used for transport, meat and milk, and yak butter is drunk in Tibetan tea with salt.

Tibetans are Buddhists and the most senior Buddhist monk, the Dalai Lama, used to be ruler of the country. In 1950 Chinese troops invaded Tibet; later they destroyed hundreds of ancient monasteries there and murdered many of the monks. The Tibetans rebelled against the Chinese in 1959 but were defeated. The Dalai Lama fled to India with many of his followers and set up a government in exile there. Most Tibetans regard the Chinese as occupiers. Since 1978 the Chinese have allowed more freedom to practise religion and some temples have been restored, but Tibetans are still leaving the country as refugees. ◆

Area 1,221,600 sq km
Capital Lhasa
Population 2,079,000
Language
Tibetan, Chinese
Religion Buddhist
Government
Autonomous region of the People's Republic of China

◀ The Potala, in Lhasa, was the Dalai Lama's residence until 1959.

▼ Find out more

Asia
Buddhists
China
Himalayas

BIOGRAPHY
Dalai Lama

Tidal power

The world's first major tidal power station was opened in 1966, on the Rance estuary, Brittany, France. Its 24 generators have a total power output of 240,000 kilowatts – about a tenth of the output of a large fuel-burning power station.

Along every coast the tide comes in and out twice a day as the sea-level rises and falls. The tides are caused by the gravitational pull of the Moon as the Earth slowly rotates beneath it. The movement of water can be used as a source of energy to generate electricity. This is called tidal power.

In a tidal-power scheme, a dam is built across the mouth of a river. When the tide comes in, water rushes through tunnels in the dam and fills a basin behind. When the tide goes out again, the basin empties, and water rushes back through the tunnels. In the tunnels, a flow of water in either direction turns huge turbines. These drive generators.

▼ In this tidal power station, each generator is turned when the tide comes in and turned again when it goes out.

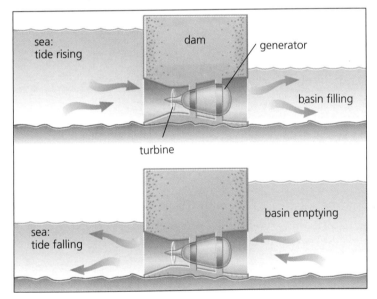

Tidal-power stations burn no fuel, so they produce no polluting gases and do not add to global warming. However, they are expensive to build and can have a damaging effect on the local environment and its wildlife. Finding suitable sites is difficult because few places in the world have a big enough height difference between high and low tides. Also, the tides occur at different times each day, so power cannot always be generated when it is most needed. ◆

Tides

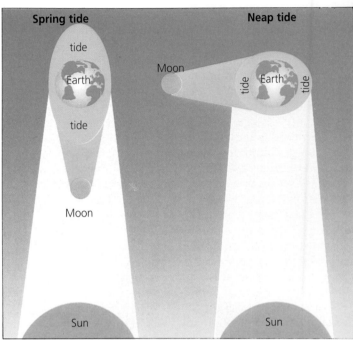

At high tide, the sea rises high up the beach. At low tide, it falls low down the beach. This happens because the Moon's gravity pulls on the Earth and its oceans.

The sea nearest the Moon is pulled most strongly so it bulges slightly towards the Moon. The sea furthest from the Moon is pulled less than elsewhere, leaving another bulge. There are high tides at the two bulges and low tides in between. As the Earth spins, places move in and out of the bulges and their sea-level rises and falls.

Most places have two high tides a day, but the shape of the coastline can affect the tides of the water. In enclosed seas like the Mediterranean the tides are very slight. Between the Isle of Wight and Portsmouth in southern England there are four high tides a day.

The Sun's gravity also pulls on the oceans, causing extra-high (spring) and extra-low (neap) tides (see the diagram above).

High tides send a tidal wave, called a bore, up some rivers. On a spring tide, the Severn bore in England can be over 2 metres. ◆

▲ Twice a month, the Sun, Moon and Earth are lined up. Then the Sun's pull adds to the Moon's, making the rise and fall of the sea more than at any other time. These are called spring tides, though they do not only happen in the spring. In between, there are neap tides, when the change in sea-level is least.

Timing the tides
High tides are 50 minutes later each day.
Highest tidal range
At the Bay of Fundy in Canada, the sea-level can rise more than 15 m between low and high tides.

Tigers

▼ **An Indian tiger threatening.** Its powerful front legs, muscular shoulders and long back legs adapted for leaping, make it a superb hunter of large prey.

Tigers are big cats of forest country. At one time they were found throughout much of eastern and southern Asia, but now they survive mainly in India and Sumatra. The biggest tigers come from the forests of Siberia.

Male tigers live alone in large territories, although these may overlap the living areas of several females. They warn other males away by roaring when they are near the boundaries of their living areas. They are chiefly active at twilight or at night, using their sight and sense of hearing rather than smell to stalk their prey. They may travel up to 20 kilometres in a night and can leap as much as 10 metres in a single bound. They are good swimmers and can climb quite well. Their main food is large mammals such as wild pigs, buffalo and deer. But in spite of their size and strength, tigers fail in about 90 per cent of their hunts. Tigers rarely attack humans, but those that do often get a taste for it.

Tiger cubs can be born at any time throughout the year. They do not hunt for themselves until the age of about 18 months, and they stay with their mother until they are two or three years old.

Although tigers are protected animals, they are often killed illegally, even in nature reserves. Unless this killing is stopped, it is likely that there will be no tigers left in the wild by the early 21st century. ◆

Timber

Timber is useful wood. Carpenters recognize two main types. These are hardwood and softwood.

Softwood comes from coniferous trees, which are mostly evergreen, have needle-like leaves, and can survive through long, cold winters. Foresters plant conifers because they grow quickly. Softwood timber is useful for building, for packaging (for example, crates) and for chipboard, which is made out of wood chips mixed with glue and pressed together.

Hardwood comes from broad-leaved trees. Temperate hardwoods include oak, beech and ash. Tropical hardwoods include teak, mahogany and rosewood. These hardwoods are very tough and make good furniture as well as special items such as boats and cricket bats. Hardwood timber can also be sliced into veneers to cover softwood chipboard for cheap furniture.

Softwood timber is obtained mostly from the huge coniferous forests of North America, Russia and Scandinavia. Hardwood timber comes mainly from the tropical forests of South America, Africa and South-east Asia.

Timber products

There are many products made from timber and these can be divided into two main groups.

Wood products are made directly from wood. They include hardboard for furniture; lumber for building materials and toys; plywood for boats, aeroplanes and doors; round timber for bridges and telephone posts; sawmill wastes for animal bedding and packing material; and veneer for furniture.

Chemical products are made by breaking down the wood using chemical processes. They include charcoal for fuel; lignin for plastics and road-building materials; and wood pulp for rayon, paper and photographic film. ◆

Wood is used for fuel more than for any other purpose. In developing countries about 90 per cent of the people rely on firewood for cooking and heating.

All of the world's hardwoods, except the eucalyptuses, grow very slowly and supplies are dwindling fast. To halt the destruction of this world resource, many areas of hardwood forest are being protected in reserves. In spite of this many trees are still cut down illegally.

Time

We all know what it means to say that time is passing by, but it is very hard to say exactly what time is. We notice natural things around us change with time – plants and animals, the seasons and weather, the Sun, Moon and stars. Anything that changes regularly can be used as a clock to keep track of time.

Now that people all round the world are in contact through telephones, television and fast air travel, it is important that everyone agrees to keep to the same standard time and measures it in the same way.

Days and hours

The day is the most important period of time for us. Our daily pattern of sleeping, eating and working is almost built-in as a kind of natural clock.

We divide days up into 24 equal hours. Hours have not always been equal. Before mechanical clocks came into use in the 14th century, an hour was one-twelfth of the period of daylight, so in winter hours were shorter than in summer. The number 24 has been handed down from the distant past. It might have been any number. The ancient Babylonians based their numbers on units of 60, rather than units of 10 like us, and it is from their example that we use 60 minutes in an hour and 60 seconds in a minute.

Days start at midnight and we use a.m. and p.m. to show whether a time is before or after the middle of the day. They are short for the Latin words *ante meridiem* and *post meridiem*. The 24-hour clock is often used instead to avoid confusion – 1.00 p.m. is called 13.00, 2.00 p.m. becomes 14.00 and so on.

Standard time

Noon (midday) at a particular place occurs when the Sun gets to its highest point in the sky. Countries further east are already into the afternoon or evening while people living further west still have not reached midday. As the Earth spins, places across the world, from east to west, have noon one after another.

If everyone measured time from when it is noon where they are, at every longitude the time would be different. People used to reckon time locally in that way, but as travel got more common, especially when the railways were built in the 19th century, having everyone using different local times became very confusing indeed. So, in 1880, the whole of Britain adopted the average local time at Greenwich (where the Royal Observatory was) as its standard time. It was called Greenwich Mean Time (GMT).

At an international conference in 1884, the world was divided up into 'time zones', each about 15 degrees of longitude wide, though the exact divisions were set to be convenient for the country and state boundaries. The standard time in each zone differs from the zones either side by one hour.

If you travel to another country you usually have to alter your watch. The further you go,

The world's first public time signal was a red ball on top of the Royal Observatory at Greenwich, put up in 1833. It was dropped from the top of a pole at 1 p.m. precisely every day.

The large publicly displayed clocks built, for example, on cathedrals from the 14th century onwards helped spread a sense of time among people.

The 24-hour clock

12-hour clock	24-hour clock
1 p.m.	13.00
2 p.m.	14.00
3 p.m.	15.00
4 p.m.	16.00
5 p.m.	17.00
6 p.m.	18.00
7 p.m.	19.00
8 p.m.	20.00
9 p.m.	21.00
10 p.m.	22.00
11 p.m.	23.00
12 p.m.	24.00
1 a.m.	01.00
2 a.m.	02.00
and so on.	

In Einstein's theory of relativity neither space nor time could exist without each other. Time became the fourth dimension (there being three dimensions of space – length, breadth and height).

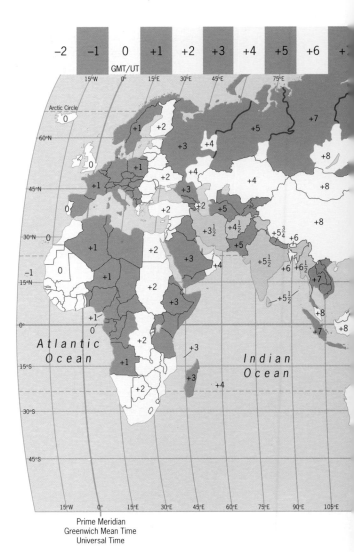

Prime Meridian
Greenwich Mean Time
Universal Time

east or west, the bigger the time change. Travelling by air, you can cross several time zones in just a few hours. When you arrive, your body has to adjust. Long-distance travellers sometimes suffer from tiredness, called 'jet-lag', as they get used to the time change.

Daylight-saving time

During World War I (1914–1918) Britain and the USA set their clocks one hour ahead of their usual standard times. The idea of this was to give extra time for working in the evening when it was light and so save electricity. It is much easier to get everyone to change their clocks than to persuade them to get up and go to work an hour earlier! Britain still goes onto British Summer Time (BST), one hour ahead of GMT, during the summer months. The government announces the days on which the clocks are to be changed.

Measuring and keeping time

Anything that happens at regular intervals or at a steady rate can be used as a clock to measure time. It could be the burning of a candle, the swing of a pendulum or the natural vibrations of tiny atoms and molecules. Quartz crystals vibrate regularly, and clocks based on them can accurately keep track of time.

The spin of the Earth gives us our day. Astronomers keep a check on the Earth's rotation speed by watching the stars travel across the sky at night. It used to be the main way of keeping standard time accurate. Today, though, 'atomic clocks' have taken over as the best time-keepers.

International atomic time is kept by special clocks in laboratories round the world. These are the clocks that are used to give the time pips broadcast by radio services and the speaking clock service on the telephone, so that anyone can set a clock accurately. ◆

In ancient Egypt short intervals of time were measured by the flow of water through a hole at the bottom of a vessel; the inside of the vessel was marked with a scale of hours. The Egyptians also used sundials to measure hours; these were more accurate than their water clocks.

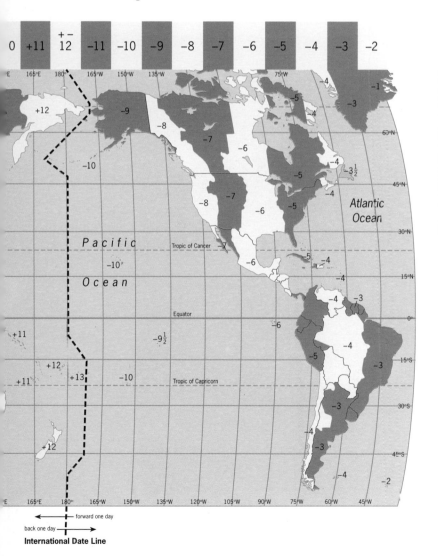

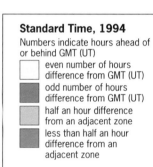

Standard Time, 1994

Numbers indicate hours ahead of or behind GMT (UT)

- even number of hours difference from GMT (UT)
- odd number of hours difference from GMT (UT)
- half an hour difference from an adjacent zone
- less than half an hour difference from an adjacent zone

◀ The world is divided into 24 time zones, each about 15° of longitude wide. The numbers on this map indicate how many hours ahead or behind Greenwich Mean Time (GMT or UT) a place is.

The International Date Line is the 180° line of longitude which marks where one day ends and another begins. Travelling from east to west across the line you go forward one day, and travelling west to east you go back a day. The line has been adjusted so that it does not cross a country.

← forward one day
back one day →
International Date Line

▼ **Find out more**
Calendars
Candles
Clocks and watches
Day and night
Latitude and longitude
Relativity
Seasons

BIOGRAPHY
Einstein, Albert

Tin

The chemical formula for tin is Sn.

Tin is a soft, silvery-white metal. It does not rust or corrode, and is mainly used in tin-plating. The 'tin cans' in which many foods are packed are not really made of solid tin but of thin sheets of steel coated with tin. The tin stops the cans from rusting. The other main uses for tin are in the solders used for joining soft metals and wires, and for making alloys such as bronze and pewter.

Pure tin is found in nature, but it is usually made from tin ores, especially cassiterite. Most of the world's tin ore comes from Malaysia, Bolivia and Indonesia. At one time Cornwall in England was an important source. ◆

▼ Find out more
Alloys
Metals

Toads

Largest
Marine toad: length up to 24 cm; weight about 1.3 kg
Number of eggs laid
About 3000 for common toad
Lifespan
May be over 30 years
Subphylum
Vertebrata
Class
Amphibia
Order
Anura (frogs and toads)
Number of species of true toads
About 380

Toads are tailless amphibians that look and live like their relatives the frogs. Before the world was as fully explored as it is today, people thought that they could tell the difference between the two sorts of animals quite easily, for in general toads have drier and wartier skins than frogs. By examining the way in which their bodies are built, scientists could see that toads and frogs had the bones in their shoulders differently arranged, and that toads had no teeth. But many more kinds of amphibians have been discovered, and they have often been named 'frogs' or 'toads' regardless of how they are built.

True toads generally have powerful poison in their warty skin. When predators touch the toad, this poison is released onto them. The fire-bellied toad shows its bright underside to an enemy to signal 'red for danger'. Usually toads are active at night, when they hunt for any small live creatures that they can catch on their long, sticky tongues, which flick in and out of their mouths in less than one-tenth of a second. ◆

▼ Find out more
Amphibians
Frogs
Newts
Salamanders
Streams

Tobacco

Tobacco is a leafy plant which originally came from South America. It was first grown commercially in Virginia in the 17th century from seeds imported from Trinidad and Venezuela. Today it is grown in any area which has a high humidity, high temperature and plenty of rainfall.

Tobacco contains the drug nicotine. This kills insects that eat the plant, but when smoked or chewed by people it acts as a drug. The leaves of the plant are harvested and tied to long sticks. They are then placed in curing barns where the leaves are heated and dried. Cured tobacco is rolled into cigars, or shredded and blended to make different brands of cigarettes and pipe tobacco. ◆

In many countries a tax is imposed on the sale of tobacco. This tax can bring in quite a lot of revenue.

Nicotine is an addictive drug, which is why smokers find it hard to give up. Tobacco smoke contains about 3000 different constituents, many of which are damaging to human health.

▼ Find out more
Smoking

▼ The flowers of the tobacco plants are pinched out at an early stage. This makes the leaves grow larger before they are picked.

Togo

The West African country of Togo is long and narrow with a short coastline. Grassy plains and hills cover much of this hot, rainy land, and these are divided by mountains which rise in the centre.

Most of the Togolese live by farming. Many northerners are Muslims, who dress in flowing white robes. The southerners usually wear western clothes. Togo produces phosphate rock (which is used to make fertilizers), cotton, peanuts and coffee for export.

Togo suffered tragedy when thousands of homes were destroyed by coastal erosion, which was the result of the damming of the River Volta in neighbouring Ghana from 1960 to 1965.

Germany ruled Togo before World War I, when it was taken by Britain and France. In 1922 it was officially divided between Britain and France by the League of Nations. The British part joined with Ghana in 1957. The French part became independent in 1960. ♦

Area
56,785 sq km
Capital Lomé
Population 4,100,000
Language
French, Ewe, Kabré, Gurma
Religion
Traditional, Christian, Muslim
Government
Republic
Currency
1 (CFA) franc
= 100 centimes

▼ **Find out more**
Africa
African history

▼ **Colourful, energetic Togolese dancers at a festival.**

Tombs

◄ The tomb of Lenin in Moscow. Thousands of people have filed past the glass-covered coffin which contains his embalmed body.

Tombs are special places for the burial of the dead. The earliest tombs were natural rock caves. Later, people cut chambers into rock, such as the tomb where according to tradition Jesus was buried.

The Egyptians built pyramids above ground as tombs for their kings and nobles. The most elaborate underground tombs were the catacombs of ancient Rome where the early Roman Christians buried their dead.

Famous tombs include those of the Unknown Soldier in Westminster Abbey, London, beneath the Arc de Triomphe in Paris, and in Arlington Cemetery, Virginia, in the USA. ♦

The tomb at Mount Li, where Zheng, the first Qin emperor of China, was buried was so large that there was room for 8000 life-size soldiers made from terracotta pottery. See China's history for a photograph of the soldiers.

▼ **Find out more**
Burial mounds
Cemeteries
China's history
Churches
Pyramids

BIOGRAPHY
Lenin, Vladimir Ilyich

Tonsils

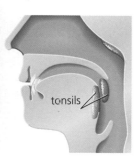

tonsils

If you open your mouth, look in a mirror and say 'aah', your tongue will flatten and you will be able to see the back of your throat. On either side of the back of your tongue you will be able to see a small, usually wrinkly, bump. These are your tonsils. They are made of lymphatic tissue. This contains large numbers of the white blood cells that protect you against germs.

When you get an infection, extra protective cells in the tonsils make them enlarge and they can become painful. This condition is called tonsillitis. If they get permanently enlarged, doctors sometimes suggest that they should be taken out. ♦

▼ **Find out more**
Human body
Immunity
Mouths

Tools

Scissors are tools. So are drills, spades and tin-openers. A tool is any device which helps you do a job. At home, people use tools for preparing food, putting up shelves, doing the gardening and mending the car. The type of tool depends on the job to be done. Hand tools use the force of your muscles. Power tools are driven by another energy source, such as electricity or compressed air, to make jobs even easier and faster. Much larger machine tools are used in factories for cutting and shaping metals, plastics and other materials. Machine tools can make lots of identical parts one after another. Often they are controlled by computer.

Power tools

Heavy drills powered by compressed air were used in the 1860s during the building of the Mont Cénis tunnel through the Alps between Italy and France. They are widely used in construction work today, for example to break up tarmac on roads.

Hand-held electric drills became popular after World War II. Extra parts enabled do-it-yourself work to be done with the drill converted into a jigsaw, circular saw or sander. Nowadays specialized electric hand tools include screwdrivers, hammer drills, chain-saws and hedge-trimmers. Most are powered from the mains, but the use of rechargeable batteries is on the increase in convenient cordless models.

Machine tools

Machine tools are generally faster, more powerful and more accurate than hand-held tools. In machine tools the piece to be worked is attached to a workbench or other fixed surface, and the tool itself is moved forwards,

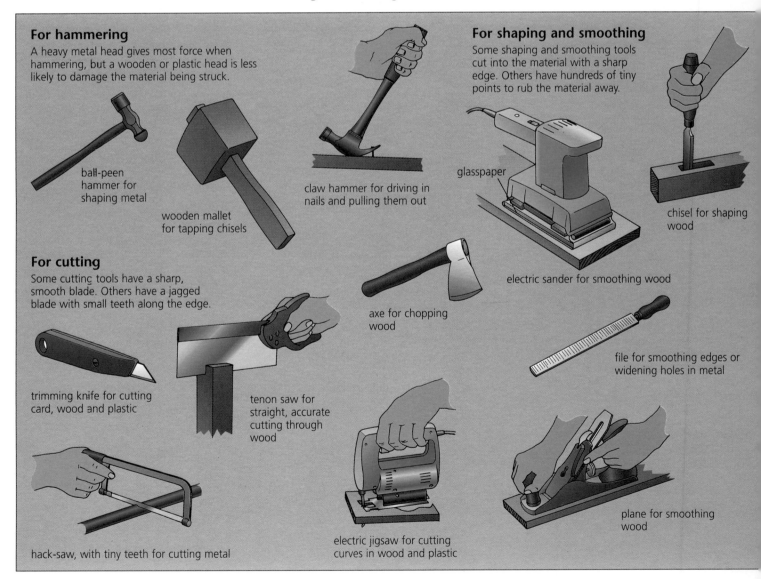

For hammering

A heavy metal head gives most force when hammering, but a wooden or plastic head is less likely to damage the material being struck.

ball-peen hammer for shaping metal

wooden mallet for tapping chisels

claw hammer for driving in nails and pulling them out

For cutting

Some cutting tools have a sharp, smooth blade. Others have a jagged blade with small teeth along the edge.

trimming knife for cutting card, wood and plastic

tenon saw for straight, accurate cutting through wood

axe for chopping wood

electric jigsaw for cutting curves in wood and plastic

hack-saw, with tiny teeth for cutting metal

For shaping and smoothing

Some shaping and smoothing tools cut into the material with a sharp edge. Others have hundreds of tiny points to rub the material away.

glasspaper

chisel for shaping wood

electric sander for smoothing wood

file for smoothing edges or widening holes in metal

plane for smoothing wood

along or across the workpiece. Specific machine tools include lathes, grinders, shapers, planers, drilling and milling machines.

Lathes were important in the growth of mass production, for example of cars, early in the 20th century. In the 1980s computerized control of machine tools and processes such as welding brought about a 'second revolution' in mass production.

FLASHBACK

In Stone Age human settlements, six basic hand tools were used: the adze (for shaping wood), auger (for boring holes), axe, knife, hammer and chisel. The saw and drill were invented in the Bronze Age. Romans used the plane. In the Middle Ages the brace, the tenon saw and the spokeshave came into use. From the 18th and 19th centuries machine tools gained in importance over hand tools. ◆

◄ Final machine polishing of a turbine blade. Turbines like this can be produced entirely by computer-controlled machine tools, directly from the engineer's computerized design.

You can find out more about early human settlements in the article on Prehistoric people.

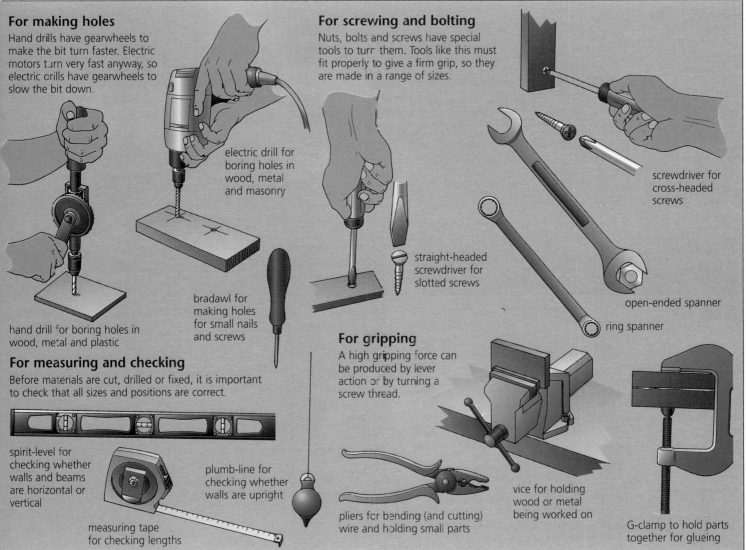

For making holes
Hand drills have gearwheels to make the bit turn faster. Electric motors turn very fast anyway, so electric drills have gearwheels to slow the bit down.

electric drill for boring holes in wood, metal and masonry

hand drill for boring holes in wood, metal and plastic

bradawl for making holes for small nails and screws

For measuring and checking
Before materials are cut, drilled or fixed, it is important to check that all sizes and positions are correct.

spirit-level for checking whether walls and beams are horizontal or vertical

measuring tape for checking lengths

plumb-line for checking whether walls are upright

For screwing and bolting
Nuts, bolts and screws have special tools to turn them. Tools like this must fit properly to give a firm grip, so they are made in a range of sizes.

screwdriver for cross-headed screws

straight-headed screwdriver for slotted screws

open-ended spanner

ring spanner

For gripping
A high gripping force can be produced by lever action or by turning a screw thread.

pliers for bending (and cutting) wire and holding small parts

vice for holding wood or metal being worked on

G-clamp to hold parts together for glueing

Torches

▼ Find out more
Batteries

The word 'torch' comes from the Latin *torquere* meaning 'to twist'. The first torches were made of twisted hemp.

▼ **A torch powered by a battery.**

People have always found it convenient to be able to carry light around with them. The Romans twisted fibrous hemp or flax into a flaming bundle or brand that could easily be held. Dipping it in oil or fat made it burn brightly. Oil lamps and lanterns replaced this simple torch, and a modern torch is powered by electricity, using electrical cells put together in a battery. Some torches use batteries that are rechargeable. Some are designed to flash, or give coloured light as a warning. Some have small fluorescent tubes, giving longer battery life. ◆

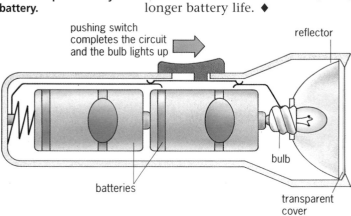

pushing switch completes the circuit and the bulb lights up

reflector

bulb

batteries

transparent cover

Tornadoes

Tornadoes are especially common in the southern states of the USA, where they are known as 'twisters'.

A tornado is sometimes called a whirlwind. It is a terrifying wind which destroys everything in its path. It looks like a violent, twisting funnel of cloud which stretches down from a storm-cloud to the Earth.

A tornado is narrow and rushes across the land at speeds of 30 to 65 km/h. The wind twists up within the funnel at speeds of up to 650 km/h. It sucks up dust, sand, even people and animals like a giant vacuum cleaner and dumps them where it dies out.

A tornado is quite different from a hurricane. It is smaller, faster and more violent. Tornadoes are most frequent far inland, unlike hurricanes. ◆

▼ Find out more
Hurricanes
Wind

Tortoises and turtles

Tortoises and their relatives are called chelonians. They are among the most ancient of reptiles, for they have survived since the days of the dinosaurs and have changed very little since then. They are easily recognized, for they carry heavy armour. Only their heads, tails and legs are outside the shell that encases and protects their bodies. Land tortoises can pull all of themselves into it, and some even have a hinged shell so they can shut themselves up completely.

A bony box

A chelonian's shell is made of bone protected on the outside with horn. It is in two main pieces. The carapace covers the back, while the plastron protects the animal's underside. The bones of the carapace are fused to those of the animal's back, shoulders and hips, so it has a very stiff body, and cannot move very fast or breathe easily. A chelonian has special muscles to draw air into its lungs.

Food

Tortoises, terrapins and turtles do not have any teeth in their mouths. Instead they have sharp-edged, horny jaws, with which they cut and tear their food. Land tortoises feed mainly on plants, terrapins chiefly on the flesh of various small creatures, and sea turtles eat sea grasses, seaweeds and some animals. The leatherback turtle feeds almost entirely on jellyfishes. Terrapins often hold food with their front feet. Tortoises also use their front feet to hold leaves down while they tug at them with their jaws.

Distribution
Mainly in warm parts of the world
Largest
Leathery turtle: over 2 m in length and weighs over 500 kg
Smallest
Striped mud turtle (terrapin): 7.5–12 cm long when full grown
Lifespan
Very long. Some large land tortoises may live for 200 years or more. Even some small species may live for over 50 years.
Subphylum
Vertebrata
Class
Reptilia
Order
Chelonia
Number of species
About 240 (there are many subspecies of some species)

In Europe, the word 'tortoise' means a land chelonian. 'Terrapin' means one that lives in fresh water and 'turtle' is one that lives in the sea. In America, the word 'turtle' is generally used to mean any chelonian.

◄ **At one time, giant tortoises, like this one from the Galapagos Islands, were found on many remote tropical islands. Most of them were hunted to extinction.**

▲ This green turtle has come ashore at night to dig a nest in which to lay her eggs.

Most chelonians are slow-moving. A few, such as the pancake tortoise, are quite agile and can scuttle away from danger and hide under rocks.

The big-headed terrapin has very long claws and may clamber into trees when it is out of the water.

Conservation of chelonians includes controlling trade in the live animals, which are often used as pets, and not allowing turtle shells or skins to be imported.

▼ **Find out more**
Endangered species
Reptiles

Eggs and young

Many terrapins are brightly coloured, and this is important in choosing a mate. A few species change colour in the breeding season. On land, some tortoises have scent glands. The males mark the area in which they live, while some females produce scent to attract the males.

After mating, the females dig a nest pit with their hind legs, and here the eggs are laid. Some species lay very few eggs – the pancake tortoise just one a season – while the green turtle lays as many as 200 in a single clutch. Some tortoise eggs are round, some oval, and some are pointed at one end, like a bird's egg. In some cases the shell is hard, and in others it is leathery. Once the eggs are laid, the female covers the nest and leaves it. Compared to birds, young tortoises and turtles usually take a long time to hatch – seven months for the Galapagos giant tortoise, smaller species usually less than half this time.

Sea turtles migrate round the oceans, travelling many thousands of kilometres before they return to their breeding beaches. Some freshwater species may make journeys of about 20 kilometres, even crossing dry land to get to suitable nesting places. In cool places they hibernate through the winter.

Tortoises and turtles are important in the folklore of many parts of the world. In spite of this, humans are now driving some kinds to extinction and most are much rarer than they were 100 years ago. ◆

Tourists

Tourists are people who travel within a country or to another country for recreation. Tourists create many jobs in the places they visit and tourism is now one of the most important industries in many countries. About three-quarters of tourists still come from the richest 20 countries, and most of them visit Europe and North America. However, a growing number of people are visiting other parts of the world, for example going on photographic safaris in Africa's game parks or back-packing through remote mountain ranges such as the Himalayas.

Although tourists help create employment, they can also bring problems to the places they visit. Many poorer countries have to spend a lot of money building roads, airports and other facilities for tourist resorts. This may mean that less money is available to spend on more essential services for the country's own inhabitants. Tourists can also cause damage and pollution to the areas they visit. The ancient monuments of Egypt and Greece attract many millions of visitors, but they are suffering damage from the traffic fumes the tourists bring with them. The Alpine mountain ranges of Austria and Switzerland are very popular with winter sports enthusiasts, but their trees, mountain plants and meadows are disappearing to make way for ski slopes and chair lifts. ◆

▼ **Find out more**
Holidays

▼ The 10 countries most visited by tourists.

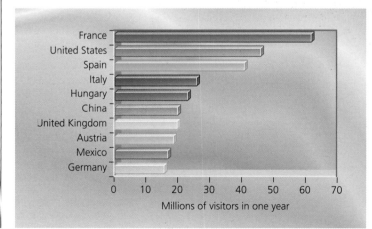

France
United States
Spain
Italy
Hungary
China
United Kingdom
Austria
Mexico
Germany

0   10   20   30   40   50   60   70

Millions of visitors in one year

Toys

The biggest toyshop in the world is Hamleys in London, which has been going for more than 200 years. It has been on its present site since 1901. The shop has 4180 sq m of floor space on six floors. During the Christmas rush, Hamleys employ over 400 people to help sell their toys.

Toys are playthings that have been used throughout the centuries by children, and adults too, for fun and entertainment. They come in all shapes and sizes. Even something as simple as a stick or a round stone can be used by children as a toy. Many toys, games and sports have developed from the use of such everyday items by children.

Some of the best-loved toys are dolls and teddy bears. These are miniature versions of humans and animals. Teddy bears were given their name after the American President Theodore (or Teddy) Roosevelt. When he was president at the beginning of the 20th century, a cartoonist drew him refusing to shoot a bear cub which had walked into his camp while he was on a bear-shooting expedition. A sweet-shop owner asked if he could call his new toy after him, and he agreed. Soon toy manufacturers saw the opportunity to make money by selling 'Teddy bears' to children. Many children keep their teddy bears or other toy animals until they are adults.

▶ This wooden rocking horse was made in the 17th century for quite a small child. It is very strong and simple. Rocking horses like this one continued to be made for many years.

▲ A traditional wooden toy village made some time between 1920 and 1930 in Germany. The children who played with it probably added other small toys when they set it out. Their grandparents could have played with a village just like it.

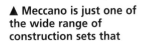

▲ Meccano is just one of the wide range of construction sets that give children the chance to build their own models.

◀ Electronic toys like these robots can be built using microchip technology.

▶ A steam locomotive stops at a model country station. Model railways have been around almost as long as the real railways and provide hours of fun for children – and adults.

Toys and learning

Some toys help children to learn skills that will help them in later life. The earliest types of play probably began as children were taught to hunt or to protect themselves. The club or stick of a child in prehistoric times would probably have been played with in much the same way as a toy sword is played with today.

Archaeological evidence suggests that children in all cultures throughout history have played with small versions of humans or animals. These miniature versions of real beings and objects, like dolls and doll's houses, encourage imaginative play and allow children to act out aspects of their own daily lives.

Puzzles and board games sharpen children's minds and teach them to think quickly. Construction kits, such as Lego and Meccano, give children the chance to use their hands to build models of vehicles and buildings.

Toys and technology

In the early days of toy-making, most toys were simply carved from wood. From the 16th century onwards, such toys were made in Germany and sold in many other countries. Quite young children were given jobs in the toy industry, assembling and painting these toys.

However, toy-making has always kept up with advances in technology and scientific

◀ Throughout the world people sell simple toys on the street. Here is a boy selling wire toys in Botswana.

knowledge. As makers of clocks and watches learnt how to use balances and counter-balances, the pendulum and springs, these ideas were introduced into toy-making. Mechanical toys were made for royal children in Europe as early as the 18th century, and later similar toys were mass-produced for many more children.

After the railways had appeared, clockwork was used to power model railways. In Britain the firms of Hornby and Triang produced very popular models, but one of the best in the world was the firm of Marklin in Germany. At the beginning of the 20th century they produced models of Stephenson's 'Rocket', the first train to run on a public railway. In 1984 one of these models was sold at Sotheby's in London for £25,500.

Later in the 20th century, batteries and electricity began to be used as well as clockwork for toys. Now there are many toys and games which use the same microelectronic technology which has been developed by the computer industry.

Where toys are made

Many of the toys sold today are made in the Far East, particularly in Hong Kong and Taiwan. In these countries toys can be mass-produced at prices that millions of families throughout the world can afford. However, there is sometimes a danger that cheap toys will be unsafe for small children, so many countries now set safety standards and have campaigns to warn parents and children about dangerous toys. ◆

▲ A lady called Miss Miles furnished this dolls' house in the 1890s. She bought the house in a toyshop and a carpenter added the small rooms to the side.

▲ A teddy bear made in about 1935 by the German firm of Shuco. It is made from fur fabric, with felt pads and glass eyes. Many others just like it would have been made in the same factory.

▼ **Find out more**
Board games
Dolls
Models

BIOGRAPHY
Roosevelt, Theodore

Tracks and signs

▶ Having cracked the nut open, this red squirrel will discard the shell. If you find empty shells, you can tell which animal has been eating the nuts by the way the shell has been opened.

▼ This owl pellet, from a short-eared owl, has been opened up to show what the owl has eaten. The small bones and grey fur are probably from a mouse or a vole.

▶ Look for tracks in wet mud (often found near gates and paths) and fresh snow. Rabbit tracks show how rabbits put their hind feet down in front of their fore feet as they hop along. Dogs and foxes make similar tracks, but dogs often have their toes spread apart. When a fox is trotting, its back feet often cover the tracks of its front feet. The thrush leaves tracks of its wings as it takes off in the snow.

Many animals are shy and distrust human beings. Often the only way to know that they are about is to find their tracks. By becoming a nature detective and studying these tracks, you will be able to find out a great deal about the animals without disturbing them.

Usually creatures take the same routes through their territories, so they make pathways through the grass or woodlands. The size of a path is often a clue to the type of animal. Obviously, the run made by a vole will be smaller than that of a badger or a deer.

Sometimes, when the ground is soft, or after a fall of snow, you will be able to see footprints. Each kind of animal makes a different sort of footprint, so you can identify the creature just from this. The first thing to do is to count the number of toe marks on each footprint. Badgers and otters have five toes on each foot. Dogs, cats and foxes have four. Cattle, sheep and deer walk on the tips of two toes, while horses and ponies leave the mark of the single toenail which forms the hoof on each foot. The distance between the footprints will tell you whether the animal was walking or running along the track. The footprints are spaced further apart when running.

When an animal leaves its den, it often grooms itself. You may find tufts of a deer's hair caught in a rubbing post, or the scarred tree that badgers have used for cleaning their claws.

When they feed, animals leave clear marks of their presence. Squirrels crack nuts with their powerful teeth, while mice and voles nibble them open. Deer and other large plant-eaters often browse on the lower branches of trees, or they may eat the bark. Each kind of animal has its own way of feeding. Look at the height from which the food was taken and see if you can find toothmarks, for these may tell you the size of the creature. Some animals make food stores. What has been hidden, where and how will again be clues to a particular species.

The tracks and signs of birds and smaller animals are usually more difficult to find. The exception is the nests of birds and some insects, but these should always be left completely alone unless you are absolutely sure they are deserted. Some birds, including hawks, owls and gulls, form pellets of the indigestible parts of their food. These are not at all unpleasant to handle and can tell you exactly what the bird has been eating. You may find that they contain the tiny bones of birds or mice and the wing cases of beetles. ◆

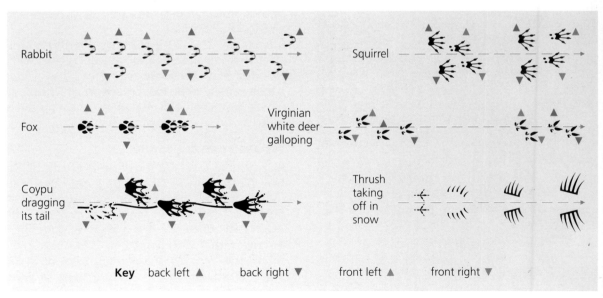

Trade

Have you ever swapped something of yours for something else your friend had? If so, you were trading. Trade takes place when people or countries exchange things. These days, most trade involves money – when things are swapped directly for other things we call it *barter*.

The last time you bought a bar of chocolate, yours was just the last in a whole series of trades. Before it was sold to you, the chocolate was probably bought from a wholesaler by the shopkeeper. In turn, the wholesaler bought it from the manufacturer, who also paid for the people and machines to make the chocolate bar. And before that, the ingredients, such as cocoa beans, sugar and milk, had to be bought by the manufacturer. It is also quite likely that the cocoa beans were brought into the country from another part of the world.

International trade

Goods and services which are sold to foreign customers are known as *exports*, while goods and services bought from another country are *imports*. The trade in exports and imports is called international trade, and it is very important to all countries in the world.

Without international trade, consumers would only be able to buy a limited variety of goods. For example, people in Britain would not be able to enjoy tropical fruits or rice because the climate in Britain is unsuitable for growing such foodstuffs. There are also countries, such as Japan, which have very few energy sources of their own. It is vital for these countries to sell exports so that they can earn the money to buy the coal and oil they need. That is one of the reasons why so many Japanese goods are available in other countries.

Free trade and protection

When all countries specialize in producing the goods and services they are most efficient at producing, they are able to increase the output of goods and services throughout the world. And if there are more goods and services being produced, then consumers will enjoy a higher standard of living. This is the main argument in favour of 'free trade', a situation where no country tries to prevent imports from another country.

Although international trade may make workers and consumers around the world better off, countries are sometime afraid of imports. They are scared that cheaper goods

from other countries will mean that people making similar goods in the home country will lose their jobs. In the past, this has often led to countries trying to keep imports out. They have used *tariffs*, which are special taxes on imported goods. Tariffs make the imports more expensive, which stops consumers buying them. *Quotas* might also sometimes be used. A quota is a limit on the quantity of imports of a particular item that a country will allow. The use of tariffs and quotas is known as *protectionism*, because the import controls are designed to protect the home industries from foreign competition.

Between World War I and World War II many countries used tariffs and quotas to keep out foreign imports. The result was that it became harder and harder to sell goods around the world. So instead of making people better off, the import controls produced the opposite effect and made them much worse off.

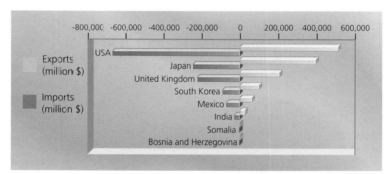

Country	Exports (million $)	Imports (million $)
USA	512,400	−666,000
Japan	395,200	−245,200
UK	204,000	−220,500
South Korea	96,000	−89,400
Mexico	57,000	−71,700
India	24,200	−26,700
Somalia	130	−225
Bosnia and Herzegovina	31	−535

After World War II, trading nations did not want to go through these problems again, so in 1948 they set up an organization known as the General Agreement on Tariffs and Trade (GATT). GATT held many meetings (or 'rounds') where trading nations negotiated to make trade as free as possible by reducing tariffs and quotas. GATT has been replaced, since the beginning of 1995, by a new, permanent organization called the World Trade Organization, with headquarters in Geneva, Switzerland. ◆

▼ This graph and the table below show the import and export figures of eight countries in 1994. The import figures are negative numbers because they show the amount of money the country has paid out. If a country's import figure is higher than its export figure then that country has a trade deficit. A country's economy cannot survive for long periods in deficit.

▼ **Find out more**
Businesses
Economics
Markets
Shops
Spices
Wool

Trade unions

One of the largest unions the world has known is Solidarnosc (Solidarity). When it was formed as a free trade union in communist Poland in 1980, it soon spread throughout the country and gained 8 million members. Even though it was banned by the government in 1981, it remained so popular that it won the free elections in 1989 after turning from a trade union into a political organization.

▼ Some trade union emblems and logos.

Teamsters (USA)

Solidarity (Poland)

the public service union

UNISON (Britain)

Workers often find that they have to band together to talk to their employers if they want to get the best possible wages and working conditions. Such groups of workers are called trade unions, or labor unions in the USA.

Employers need their workers if their firms are to make a profit, since without workers they would not be able to produce goods and services for sale to the public. Workers need employers to pay their wages. Both sides make use of this fact when they bargain about wages or working conditions. Usually employers and unions will reach an agreement that is acceptable to both sides, but if talks break down, trade unions may take action to support their demand for better wages or improved working conditions. They may even threaten to stop working (strike) to make employers agree to their demands. Trade unions also support their members in other situations, for instance where the safety of workers is at risk, or in cases of wrongful dismissal.

Different kinds of union

Craft unions are for workers who have the same skill, such as printers or electricians. There are many unions of this type in Britain. *Industrial unions* recruit all the workers in a particular industry, such as coal miners or metal workers. Such unions are the usual type in Germany. *General unions* represent workers in many different industries, and may also concentrate on recruiting less skilled workers. They are common in many developing countries, and the largest unions in Britain are of this type. Finally, *white-collar unions* represent non-manual workers in administrative, clerical, supervisory, professional or technical jobs. These have been the fastest-growing unions in recent years in those countries where jobs have become more skilled.

Federations of unions

It is often useful for unions to act together, so they have formed both national and international associations. In Britain the national association is the Trades Union Congress (TUC), founded in 1868. Most British unions are members, so the TUC represents millions of workers. The American Federation of Labor and Congress of Industrial Organizations (AFL-CIO) and the Australian Council of Trade Unions (ACTU) are similar. In France the main federation is the Confédération Générale du Travail (CGT), which sometimes organizes street demonstrations to persuade the French government to change its policies.

FLASHBACK

Life was particularly hard for workers in Britain during the early part of the Industrial Revolution. Many workplaces were dirty, badly lit and poorly ventilated. Men, women and children were expected to work for up to 16 hours a day, six days a week. Conditions like these encouraged workers to form the first trade unions.

At first, trade unions were banned by law in Britain. In Tolpuddle, Dorset, six farm labourers formed a trade union and swore an oath to be loyal to each other. In 1834 they were sentenced to seven years' transportation to Australia. A public outcry brought an early end to their sentence and helped to convince people that trade unions should be allowed. A major step forward came when the trade unions helped to form the Labour Party at the beginning of the 20th century.

Although they grew in power and influence during the 20th century, trade unions still had to struggle to make their voices heard. Some governments, including the Conservative government in Britain in the 1980s and 1990s, have made changes in the law designed to limit their strength. ◆

The Tolpuddle Martyrs were the farm labourers George Loveless, James Loveless, James Brine, Thomas Stansfield, John Stansfield and James Hammet. Public outcry over their deportation to Australia brought about their return to England two years after their trial. Five of the six later emigrated to Canada.

George Loveless at his trial said: 'My Lord, if we have broken the law, it was not done intentionally. We have injured no man's character, reputation, person or property. We were uniting together to preserve ourselves, our wives and our children from utter degradation and starvation. We challenge any man to prove that we have acted different from that statement.'

▼ **Find out more**
British history since 1919
Industrial Revolution
Poland
Victorian Britain

BIOGRAPHY
Hardie, James Keir
Marx, Karl

Trams

Trams are passenger-carrying vehicles that run on rails laid in the street. The top of each rail is level with the surface of the road so that other vehicles can cross the rails without any difficulty. Today there are trams in many European towns. Modern trams are quiet, comfortable and fast, but the old trams were noisy and slow and got in the way of other vehicles. Most British towns replaced trams with buses in the 1940s.

Horse-drawn trams were first used in the USA in about 1830 and in Britain in 1858. Within about 15 years almost every city in Europe was using them. Two horses could pull a tram carrying about 40 passengers. In some places, the horses were replaced by steam tram locomotives pulling up to four tramcars. Since about 1900, trams have been driven by electricity collected from rails below ground, or from overhead wires by an arm on the top of the tram. ◆

◀ Trams, like this one in Amsterdam, the Netherlands, are used in many European cities.

▼ **Find out more**
Transport

Transformers

Transformers are devices which change an alternating current of one voltage of electricity into a different voltage. Electric model train sets run on low-voltage electricity. Mains electricity is high voltage and is pushed out with too great a force for a train set. A transformer reduces the mains voltage to the right level for the train set. Transformers for reducing mains voltage are also used in radios, television sets, cassette players, battery chargers, and mains adaptors for computers.

Some transformers increase voltage. There are huge transformers like this at power stations.

They increase the voltage before the power is fed to the overhead lines. When a transformer increases voltage, it reduces the current. In other words, the electricity is pushed harder but less of it flows. This means that thinner power lines can be used. ◆

How a transformer works

Transformers only work with alternating current (a.c.); the sort of electricity you get from the mains. It flows backwards and forwards. Inside a transformer, there is a core of iron with two coils of wire wrapped round it. When alternating current is passed through one coil (the primary), it sets up a changing magnetic field in the iron. This generates a voltage in the second coil (the secondary). The more turns there are on the secondary, the higher the voltage produced.

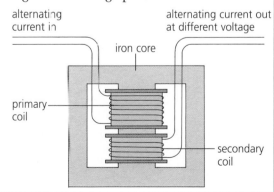

alternating current in

alternating current out at different voltage

iron core

primary coil

secondary coil

A step-down transformer is one which *decreases* voltage (and increases current). It has *fewer* turns on the secondary coil than on the primary.

A step-up transformer is one which *increases* voltage (and reduces current). It has *more* turns on the secondary coil than on the primary.

◀ **Step-up transformer at a power station. It transfers power to overhead cables in the form of a much smaller current at a greatly increased voltage.**

▼ **Find out more**
Electricity
Electricity supply

BIOGRAPHY
Faraday, Michael

Transplants

Before making a transplant, tests must be made on both the donor organ and the recipient's body to make sure that they are similar. This is called finding a good tissue match and reduces the risk of rejection.

Everyone has two kidneys but can survive with only one. It is possible to donate a kidney for transplant to a close relative.

Research is being carried out into the possibilities of transplanting animal organs into humans. Scientists are also trying to grow organs for transplant in laboratories.

▼ **Find out more**
Artificial limbs
Immunity
Kidneys
Operations

Transplant surgery usually means organ transplantation, which is the replacement of a damaged or diseased organ in the human body by another from someone else's body. A transplant can also mean moving tissue within the same body as, for example, in a skin graft. In organ transplantation, the replacement organ is taken from the body of one person (the donor) and put into the body of another (the recipient). Living donors are occasionally used (for example, in bone-marrow and kidney transplants), but usually they are dead, often as the result of an accident. The organs that can be transplanted in this way include the heart, lungs, liver, kidney, pancreas, bone marrow and the cornea (transparent front of the eye). Blood can be transplanted by transfusion.

Rejection

When a patient receives a transplanted organ, their immune system, which defends the body against disease, is likely to attack the new organ as a 'foreign body' or invader. This can cause the transplant to fail and is called rejection. Scientists and doctors have to try and stop this happening. One way is to make sure that the cells of the donor are as similar as possible to those of the recipient. Another way is to use drugs which suppress the recipient's immune system so that it does not reject the transplant. An anti-rejection drug called cyclosporin has been used successfully since the 1980s. People who have received transplanted organs can lead normal lives and often live for many years after the operation.

There is a worldwide shortage of organs for transplant. In some countries, people carry cards saying they wish to donate their organs after death. This is necessary because the organs must be removed from the donor's body without delay so that they are in good condition for transplant. If doctors have to take the time to trace the family of an accident victim to ask permission to use their organs, the organs may no longer be in a good enough state to use.

FLASHBACK

The first human heart transplant was carried out in South Africa by Dr Christiaan Barnard in 1967. A patient who received a transplanted heart in 1971 lived for more than 23 years after the operation. ◆

Transport

▼ Apart from walking, the bicycle is probably the most common form of transport in the world. Bicycles are very versatile, having the ability to cope with rough terrain and heavy loads. They are also cheap, and so are widely used in countries where most people cannot afford a car.

Transport keeps the world on the move. It takes children to school, workers to offices and factories, and business people and tourists around the world. It carries goods from factories to shops and from country to country, and raw materials for industry around the world.

The main forms of transport are road, rail, air and water. Cars, buses, trucks, motor cycles, bicycles and horse-drawn carts all travel on the roads. On railways, locomotives pull carriages carrying passengers, or wagons carrying goods. In the air, there are passenger and cargo aircraft. On the water, there are ocean-going cargo ships, car and passenger ferries, and a huge variety of smaller craft.

All transport vehicles need to be part of a system of transport, using what is called the transport *infrastructure*. Cars, buses and other road vehicles would be useless without roads. Road bridges and tunnels make the roads shorter and easier to travel on. Traffic lights, roundabouts and flyovers are some of the things which help to keep traffic flowing smoothly. In the same way, trains need tracks, stations, signals, crossings and tunnels. Aircraft need runways, airport buildings, and air-traffic control centres. Ships need ports, navigation buoys and cranes to load and unload them.

Transport in cities

Every morning, in almost every major city in the world, thousands of commuters travel from their homes in the city suburbs to the city centre. And every evening they travel home again. During these 'rush hours', there must be enough transport to move them all.

Commuters choose the form of transport which is the cheapest, quickest or most convenient. They might drive themselves by car or motor cycle, or catch a bus, train or tram.

Many commuters use two or three types of transport during their journeys.

Most large cities have bad traffic problems. There are always queues of traffic, with vehicles pouring unpleasant exhaust gases into the streets. Traffic queues also waste people's time and money.

There are several ways of reducing city-centre congestion. One way is to ban cars, or make drivers pay to enter the city-centre area. Another is to make it easier for them to use other forms of transport. For example, road lanes reserved for buses can let buses travel quicker than cars, and cycle tracks make it safer for people to cycle through the busy traffic.

Elevated expressways, tunnels and ring roads all help to get vehicles in and out of city centres more quickly. Some cities have traffic surveillance cameras. They send pictures to a traffic control centre. Warnings can then be given to drivers to avoid congested areas.

Underground railways carry people right into city centres from city suburbs and main-line railway stations. Trams travel along rails in the city streets, but make less pollution than buses, and travel quickly into the suburbs along rail lines. Underground trains, trams and other commuter trains have carriages with plenty of doors and standing room.

Long-distance transport

To travel between towns and cities, most people use road and rail networks. A road network is made up of different types of road. Motorways link towns and cities together, and are fast to drive on. Major roads also link towns, while minor roads link villages to the major roads. Railway networks are similar, with main lines, commuter lines and branch lines. Going by train is quicker than travelling by car, but it is often less convenient. In countries which have good road networks, most goods are carried by trucks.

To travel between different countries or continents, most passengers travel by air. Airlines operate services between the world's major cities, using large jet aeroplanes. Flights between the major cities and regional airports are made by smaller aeroplanes. Airports are often many kilometres outside city centres, and fast train or bus links to and from the city are provided.

Most goods which travel around the world are carried by ship. Ships are not very fast, but a single ship can carry as much cargo as thousands of trucks or aircraft. Most cargo ships are specially designed to carry one sort of cargo,

▼ In a modern city there is a wide range of transport systems operating at many different levels.

such as oil, grain or natural gas. Container ships can carry hundreds of rectangular metal containers. The containers can be filled with any sort of cargo, and can also be carried by trucks and trains. Most ports have container handling areas for transferring containers from ships to trucks or trains.

Transport around the world

If you visit another country, in a different part of the world, you might be surprised by the forms of transport you see. In developed countries, most families can afford cars, and travel on complex road networks. They can also catch fast trains to any town or city.

In less developed countries, there are fewer cars. In the cities, many more people use public transport, or ride bicycles or motor cycles. In the countryside, transport has not changed for hundreds of years. People walk short distances. Farmers transport their crops to market in carts pulled by animals. Only a few can afford tractors. Only the city streets and main roads have a tarmac surface.

In some cities, where there are lots of waterways, boats are the most important type of transport. Boats are used as floating markets and taxis. They also carry goods along rivers and canals between towns and cities.

FLASHBACK

Ten thousand years ago people lived by hunting for food. They walked from place to place, and carried their few belongings on their backs. In the next few thousand years, people began to settle in different places, grow crops, and trade. Around 7000 years ago, they started to train donkeys and oxen to carry goods. People who lived on rivers, or next to the sea, travelled in small, simple boats, such as dugout canoes.

The wheel was invented around 3500 BC, in Mesopotamia (modern-day Iraq). It allowed people to build carts. A few hundred years later, the first sailing ships, made from reeds, appeared on the River Nile in Egypt. Sailing ships were also developed in Asia.

Two thousand years ago, the Romans built a huge network of excellent roads, linking Rome with other parts of their empire. They built long-lasting masonry bridges over rivers and valleys. The Roman citizens also relied on goods from other parts of Europe, Africa and Asia, which were transported by ship to specially built ports.

By AD 1400 European sailors were making long ocean voyages, and opening new trade routes. It was often quicker to travel by sea than overland, even when the sea route was longer.

During the 1800s steam engines were developed which could power vehicles and ships. In 1825 the first railway was opened in the UK. Railways spread rapidly through Europe and the USA. Iron and steel replaced wood for building ships, and ships became bigger and faster.

In the 1880s, the first internal-combustion engines were developed. They were much lighter and easier to run than steam engines. Soon after, the first cars appeared, followed by buses, trucks and motor cycles. Early in the 20th century, road networks began to spread, and the first motorways were built.

The internal-combustion engine also made it possible to build aircraft. The first powered flight was made in 1903, and by 1920 there were regular passenger and air-mail services in Europe and the USA. ◆

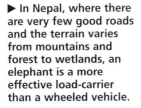
▶ In Nepal, where there are very few good roads and the terrain varies from mountains and forest to wetlands, an elephant is a more effective load-carrier than a wheeled vehicle.

Trees

Trees are the largest land plants. They have a strong, woody stem with a mass of branches supporting leaves, the food factories of a tree. Usually, they have a single massive trunk, but if they are grazed or cut, many stems can grow from their base. By growing tall, trees can reach above other plants to the sunlight they need for growth. Their height also helps protect their leaves from ground-living grazing animals.

In strict scientific terms, a tree is simply a tall shrub (a woody-stemmed plant). Generally, a shrub is said to be a tree if it is more than 7.5 metres tall. However, species that we think of as trees, such as oak or pine trees, can grow much lower than this height and look distinctly shrubby when they grow in windy places on coasts and mountains, or in the Arctic.

Types of tree

The term 'tree' refers to a form of growth, rather than a family of plants. In fact, trees belong to two main groups of plants. Conifer trees, which have cones and needle-like leaves, belong to a division of the plant kingdom called the cone-bearing plants or *gymnosperms*. They are only distantly related to trees belonging to the flowering plants or *angiosperms*. Angiosperm trees generally have wide, flat leaf-blades, and so are called broadleaves.

Some trees shed all their leaves for part of the year (generally the winter, but it can be the dry season in hot countries); they are said to be *deciduous*. Shedding leaves helps protect the tree from frost damage or from drought. Other trees are *evergreen*, keeping some leaves on their branches throughout the year. Evergreens usually have tough, leathery leaves to protect them from the cold or save water.

Leaves

The leaves of trees form a leafy crown. In forests, the crowns of many join together into a continuous canopy. Each leaf plays its part in making food for the tree by photosynthesis. Light energy from the Sun powers this process,

male flowers (catkins)

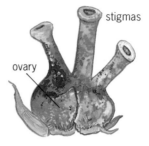
stigmas
ovary

female flowers, enlarged

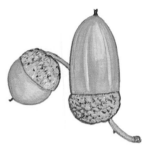

acorns

so the leaves are arranged to receive as much light as possible.

Fruits and flowers

All trees reproduce (multiply and spread) by seeds. Conifer trees contain their seeds in a cone. When ripe, the seeds are shaken out and spread by the wind. The fruits of broadleaved trees can be berries or nuts, as in hawthorn and hazel trees, or dry, papery fruits which are spread by the wind, as in elm and sycamore trees.

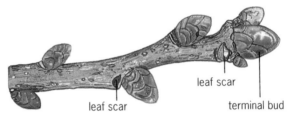

leaf scar
leaf scar
terminal bud

Perhaps the best-known tree fruit is the acorn of an oak. Oak flowers are less familiar. They dangle in yellowy-green catkins, which appear in early May before the leaves. Catkins of male and female flowers grow separately on the same tree. The male catkins produce clouds of yellow pollen. Female flowers, each with three dark red stigmas, develop on spikes growing from buds at the end of a shoot. After pollination by the wind, each ovary grows into an acorn, held in its own little cup and containing the oak seed.

Some trees also spread using creeping underground stems which give off new trunks at regular intervals. All the elm trees in a hedgerow, for example, may have spread from a single tree.

Buds and twigs

Buds form on the twigs of deciduous trees at the end of each growing season. They contain tiny leaves or flowers, protected by scales. These buds survive the harsh weather of winter or the dry season, ready for the leaves and flowers inside to swell and begin growing in the next year. At the tip of each twig is a large terminal bud. This will produce the new growth of the twig in the following season.

▲ The male flowers of the oak are catkins, which produce pollen. The female flowers have red stigmas to catch the pollen. After the ovary has been fertilized by the pollen, it swells and grows into an acorn.

◄ Twig from an oak tree in winter.

◄ An oak leaf, one of thousands that cover an oak tree in summer. Each one plays a part in making food for the tree.

oak bark

ash bark

beech bark

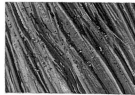

sweet chestnut bark
▲ **One way of recognizing different species of tree is by the patterns made by grooves in the bark.**

▶ **The left half of the illustration shows an oak tree in the summer months when the twigs are covered in leaves. The right half of the same picture shows the tree in winter when the leaves have fallen. Note the mass of roots in the soil.**

Smaller buds along the length of the twig will grow into side shoots.

Roots

Usually there is as much mass of tree beneath the soil as above ground. Roots spread through the soil like underground branches. They have two basic functions. One is to form an anchor to stop the tree being blown over. The other is to absorb water and minerals from the soil. Most trees have a fungus partner that lives in their roots and helps them take the goodness from the soil.

Bark

Bark is the rough, grooved layer which covers the surface of tree trunks and branches. It is made of dead, corky wood, and protects the living wood deeper inside the trunk. New bark is produced by a ring of living cells beneath the bark, called the *bark cambium*. The bark dies as it is pushed outwards by the expanding trunk. As this happens, the bark often cracks, and the pattern of cracking is one way of telling tree species apart.

How a tree works

Most of a tree trunk is made of dead wood, which supports the tree, even in strong winds. However, immediately beneath the bark is a zone of living cells, called the *sapwood*. A band of tubular cells in this zone transport water and mineral salts up and down the height of the tree.

The tubes are of two types. *Xylem tubes* carry water and minerals up the tree from its roots. In the crown of the tree, its leaves continuously leak water into the air by a process called *transpiration*. This sets up a suction, which draws water up through the xylem tubes from the roots. Because no energy is involved in this process, xylem can go on carrying water after the cells have died. However, over time, a tough material called *lignin* builds up inside the tubes, blocking them off. The old, dead xylem tubes form the heartwood supporting the tree, and it is lignin which gives trees their rigid strength.

Sap, carrying sugars made in the leaves, is transported down the tree in another set of tubes called the *phloem*. The sugars provide energy where the tree needs it, or can be stored as starch in the trunk or roots. Each spring, the tree produces new sapwood to carry sap to the opening buds.

How trees grow

As the branches and roots spread, the trunk and branches must increase in girth (diameter) to

Oak tree in summer

Oak tree in winter

support them. This is made possible by a ring of living cells, called the *vascular cambium*, found in the sapwood between the phloem and xylem. The cambium cells divide, producing new xylem towards the inside of the trunk and new phloem on the outside. Early in the season, the xylem tubes produced by the cambium have a wide diameter to carry water and stored food rapidly to the opening buds. Later in the year, the tree needs less water, so smaller xylem tubes are produced, resulting in denser wood which looks darker.

These bands of spring and summer xylem show up as rings through the wood, with the dark band of small late-summer tubes marking each year's growth. By counting these 'annual rings', it is possible to tell the age of a tree.

In good summers, when trees grow rapidly, their annual rings are wide. In bad years, the rings are narrow. The width of the growth rings in old trees can therefore provide scientists with a valuable record of past weather from year to year.

bark
bark cambium
phloem
cambium ⟩ sapwood
xylem
heartwood (dead xylem)
annual ring (the 14 rings show that the tree is 14 years old)

◀ Only a small part of a tree trunk is alive: a layer of dividing cells called the bark cambium, which makes new bark, and another layer of cambium, which produces new sapwood each year. The yearly cycle of growth gives rise to the annual rings.

Growth rates

Broadleaved trees like oak, beech and ash are quite slow-growing. They may take 150 years to reach their maximum height of 13 metres. Conifers grow much more quickly, reaching a height of 10 metres in 30 years. Because of their rapid growth, conifers produce a much softer type of wood, which has fewer uses in building than the 'hardwood' of broadleaved trees.

The value of trees

Trees are valued by humans for their timber. In nature, their leaves and fruits provide food for many animals, supporting a complete food web. When growing as forests, trees form an entire ecosystem, providing food high above the ground and creating a damp, shady woodland floor where other plants and animals can live. ◆

▼ **Find out more**
Conifers
Flowering plants
Flowers
Food chains and webs
Forests
Fruit
Leaves
Photosynthesis
Plants
Pollination
Roots
Shrubs
Timber
Wood
Woodlands

Trigonometry

Trigonometry is of great practical importance in navigation and surveying.

Trigonometry is the branch of mathematics which deals with the links between lengths and angles in triangles and other figures. When some measurements are known, others can be calculated.

One important idea in trigonometry is that similar triangles have sides whose lengths are in proportion. The red and green triangles here have the same angles even though the red triangle has a base twice the length of the green triangle and it is twice the height.

The idea of proportion is very useful for measuring the height of something whose top you cannot reach. Try using it to find the height of a lamp-post. Stand exactly 10 metres from the lamp-post. Ask a friend to hold a stick upright exactly 1 metre in front of you. Make two marks on the stick so that, looking with one eye, the top mark lines up with the top of the lamp-post and the bottom mark lines up with the base. Measure the height between the marks. The lamp-post is 10 times this height. ◆

▼ **Find out more**
Geometry
Mathematics
Surveying

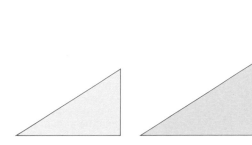

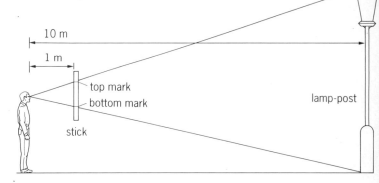

Trinidad and Tobago

Tobago became a British colony in 1763 and Trinidad in 1802. They became a republic within the British Commonwealth in 1976.

▼ A bitumen lake in Trinidad. Bitumen is a tar-like substance which can be used for road surfacing and roofing.

Trinidad and Tobago is a twin-island country in the Caribbean, and it is a member of the Commonwealth. Oil and natural gas are extracted in Trinidad and from the shallow seas around the island. Money from oil exports made Trinidad and Tobago into a prosperous country in the 1970s. Some of the oil wealth was used to build up other industries, making steel, chemicals and other goods, and to modernize farming.

Tobago is much quieter than Trinidad. It has a beautiful coastline with fine coral reefs, and attracts many tourists from Trinidad and elsewhere.

Trinidad and Tobago is sometimes called the 'Rainbow Country', because so many different peoples have made up one nation. First there were Native Americans from South America, then Spanish, French and British settlers, who brought in slaves from Africa to work on their sugar and cocoa plantations. In the 19th century contract labourers arrived, mostly from India, but also from China and the Portuguese island of Madeira. In the 20th century, there have been many migrants from other Caribbean islands. This mix of cultures can be seen in the annual carnival, with its calypsos, steel bands and costume bands. ◆

Area 5130 sq km
Capital Port of Spain
Population 1,300,000
Language
English, Hindi,
French, Spanish
Religion
Christian, Hindu, Muslim
Government
Parliamentary republic
Currency
1 Trinidad and Tobago
dollar = 100 cents

▼ **Find out more**
Caribbean
Caribbean history
Carnivals
Commonwealth of
Nations

Trojan War

In the times of the ancient Greeks there was a city of Troy on the eastern coast of the Aegean Sea in the land that is now Turkey. About a hundred years ago the ruins of this city were discovered and excavated. It had probably been destroyed by Greeks about 1210 BC. There is a legend that the city states of Greece combined to send a vast fleet to attack Troy. Many stories grew up around this Trojan War and some of them have come down to us through the poems of Homer and Virgil.

How the war began

Three goddesses argued about who was the most beautiful and asked a mortal, Prince Paris of Troy, to choose. Paris chose Aphrodite and she rewarded him by saying that he could marry Helen, the loveliest mortal woman in the world. But Helen was married already, to King Menelaus of Sparta in Greece. Paris kidnapped her and took her to Troy. The Greeks sent an army to win her back, and the Trojan War began.

Hector and Achilles

The war lasted for 10 years. Neither side could win. The two most powerful warriors were Achilles of Greece and Hector of Troy. No one else could beat them, and they refused to fight each other. Then Patroclus, a friend of Achilles, put on Achilles' armour and challenged Hector, pretending to be Achilles. Hector killed Patroclus, and Achilles was so angry that he fought Hector, killed him and dragged his body behind a war-chariot, three times round the walls of Troy. Achilles was later killed by an arrow in the one unprotected spot on his body: his heel.

The wooden horse

Not even Hector's death ended the war. The walls of Troy were too strong for the Greeks, and the Greek army was too big for the Trojans to defeat. Then a Greek warrior called Odysseus thought of a trick to beat the Trojans. The Greeks built a huge wooden horse, and filled its hollow inside with soldiers. Then they left the horse outside the walls of Troy and pretended to sail away. The Trojans were overjoyed. Thinking that the Greeks had fled, they dragged the horse into Troy as an offering to the goddess Athene, who had helped them in the war. That night, the Greeks sailed back to Troy, and Odysseus and the other soldiers in the horse slid down on ropes and threw open the city gates. The Greeks poured in, and captured the city.

Aeneas and the survivors

The Greeks killed all the Trojan men they could find, took the women prisoner, and burned the city. But that was not the end of Troy. A band of Trojan refugees escaped. Led by Prince Aeneas, they sailed south to found a new city. But they were blown off course by storms and faced terrifying supernatural monsters. Eventually they landed at Carthage in North Africa, where Aeneas fell in love with Queen Dido. The gods led them at last to Italy. Here they settled on the banks of the River Tiber, not far from the place where Romulus later built a new city, called Rome. ◆

'Achilles' heel' is an expression we use today. It means a person's weak or vulnerable point.

Trojan War heroes
Greeks
Agamemnon (leader of the army), Achilles, Ajax, Diomedes, Menelaus, Odysseus
Trojans
Priam (King of Troy), Aeneas, Antenor, Glaucus, Hector, Paris

Homer's long Greek poem, the *Iliad* (which means 'poem about Troy'), is nearly all about a few days in the last year of the war. Virgil's long Latin poem, the *Aeneid* (which means 'poem about Aeneas'), describes the fall of Troy and Aeneas' later adventures.

◄ The climax of Homer's *Iliad* is the single combat between Achilles and Hector. Here Achilles, wearing helmet, shield and sheathed sword, lunges forward with his spear to deal a finishing stroke to Hector who, already wounded, gives ground.

▼ **Find out more**
Greek ancient history
Greek myths
Legends
Myths
Odysseus

BIOGRAPHY
Homer
Virgil

Tropics

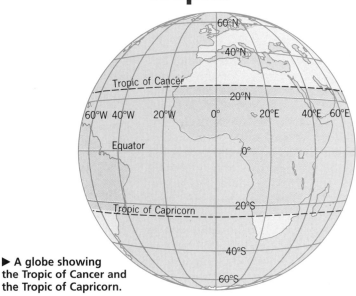

▶ A globe showing the Tropic of Cancer and the Tropic of Capricorn.

You will find two tropics marked on any globe or map of the world: the Tropic of Cancer at 23½° north of the Equator; and the Tropic of Capricorn at 23½° south of the Equator. These imaginary lines mark the places furthest away from the Equator where the Sun is overhead. It is directly overhead at the Tropic of Cancer at midday on 21 June, and at the Tropic of Capricorn at midday on 22 December each year. The area between these two lines is called the tropics.

Tropical areas are hot all through the year. It is the rainfall that varies, and gives the seasons. At the Equator, there is plenty of rain every month. At the edges of the tropics, some areas are desert. In between, there are large areas with a wet season at the hottest time of the year, and a dry season when it is slightly cooler.

Places nearer the Equator have a long wet season and a short dry one. Tall trees grow as well as grass. But nearer the deserts, there is a short wet season and a long dry one. Trees get fewer and further apart, and there is more grass. It grows tall and lush in the wet season, but it is brown and dry when there is no rain. This landscape of tropical grassland and trees is called *savannah*. ◆

It does snow in the tropics. Kilimanjaro, Africa's highest mountain, has snow all year. So do the highest peaks of the Andes in tropical South America.

Trees lose their leaves in the dry season in the savannah.

▼ **Find out more**
Climate
Equator
Grasslands
Latitude and longitude
Seasons

Trucks

Trucks (lorries) are large vehicles used for carrying goods by road. The heaviest can weigh 40 tonnes or more. Most are powered by diesel engines and can have as many as 16 gears.

Trucks are often built with the same basic cab and chassis (frame), but different bodies are bolted on depending on the load to be carried. Special trucks can tip, carry liquids in a tank, or keep food refrigerated.

Some trucks are in two parts. The front part, with the engine and cab, is called the tractor unit. This pulls the rear part, a trailer which carries the load. Trucks like this are known as *articulated trucks,* because the whole unit bends where the two parts join. As the parts can be separated, the trailer can be loaded before the tractor unit comes to collect it. In Australia, 'road trains' – trucks in which one cab is used to pull two or three trailers – are used for long-distance haulage on straight, little-used roads.

flat bed truck

truck with rubbish skip

tipper

tanker for bulk liquids, powder or grain

truck with drawbar trailer

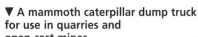
articulated truck with container

▼ A mammoth caterpillar dump truck for use in quarries and open-cast mines.

The longest truck is the Arctic Snow Train, which was originally built for the US Army. It is 174 m long and has 54 wheels.

Very large trucks are sometimes called 'juggernauts'. Juggernaut is the name of a Hindu temple and god, whose image is traditionally carried in a huge, unstoppable chariot.

▼ **Find out more**
Docks
Petrol and diesel engines
Transport

▼An American articulated truck made by White's.

Most trucks are owned by haulage companies and hired out with their drivers. Some travel abroad or carry containers to and from the docks. Bigger trucks may have a bed, a basin and even a microwave oven so that the driver can live in the cab on long journeys.

FLASHBACK

Trucks, powered by steam or electricity, first appeared in the 1890s. Trucks with petrol engines were introduced in the early 1900s and were widely used for carrying supplies during World War I (1914–1918). During the 1920s, reliable diesel engines became available. These proved to be more economical and longer-lasting than petrol engines and have been used on trucks ever since. ◆

▼ Special trailers are made to carry very long loads. The longest load ever moved was a gas storage vessel, 83.8 m long.

Tubers

Tubers are underground stems or roots which swell up to store food. With stored food the plant can survive the winter. Some perennial flowering plants, such as dahlias, produce root tubers which can be dug up in autumn and stored through winter. The following spring they can be split and planted to increase the number of plants grown.

◄ Potato tubers.

Other tubers, like potatoes, develop from special underground stems. Gardeners encourage these to grow by piling up the soil around the potato plants. This keeps out the light and stops them becoming green and poisonous. Extra food produced by the leaves in summer travels down the veins into these special stems. The tips swell with stored food to form potatoes.

Many tubers provide animals, including humans, with a vital part of their diet. ◆

Looking at potatoes

Look carefully at a potato and see if you can recognize the features that make it part of a stem. At one end there is a group of 'eyes'. The central one has a larger bud, the terminal bud. With a closer look at the 'eyes' you will see that the 'eye' is a bud and the 'brow' above is a scale leaf scar.

▼ **Find out more**
Bulbs and corms
Flowering plants
Roots

Tudor England
1485–1603

▶ A Flemish painter, called Joris Hoefnagel, painted this picture in 1571. The tall man dressed in black and standing behind the two violinists may be his self-portrait. In the background on the left you can see the River Thames and the Tower of London.

The picture above shows a party going on in the village of Bermondsey in the time of Elizabeth I. It gives us many clues about what it was like to live in Tudor England. Most people lived in villages. Although Bermondsey was near London, it was right in the country then; now it is just part of the great city.

Houses were generally built of wood and plaster. Poor cottages were often much smaller than the ones in this picture. Only the church and the manor house were made of expensive stone or brick.

Knowing your place

In Tudor England, people accepted that they had their place in the world. The powerful ruling classes who owned land were the most important. The landowners in this village are probably the serious-looking group on the right, coming out of the church. They employ most of the other people in the picture. Rich people at court wore grander clothes in bright colours, like the important visitor arriving on horseback on the left. The well-dressed

musicians are probably a travelling group. Like almost everyone else in the picture they have to work for their living. The plainly dressed men, and women with aprons, may run small farms or be skilled cobblers, thatchers or carpenters. The busy servants (four carry huge pies) are the poorest people in this picture.

Women in Tudor England

Girls were not free to run their own lives, and parents expected to choose their daughters' husbands. However, widows could have more independence, especially if their husband left them money or a thriving business. If they decided to marry again, they could often choose a husband for themselves.

Growing up in Tudor England

Rich children's clothes were heavy and complicated. Toddlers (both boys and girls) wore long dresses until they were about six. From then on, in portraits at least, they looked like miniature adults. Boys in towns often went to 'grammar' schools, where they learned a great deal of Latin grammar, religion, and usually arithmetic and geography. Some high-born girls, like the Tudor princesses, were well educated. Most girls, however, did little more than learn to read. Then they prepared for marriage by helping their mothers at home. Some villages had schools, but many country children worked alongside their parents as soon as they were old enough, at home and in the fields. Parents and teachers were very strict, and beating was a common punishment.

Health

Diseases were often killers. Many children died young; about one baby in five died before its first birthday. Outbreaks of bubonic plague spread by rat fleas were common (London had a bad one in 1563). In wartime many more soldiers and sailors died from diseases like typhus than from battle wounds. A dangerous kind of influenza called the sweating sickness swept through Tudor England several times. Doctors were expensive. They usually treated disease by bleeding the patient, or giving purges (medicines to cause vomiting and diarrhoea), which cannot often have helped to cure them, though some medicines made from herbs were very good. People who had survived all these dangers were often tough and energetic.

Crime and punishment

There was no police force in Tudor England, so catching criminals was usually a matter of luck. The worst crime was treason, plotting against the king or queen. The punishment for this was public execution: beheading by an axe if you were a noble, or hanging, drawing (pulling out the intestines) and quartering (cutting off the legs and arms) if you were unlucky enough to be an ordinary person. Death was the punishment for many crimes, including stealing. Poverty was a great problem, and there were harsh punishments for wandering beggars, especially in towns. At best they were

put in the stocks, or whipped out of the town so that they became someone else's problem. But by 1601 the new Poor Laws gave some help to people who were poor because they were too old, too young, or too ill to earn a living.

Entertainments

Going to the theatre was new and fashionable. Earlier, plays had been acted in the street or in rich people's houses. The Globe Theatre was a very exciting place to visit in Elizabeth I's time. Both rich and poor marvelled at the comics, the ghosts, murders and tragic deaths in plays by an actor called William Shakespeare.

A kind of football was a terrifying game played in the streets, with no rules and goals often more than a kilometre apart. Stool-ball was rather like cricket, and archery, wrestling and bowls were popular. The rich enjoyed hunting, jousting and real (royal) tennis. Quieter games were chess, nine men's morris, backgammon (found amongst sailors' belongings on the shipwreck of the *Mary Rose*) and different kinds of card games.

Tudor rule

The first Tudor king, Henry VII, won his crown by defeating the unpopular Richard III at the battle of Bosworth in 1485. His victory ended the 'Wars of the Roses' which began in 1455. The wars were a power struggle for the throne between the families of York (one of whose badges was a white rose) and Lancaster (often represented by a red rose); there had been five different kings in the 30 years of war.

Henry VII was descended from the Lancastrians. He had luck on his side, for the Yorkist Richard III was killed at Bosworth, and there were no other adult male Yorkists to claim the throne. He married Elizabeth of York, Richard III's niece. Henry faced plots and rebellions, and in 1502 his son and heir Arthur died young. But by the time he died in 1509, his second son Henry VIII was old enough to rule, and the Tudor family was secure.

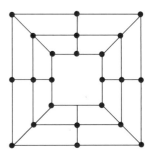

Nine men's morris is a board game for two players. Each has nine counters and takes it in turn to put a counter on one of the circles. The aim is to get three counters in a straight row, and to stop your opponent doing so. When you make a row of three, you can remove one of your opponent's counters, as long as it is not already in a row of three. When you have used all your counters, you must move one of your counters from circle to circle along the lines, even if it means breaking up a row of three. (Still play in turns.) If you can remove all your opponent's pieces, you have won.

▼ **London in 1600: a much bigger and more crowded city than in 1500. The circular Globe Theatre is near the middle in the foreground. Old St Paul's is the biggest church in the background, and London Bridge with its narrow arches is on the right. People often preferred a boat trip to a journey along the city's dirty, crowded streets.**

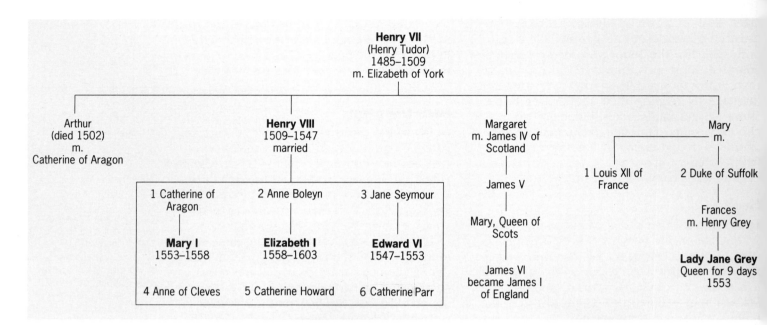

Henry VII
(Henry Tudor)
1485–1509
m. Elizabeth of York

Arthur
(died 1502)
m.
Catherine of Aragon

Henry VIII
1509–1547
married

1 Catherine of Aragon
2 Anne Boleyn
3 Jane Seymour

Mary I
1553–1558

Elizabeth I
1558–1603

Edward VI
1547–1553

4 Anne of Cleves
5 Catherine Howard
6 Catherine Parr

Margaret
m. James IV of Scotland

James V

Mary, Queen of Scots

James VI
became James I
of England

Mary
m.

1 Louis XII of France

2 Duke of Suffolk

Frances
m. Henry Grey

Lady Jane Grey
Queen for 9 days
1553

▶ Catherine Parr, Henry VIII's sixth and last wife. Unlike Henry's previous wives, she had a soothing effect on the king.

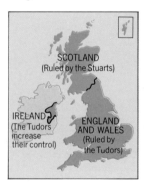

SCOTLAND
(Ruled by the Stuarts)

IRELAND
(The Tudors increase their control)

ENGLAND AND WALES
(Ruled by the Tudors)

▲ The British Isles in Tudor times.

▼ **Find out more**

Armada
Explorers
Ireland's history
Protestants
Puritans
Reformation
Scotland's history
Theatres
Wales's history

BIOGRAPHY
Drake, Francis
Elizabeth I
Henry VII
Henry VIII
Mary I
Mary, Queen of Scots
More, Thomas
Raleigh, Walter
Shakespeare, William
Wolsey, Thomas

The Tudors were effective monarchs, but from 1509 each ruler faced a problem over who was to succeed to the throne. People feared a return to the upsets of the Wars of the Roses, and believed that England could only be secure if there was a grown-up male heir.

Henry VIII went through three marriages and a major quarrel with the Pope before his son Edward was born, 27 years after he became King. Edward VI was only 9 when his father died in 1546, and too young to rule himself. Then he died in 1553.

Edward's heirs were his two older sisters, Mary and Elizabeth. No one expected a woman to rule effectively. Mary I married Philip of Spain but she died five years later without having children. When Elizabeth I became Queen in 1558, everyone expected her to marry and produce an heir. However, she proved that a woman could be a successful ruler, and she never married. She was the last Tudor monarch.

Ambitions beyond England

The Tudors ruled England reasonably successfully. They also tried to control more of the British Isles. Their family came from Wales, and under their rule Welsh landowners had a better chance of doing well in England. In 1536 the Act of Union gave Wales the same local government as England, and made English the official language there, which made life difficult for the ordinary Welsh-speaking people.

Henry VIII made himself King of Ireland in 1541 (until then English kings had been only 'Lords of Ireland'). Mary I and Elizabeth I tried to strengthen English control by giving Irish land to English settlers. There were six serious rebellions in Ireland in Elizabeth I's reign.

Scotland was an independent kingdom ruled by Stuart kings. The Scots had long defended themselves against English attempts to conquer them. Henry VII tried to make peace by marrying his daughter Margaret to the Scots king, James IV, in 1503. The marriage did not bring peace, for Henry VIII tried unsuccessfully to conquer Scotland. However, when Elizabeth I died, Margaret Tudor's great-grandson James VI became James I, the first Stuart king of England.

Tudor England: time of change

As the population increased, food prices went up because there were more people to feed. Wages did not go up because employers had no difficulty in finding people to work for them. There was more unemployment because there were not enough jobs for everyone.

Printed books first appeared in England when William Caxton set up his printing press in Westminster in 1476. Books became cheap and easy to buy, and ideas and information spread more quickly. There were probably more people who could read. Printed pictures began to appear too. By 1600 most English villagers had probably seen a picture of Elizabeth I.

The Church changed as the Reformation spread to England. Henry VIII quarrelled with the Pope and in 1534 made himself Supreme Head of the Church of England. Between 1536 and 1540 he destroyed all the monasteries (over 800) and sold most of their lands.

The English Bible was printed, and became a bestseller. Under Edward VI, Protestant changes altered the parish church. Statues and pictures disappeared, and there was a new English service.

Mary I brought back the old Catholic faith, and persecuted Protestants. Elizabeth's Church of England aimed to be a 'middle way'. In reality, people's beliefs probably changed much more slowly. In Elizabeth I's reign, the Catholic Mary, Queen of Scots, had ambitions to retake the English throne, and the Spanish Armada sent by the Catholic King Philip II threatened to invade. As a result there were harsh laws against English Catholics, and Catholics became very unpopular.

New goods like tobacco and potatoes appeared as English sailors and explorers travelled new routes, and trade increased. Rich people could buy luxuries such as silks, spices, cotton, furs and carpets more easily. Some explorers went to make a new life in North America; this was the beginning of colonies. But for ordinary people, work, food, houses and entertainments were much the same as they had been for centuries. ◆

The Mary Rose

On 19 July 1545, King Henry VIII proudly watched his warships sail out from Portsmouth to face an invading French fleet. It was a calm, sunny day.

The *Mary Rose* was one of the king's biggest ships. Its 91 guns were ready to fire, many of them through the open gunports cut in its sides. As well as its crew of 415 sailors, there may have been up to 300 soldiers on board.

As the crew hoisted its sails, the ship suddenly heeled over. Water poured through its gunports and it capsized. It sank so quickly that only about 40 people managed to escape. The king could hear the cries of the drowning men from the shore.

Some objects found

Guns
Bows and arrows
Beef, pork and mutton bones, some cut into serving portions
Herbs and spices
Cauldrons and cooking pots
Leather bottles with wooden stoppers
Leather jerkins
A pair of fashionable knee-length leather boots
Combs to deal with lice
Dice
Backgammon set
Trumpet
Tabor pipes (like recorders)

A moment in Tudor time

For over 400 years, the *Mary Rose* lay deep in the mud of the Solent. In 1971, a team of diver archaeologists found it. For 11 years they worked underwater, recording and measuring. They brought up to the surface as much as they could: heavy iron guns, the equipment, possessions and bones of the men who died, and even Tudor lice and fleas. In 1982 the ship itself was raised. So that moment in 1545 when the *Mary Rose* sank is now captured for ever.

▼ The *Mary Rose* in dry dock at Portsmouth. The salt from the sea water has been washed out by years of spraying with cold, fresh water. Now the hull is being sprayed with water containing a chemical wax to preserve the wood. After many years of treatment, the *Mary Rose* will eventually be allowed to dry out.

Tundra

▶ For much of the year, tundra is covered by snow. During the short summer, temperatures rarely rise above 10 °C. This melts the surface ice and snow, but 50 cm beneath the surface the soil stays permanently frozen, as permafrost. This stops water draining, so the tundra is boggy in summer, with many lakes and pools.

Musk oxen survive the winter by pawing beneath the snow to find plants to eat. In summer, they gorge themselves on the rich plant growth, laying down a thick layer of fat to help them survive the winter. They protect themselves from wolves by bunching together in a circle, with their massive horns outwards.

Tundra is the name given to Arctic areas which are free from snow and ice for only a few months of the year. The word comes from the language of the Sami (Lapp) people, who live in the far north of Scandinavia, and means 'treeless', which describes the area rather well. Tundra forms a broad belt running through the far north of Europe, Asia and America, between the Arctic ice sheet and the region further south where trees are able to grow. Another zone of tundra occurs on the edge of Antarctica, and in high mountains beneath the height at which snow lies constantly.

Tundra plants

Because of the cold, winds and frozen soil, trees cannot grow here. Lichens, mosses, grasses and sedges are the main plant cover, amongst which grow a few flowering plants that are able to withstand the winter cold and can flower and set seed in the brief summer. Although summer may last only two months, the Sun shines for 24 hours a day at this time of year, so plants are able to photosynthesize (use light as a source of energy) continuously and grow rapidly.

Saxifrages, buttercups and poppies are amongst the colourful flowers that briefly bloom in summer, providing food for the few insects that live in the tundra. Ankle-high shrubs also grow in parts of the tundra, and their berries provide a late-summer feast for Arctic animals.

Tundra wildlife

Voles, shrews and lemmings live in the tundra all year round. They tunnel beneath the winter snow and dig up plant roots for food. Arctic foxes also live here, chasing the smaller animals when they come to the surface. Polar bears hunt more widely, wandering out onto the ice-sheets to catch seals and walruses.

One of the largest tundra animals in Canada and Greenland is the musk ox. Half-way between cattle and goats, these pony-sized animals have a massive woolly coat to protect them from the cold.

Summer visitors

When summer arrives, animals from further south come to the tundra to benefit from the rich feeding that is briefly available. Huge herds of reindeer (caribou) wander north from the forests in which they spend the winter, to feed up and produce their calves. Packs of wolves follow them north, to hunt weak animals or unprotected calves. Sometimes Sami herdsmen may also follow the reindeer, although few people live permanently in the tundra.

Many birds migrate to the tundra – they fly north from their winter homes to breed. Willow grouse, geese, swans, plovers and other shorebirds nest amongst the peaty pools, feeding on grasses and sedges or on the mosquitoes and other insects that hatch from the pools. However, before winter returns, the birds and their young migrate south once more. ◆

Tunisia

Tunisia is a small Arab country in North Africa on the Mediterranean coast. Most of the country is lowland, rising to the Atlas Mountains in the north-west. Evergreen oaks and cork trees grow on the hills. Wheat, grapes and olives grow well in the Mediterranean climate in the north where the majority of the people live.

To the south lies the Sahara Desert. Here date-palms grow in the oases, and phosphates are dug from ancient dried-up lakes. Both are valuable exports. Oil and natural gas are found deep under the desert and are more than enough for Tunisia's own needs.

FLASHBACK

Carthage, now a suburb of Tunis, was once the home of Hannibal, who in 218 BC took elephants as well as an army from Spain over the Alps to try to conquer Rome. Later Tunisia became part of the Roman empire. In the 7th century AD Muslim Arabs conquered North Africa, and from the 16th century Tunisia was part of the Ottoman empire. It was ruled by France from 1881 until 1956, when it became independent. ◆

▼ **Find out more**
Africa
Muslims
Sahara
BIOGRAPHY
Hannibal

Area 164,150 sq km
Capital Tunis
Population 8,600,000
Language Arabic, French
Currency
1 dinar = 1000 millimes

Tunnels

Tunnels are underground passages that have usually been built for a particular purpose. In cities, tunnels beneath the streets and buildings allow road vehicles and railway trains to travel quickly through the city. People can cross busy roads in safety by using subways (short tunnels) under the roads. City tunnels also carry water, bringing water supplies to all parts of the city and taking away waste water or sewage. Small rivers may be diverted to flow through tunnels. Narrow tunnels may contain cables for telephones and other kinds of communications.

In the country, tunnels are built to carry road and rail vehicles under rivers and through hills or mountains, avoiding long journeys around these obstacles. Tunnels also carry road and rail traffic under sea channels or straits, connecting islands or countries where a bridge would be hazardous to passing ships. Sea tunnels can be built over much longer distances than bridges.

Underground mines consist of tunnels dug into deposits of coal or minerals. Mines are by far the deepest tunnels of all.

Constructing tunnels

Tunnels that are to lie just beneath the surface of the ground may be built by the cut-and-cover method. A large long ditch is dug, and then covered over to form a tunnel. Underground railway lines that run beneath city streets are often constructed in this way.

Most tunnels have to go deeper and are dug down into the ground. The tunnellers may use cutting machines to gouge out soft rock or soil, or they may drill holes into hard rock and fill the holes with explosives that then blow out the rock. Conveyor belts or trucks carry away

▲ A tunnel cutter used in making the Channel Tunnel that links Britain and France. The rotating head carries 'picks' made of hard tungsten carbide.

the debris, and the tunnellers put up supports or a tunnel lining of steel or concrete to prevent the tunnel collapsing. A tunnel through hard rock may need no supports or lining.

A tunnelling machine is often used to build a tunnel. The machine has a cylindrical shield with a head containing cutting tools or teeth. Powerful motors rotate the head and push it forward, and the cutting teeth or tools excavate the rock or soil. Conveyors remove the debris, and segments of tunnel lining are fitted into place behind the head. The machine can dig its way through the ground automatically, advancing several metres a day through soft rock or soil. It may use a laser beam for guidance so that it steers a straight course through the ground. ◆

The longest tunnel in the world is in the United States. It carries water 169 km from a reservoir to New York City, and was completed in 1944.

The longest road tunnel in the world is the St Gotthard tunnel in Switzerland. Completed in 1980, it is 16.3 km long.

▼ **Find out more**
British history since 1919
Canals
Channel Tunnel
Explosives
Mining
Railways
Roads
Tools
Victorian Britain

Turbines

A windmill is a type of turbine. So is a water-wheel. Turbines are huge wheels with fanlike blades or vanes on them. When a stream of moving liquid or gas strikes them, they spin round. Most turbines are turned by air, water, steam or hot

◄ A low-pressure steam turbine rotor to be used in a power station.

gas. They have a shaft through the middle which is used to drive other machinery.

Types

There are two main types of turbine. Radial-flow turbines work like water-wheels, where the water hits the edge of the wheel. Axial-flow turbines work like windmills, where the blades face into the wind. Modern axial-flow turbines can have hundreds of blades.

Uses

Turbines have many uses. Water turbines drive the generators in hydroelectric power stations. They are turned by water rushing from a river or dam. Steam turbines are spun round by jets of steam from a huge boiler. They drive the generators in coal, oil, gas and nuclear power stations. They also turn the propellers in some ships. Gas turbines are used in jet engines. They are pushed round by the jet of hot gas which shoots out of the back of the engine. They are used to turn the compressor which sucks in air at the front of the engine. Some people call the whole engine a 'gas turbine'. ♦

The first practical steam turbine was built by Charles Parsons in England in 1884.

More than 95 per cent of the world's electricity is made in power stations which use turbines.

▼ **Find out more**
Hydroelectric power
Jet engines
Power stations
Steam engines
Water power

Turkey

Turkey is a country at the eastern end of the Mediterranean Sea. A small part, called Thrace, is in Europe, but most of the country is in Asia. Dividing the two parts is a strait called the Bosporus. The Asian part, called Anatolia, has a high central plateau surrounded by mountains. Mount Ararat, the highest peak at 5165 metres, is supposed to be the resting place of Noah's Ark, as told in the Bible. The central area is largely agricultural, growing cereal crops, but many

small boys watch over sheep grazing in the dry countryside. The shepherd boys have dogs that help drive off the wolves. Nearly 90 per cent of the people are Turkish, but Arabs and Kurds live in Turkey as

Area
779,452 sq km
Capital
Ankara
Population
60,900,000
Religion
Muslim
Government
Parliamentary republic
Currency
1 Turkish lira = 100 kurus
(piastres)

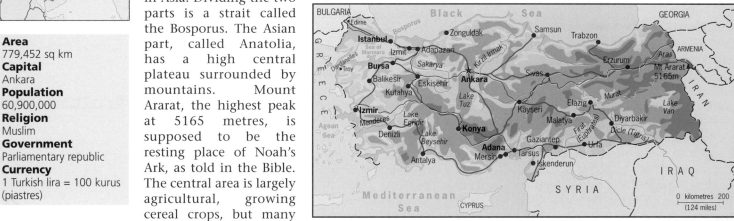

well. Nearly 40 per cent of the population are less than 15 years old. Primary education is free, and pupils can go on for six years of secondary education, then on to higher education.

Turkey's biggest city, Istanbul, bridges the Bosporus and is the only city to be built in two continents. It is a lively city with a busy port. Turkey is a Muslim country, and on Istanbul's skyline you can see many towers and minarets of mosques such as the Blue Mosque and the Mosque of Suleiman the Magnificent.

The hot climate and the culture of Turkey make tourism an important industry for the country.

FLASHBACK

From the 15th century, Turkey was ruled by the Ottomans, a Turkish tribe. By the 16th century the Ottoman empire included a large part of Europe and the Middle East and most of North Africa. The capital was Constantinople, today's Istanbul. The Ottoman empire slowly declined over the next 400 years and finally came to an end after World War I. Then, in 1923, General Mustafa Kemal Atatürk founded the modern republic, becoming its first president. He changed the alphabet to a Latin script and made Turkey a more westernized country. ◆

▲ The Hagia Sofia, Istanbul, was originally a church, then a mosque. It is now a museum.

Turkmenistan

Turkmenistan is an Asian country to the east of the Caspian Sea. Most of its area is made up of a desert known as Kara Kum, which means 'black sands' in the Turkmen language. It is a great sandy desert with dark-coloured dunes. Most people in Turkmenistan live in oases along the country's rivers. They grow cereals, fruit and cotton and rear Karakul sheep, whose fleece is made into carpets. Water is so scarce in Turkmenistan's arid climate that a great canal was built in the 1950s to bring water 800 kilometres from the Amu Darya river for the purposes of irrigation and hydroelectric power. In the city of Krasnovodsk, on the Caspian Sea, they use atomic power to remove the salt from sea water so that it is fit for general use.

Most of the population of Turkmenistan are Turkomans, a Muslim people who speak their own Turkic language, but there are also Uzbeks and Russians living there. Some Turkomans are partly nomadic, wandering the desert with their animals living in tents.

FLASHBACK

About 2500 years ago Turkmenistan was part of Persia (today's Iran). Since then the country has been invaded by Alexander the Great of Macedon, and many centuries later by the Mongols. It was ruled by Russia from 1881 and then became a part of the Soviet Union (USSR). In 1991, when the USSR broke up, Turkmenistan declared its independence, and later in the year joined the Commonwealth of Independent States. ◆

Area
488,100 sq km
Capital
Ashkhabad
Population
4,000,000
Language
Turkmen
Religion
Muslim
Government
Parliamentary republic
Currency
1 rouble = 100 copecks

▼ A woman spinning wool to be dyed and woven into a carpet.

Twentieth-century history

By the 1990s a supersonic aircraft could fly from New York to London in less than three hours. Even the journey from America to Australia can be done in less than 15 hours.

The world has changed more in the 20th century than at any other time in history. Since 1900, the human race has conquered the air and explored space. Radio and television have brought distant peoples together. Many disabling and fatal diseases have been brought under control. More children are now educated. However, despite the wonderful inventions and discoveries, millions still live in poverty. Famine and disease are widespread. Slums spread like cancers on the fringes of many major cities. In 1990 about 30 million children were living on the streets. Throughout the century, wars and disputes over land have thrown countless people out of their homelands to live in squalid refugee camps. For every person who has a car, a television and a comfortable home, there are many more for whom such things are unimaginable luxuries. And our great inventions have brought death and destruction as well as health and happiness.

Population
The world's population in 1900 was 1550 million. A quarter lived in Europe. Now only a fraction of the world's population (estimated to reach over 6000 million by the year 2000) are Europeans. Over 1000 million people live in China alone. This population explosion has brought enormous problems. We urgently need to find a way of limiting population growth, for the world cannot get bigger. We also have to control pollution and find a fair way to share the Earth's resources.

Cities
In 1900 most people lived in small villages. Even important cities were much smaller than they are today. Throughout the century people have moved into towns and cities. Nearly

▶ The waterfront of Singapore in the early years of the 20th century.

Industry
In 1900 many millions of men and women laboured long hours at heavy jobs in mines, quarries and factories. Conditions were often dangerous. Many such jobs are now done by machines.

Travel
In 1900 long-distance travel had to be done by rail or by ship. In towns there were trams or horse-drawn vehicles, and some travelled by bicycle. For many families a long journey was a rare and exciting event.

Communications
At the beginning of the century all contact between separated families and friends was by letter. Telephones and telegraph were already being used by businesses.

▶ By 1987 Singapore city had grown enormously and the skyline had completely changed.

everywhere cities have spread into the surrounding countryside and upwards into the sky. Better transport and building methods have encouraged urban living. For some town dwellers, life is convenient and pleasant, with plenty of shops and places of entertainment. For the poor, though, town life can be grim and violent.

Technology

Today, the well-off can take a meal from the freezer, cook it in seconds in the microwave and put the dirty plate in the dishwasher. They can then phone a friend and choose whether to go to a film or stay in and watch TV or a video.

All this is possible because of the startling advances in technology made this century. In 1900, in the West (broadly speaking, Europe, North America and similar societies) the family washing was done by mother or – if they could afford it – by a woman servant. She washed by hand, in tubs, using water heated on a stove and carried in buckets. Food was prepared in the house and cooked on a coal or wood stove. In many parts of the world, life is still like that.

It is now possible to live far from one's place of work. Quick and easy transport and new methods of communication make this possible. Many people travel at least 20 miles to work each day, and some travel over 100 miles. Computers, telephones and faxes allow growing numbers of people to work from home. For example, accountants can work on a personal computer and e-mail or fax what they have done to their office or another home.

In some parts of the world, particularly Europe, the triumph of science has affected religion. Many fewer people go to a place of worship than did so in 1900. They prefer to stay at home or go out and enjoy themselves. This is not the case everywhere. In the Americas, the Muslim world and even in parts of Europe, such as Northern Ireland, religion is just as important as ever. Over the last quarter of the century, religious terrorism has grown alarmingly.

The global village

In 1900, most people knew little about those living on the other side of the world. They were strange folk who appeared only in books and magazines. Long-distance travel was expensive and time-consuming. America was a week away from Europe by ship; the journey to Australia took five weeks. Now all nations are bound closely together by air travel, telephone, radio and television. We know much more about each

other, too. Peoples from distant nations come together for international sporting events, such as the Olympic games. In 1945 the United Nations Organization was set up to help countries settle their differences peacefully and tackle such problems as poverty and racism. Huge companies, known as *multinationals*, operate in dozens of different countries. This ought to make human beings friendly and united: one people on the Earth. But sadly this is not always the case. Powerful nations still threaten weaker ones, and minority groups are afraid of disappearing altogether.

Women, children and teenagers

In 1900 few people went to school. Even in the West, most children had only a few years of elementary schooling. Now, all over the world, there are schools for most children, and in the wealthier countries they stay at school well into their teens. In poor countries, education is highly valued, and governments try hard to provide it. As the world becomes much more complicated, people need to be educated to cope with modern life. In 1900 a person could get by without being able to read. In many parts of the world today a non-reader is at a great disadvantage.

The spread of education has encouraged people to stand up for their rights. Women have benefited more than any other group. In 1900 women were largely seen as second-class citizens, without education or paid work. Nowadays, most governments accept that men and women have the right to be treated equally and be given the same opportunities in life.

Empires break up

The map of the world has changed dramatically since 1900. During the first half of the century, Britain, France, the Netherlands and other European countries had empires stretching across the world. Europeans ruled most of

◀▲ The photograph on the left was taken in a West African village in 1911. At that time, the vast majority of Africans lived in villages and worked on the land. The photograph above shows that by the end of the 20th century, living conditions for African villagers were still basic. But high technology, in the form of televisions run on car batteries, brought images of the rest of the world into their homes.

In 1900 you were either a child or an adult. Now people from 13 to 18 have their own entertainment scene: music, clothes, films, clubs. Although the idea of the 'teenager' is a western one, television and travel have spread it throughout the world, even into countries where adults are still faithful to their traditional way of life.

Africa, the Caribbean, Oceania, and huge areas of Asia. Before 1914 much of the Middle East was part of the Ottoman empire. Gradually these empires fell apart as the power of the European states grew less.

New nations

Dozens of new nations have appeared and some ancient ones have got back their independence. In 1947 India and Pakistan became independent countries within the Commonwealth. Morocco and Tunisia won independence from France in 1956. Over the following years many more independent states were created, sometimes after periods of bloody conflict.

The terrible racist persecution of the Jews by the Nazis during World War II led to the creation of the Jewish state of Israel in 1948. Racism has haunted the 20th century. The Nazi

destruction of millions of Jews was the worst example, but the massacre of the Tutsi people of Rwanda in 1994 was equally horrifying. In South Africa until 1994, a white minority governed, and black and Asian people were persecuted. Some governments have tried to stop persecution of racial minorities by making racism illegal.

Conflicts and war

The 20th century has seen two world wars. Each of them deeply affected the nations which took part. World War II, particularly, showed how tremendously strong the USA and the USSR had become. By 1945 these two countries had replaced Europe as world leaders.

After World War II, the capitalist USA and the communist USSR became deeply suspicious of each other. Each believed the other wanted to

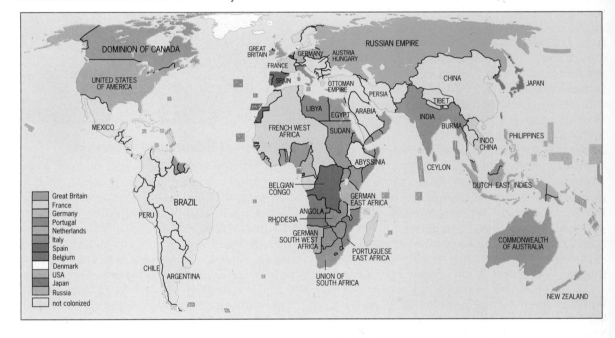

► In 1900 the European powers ruled over large parts of the world. The French, Dutch, Belgians, Germans, Portuguese, Spanish and British all controlled colonies overseas.

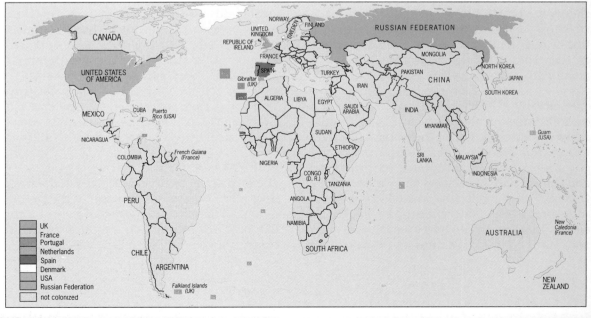

► By the 1990s there were many more independent countries. The European empire had gradually broken up. New nations had formed and ancient ones regained their independence.

dominate the world. From 1946 to 1989, the world was gripped by a dangerous Cold War (so called to distinguish it from a 'hot', or shooting, war) between capitalists and communists.

When the atomic bomb brought World War II to an end, another world war seemed unthinkable. There were many smaller conflicts, however. The Korean War (1950–1953) and the Vietnam War (1963–1975) were both caused by suspicion between the communists and their enemies. The same suspicions have affected most recent conflicts. For example, in the series of wars between Israel and its Arab neighbours between 1948 and 1973, the USA supported Israel, while the USSR backed the Arabs.

The Cold War caused billions of pounds to be spent on weapons. It led to concrete and barbed-wire barriers going up between countries. It split Europe into two blocs: the capitalist western countries and the communist eastern bloc. Only with the collapse of the communist USSR in 1991 did the Cold War finally cease.

For a brief period, there was hope that the ending of the Cold War would put a stop to all international conflict. There were some advances, such as the break up of the racist regime in South Africa. But once the balance of fear between the USA and the USSR was broken, minor wars flared up in many regions. Horrific civil wars gripped Yugoslavia and Somalia, for example, and several parts of the former USSR fought for independence.

Democracies, dictators, communists and capitalists

Throughout the century, countries have changed the ways they are governed. Democratic countries, such as the USA and the United Kingdom, improved their democracy by giving all adults – male and female, black and white – the right to vote for their government. Other countries, like Italy and Spain and Germany, moved between democracy and dictatorship.

Many countries, particularly the USSR and China, adopted a communist system of government. They often called themselves democracies, but they gave their people little freedom. The government controlled all aspects of life, including industry, transport, education and the media. Each country thought its own system of government was best. This often led

to conflict and sometimes to war. By the 1990s, however, communism was out of favour. Most countries were capitalist and democratic, at least in name.

Energy and food

Since 1900 the world has used more and more energy. Much of it comes from fossil fuels – coal and oil taken from the earth. The growing population has needed more food, too. As the century comes to its close, the struggle for food and energy is perhaps the most pressing of all problems. Oil-producing states, such as Saudi Arabia, have grown rich. Countries in which it is difficult to grow food have become poorer. However, new crops and methods of farming allow us to produce enough food for everyone. The problem is how to distribute and pay for it. Technology has given us alternatives to fossil fuels, including nuclear, wind, water and tidal power. Because at the moment they are expensive or inefficient, we are reluctant to use them. But before long, we will have no choice.

Unsolved problems

A hundred years ago, some people dreamed of creating a better world in which there would be no more disease and no more war. Now we are more realistic. We see that, as some problems are solved, others take their place. New diseases, like AIDS, claim thousands of lives. Famine still strikes. Pollution threatens to poison the planet. Despite the United Nations, wars still break out when people cannot solve their problems peacefully. We are not perfect, and our world will probably never be perfect. But, as the history of the 20th century has shown, we go on striving. ◆

◀ World War II brought changes in the role women had in society. This American magazine cover shows Rosie the Riveter, who worked for the war effort in a factory while the men were away fighting the enemy.

By the fourth quarter of the 20th century, oil-rich countries such as Saudi Arabia had an income per person as high as that in Europe, America or Japan.

The phrase 'Cold War' was first used in 1947 by Bernard Baruch, an adviser to the American president.

▼ After World War II, Berlin in Germany was divided into two sectors. West Berlin was under the control of the USA, Britain and France, and East Berlin was controlled by communist Russia. In the 1960s the communists built a wall to stop East Berliners from moving freely into the western sector. This picture shows the beginnings of the movement which brought down the wall in 1989.

Type

This encyclopedia has been set in three typefaces. The main text has been set in 9.5 pt Stone Serif. The headings have been set in Stone Sans, and the marginal notes and captions in Frutiger, both sans serif faces. The main headings are set in bold in 19 pt. The margin notes are set in 8.5 pt.

Type is the term used to describe letters, numbers or any character used in printing. Originally each letter was cut out of a piece of wood or metal, but today most type is produced using a type-setting machine which is very similar to a word processor.

There are hundreds of different typefaces, but most fit into three categories: serif, sans serif (without serifs) and script.

Serif is a slight projection finishing off a stroke of a letter. Sans serif is a form of type without serifs. Script is a form of type which imitates handwriting.

serif   sans serif   script

typo graphy

Typography is the design and layout of the type. Each typeface can be set in a range of different styles:

Roman   *Italic*
Bold   ***Bold Italic***

They can also be set in different sizes. Type is measured in points; there are 72 points in 25.4 millimetres (1 inch). The different parts of letters used in type have their own names. For example, an ascender is the part of a letter that extends above the main part, as in *b* or *d*. A descender is the part of a letter that extends below the line, as in the letters *g* and *y*. ◆

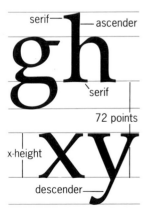

serif — ascender
serif
72 points
x-height
descender

▼ **Find out more**
Printing
Typewriters
Word processors

Typewriters

Typewriters let you write letters and articles as if they were printed. Some typewriters are powered by electricity. Others are manual; they work using the downward force of your fingers. A manual typewriter has lots of long, thin hammers (called type bars) with the shape of a different letter on the end of each one. When you press a key, the hammer flips up and hits an inky ribbon against the paper. In some electric typewriters, the letters are all on a single 'golfball' which rotates into position before hitting the ribbon. Most typewriters have now been replaced by word processors. ◆

▼ **Find out more**
Word processors

The first typewriters to go on sale were made by the Remington company in the USA in 1874.

The world's smallest typewriter was only 16 cm square and weighed 90 g.

▼ **Most typewriters, computers and word processors have a 'qwerty' keyboard like this. The name comes from the first six letters on the top row.**

Tyres

A tyre is a band of rubber or metal, put around a wheel to strengthen it, to prevent it jarring, and to help the wheel grip the road. Most tyres are air-filled and are made of rubber or synthetic plastics that behave like rubber. They are strengthened with cords.

FLASHBACK

Metal cart tyres were heated to expand them, and slipped onto wooden cartwheels. When the wheel was plunged into water the metal shrank onto the wheel, holding it together. Solid rubber tyres were used on early cars and bicycles. Pneumatic (air-filled) tyres were invented by the Englishman Robert Thompson in 1845. However, solid tyres remained more popular until in 1888 the Irishman John Boyd Dunlop sucessfully developed pneumatic tyres for bicycles. ◆

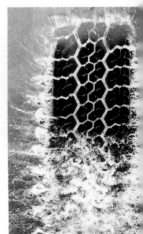

▲ **A tyre's tread pattern is designed to spray away water, so that the rubber can grip the road.** In snowy countries, tyres have studs in the tread for grip; or the driver may fit a chain belt over the tyre.

▼ **Find out more**
Motor cars
Wheels

BIOGRAPHY
Dunlop, John Boyd

UFOs

The name 'unidentified flying object', or UFO, was first used by the United States Air Force in 1953. Before that time most people spoke of 'flying saucers' or, in Russia, 'flying sickles'.

The letters 'UFO' are the initials of the words 'unidentified flying object'. A UFO might be anything someone sees in the sky and cannot explain. The kinds of things people claim to see are mysterious lights or 'flying saucers'.

Most sightings can probably be explained quite easily, either as natural things such as clouds or lightning, or as man-made things such as aircraft, satellites or scientific balloons.

Some people imagine that UFOs are signs of living visitors from space. Others have deliberately set out to create a hoax by faking photographs and telling lies. So far, no one has been able to produce evidence that will satisfy the majority of scientists that life exists beyond the Earth. ♦

▼ **Find out more**
Satellites
Space exploration

Uganda

Water covers about a sixth of Uganda. The largest area of water is Lake Victoria, Africa's largest lake, which Uganda shares with Kenya and Tanzania. The northern outlet of the lake is part of the River Nile.

Most of the north consists of high plains, the central region is marshy, and the south contains Lake Victoria. In western Uganda there are high mountains and a long, deep valley, containing several lakes.

About 40 languages are spoken in Uganda. One of them, Luganda, is spoken by the Baganda of central and southern Uganda. Most of the Baganda are farmers, and the women do most of the farm work. They grow plantains, a type of banana, which are picked when green, and eaten in spicy stews. Many farmers also grow coffee, cotton and tea to sell. Some of the people in the dry north are nomads who rear cattle.

Area
236,036 sq km
Capital
Kampala
Population
19,000,000
Language
English, Kiswahili, Luganda, Nyankole, others
Religion
Christian, Muslim, Traditional
Government
Republic
Currency
1 Uganda shilling = 100 cents

FLASHBACK

When Europeans first came to East Africa, Uganda consisted of several kingdoms. The most powerful was Buganda, which was ruled by a king called the Kabaka. Britain ruled Uganda from 1894 until 1962. In 1963 the Kabaka of Buganda became president of Uganda, but later he was dismissed. In 1967 all the old kingdoms, including that of Buganda, were abolished, only to be restored by President Museveni in 1993. ♦

▼ **Find out more**
Africa
African history

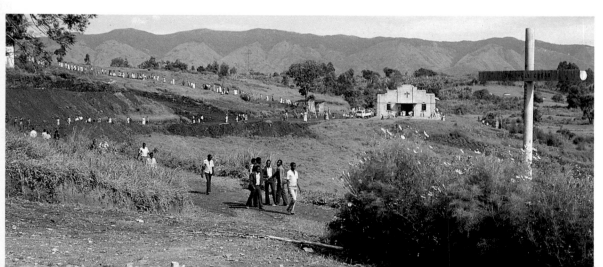

◀ Ugandans leaving church on a Sunday at Fort Portal, in a hilly region in the western part of the country.

Ukraine

Area 603,700 sq km
Capital Kiev
Population
52,000,000
Language
Ukrainian, Russian
Religion Christian
Government
Parliamentary republic
Currency
1 hryvna = 100 kopiykas

▼ **Find out more**
Choirs
Europe
Nuclear power
Russia's history
Soviet Union

BIOGRAPHY
Prokofiev, Sergei
Trotsky, Leon

Ukraine is the second largest country in Europe (after Russia). From 1922 to 1991 it was part of the Soviet Union. The Ukraine is an area of vast treeless steppes to the north of the Black Sea. Much of the country is dominated by the lowlands of two great rivers, the Dnieper and the Donets. To the south-west are the foothills of the Carpathian Mountains and in the extreme south are lowlands bordering the Sea of Azov and the Black Sea. The region called the Crimea has a hot, dry climate which makes it very popular with tourists from eastern Europe and Russia.

Many Ukrainians work on farms, which cover the fertile soils of the countryside. Wheat, barley, rye, maize, sugar beet and sunflower seeds are all major crops. The eastern part of the country has some large industrial cities, including Donetsk, Dnepropetrovsk, Kharkov and Krivoy Rog. Beneath the basin of the River Donets is an important coalfield.

The Chernobyl disaster

In April 1986 a leak at a nuclear power station at Chernobyl, near Kiev, caused radioactive clouds to escape and spread west as far as western Europe. Some 31 people were killed immediately and people were moved out from thousands of square kilometres of contaminated land. Deaths and other casualties from cancer are expected to increase in the coming years, as a result of the accident.

▲ The cathedral of Odessa, a city on the Black Sea, stands among tree-lined streets.

FLASHBACK

Kiev, the capital, is one of the oldest cities in eastern Europe. It was a commercial centre as early as the 6th century AD, and 400 years later became the capital of a state called Kiev Rus, which eventually became Russia. When the Tartars conquered Kiev in the 13th century, the rulers of Kiev Rus moved north-east to Moscow. Ukraine was later conquered by Poland, and then by the growing Russian empire.

Under Soviet rule in the 1930s, the Ukrainians suffered a terrible famine. It was caused deliberately by the Soviet dictator Joseph Stalin who wanted to persecute the Ukrainians. More than 6 million people died of starvation.

During World War II Ukraine suffered heavily from the invading Germans. Kiev, which has been badly damaged by fighting several times in its history, was occupied by the Nazis for four years. In 1991 the Ukraine declared independence from the Soviet Union; this was confirmed the same year by a referendum of the people. ♦

Land height in metres
more than 1000
500–1000
200–500
less than 200
main roads
railways
0   kilometres   300
(186 miles)

Ulster

The Celtic stories of Cuchulain, 'the hound of Ulster', and other Ulster heroes, give Ulster an important place in Irish legend and literature.

Ulster is a former province in the northern part of Ireland. It consists of the nine counties shown on the map. It is a beautiful land of mountains, lakes and, in Donegal, rugged cliffs, bays and islands.

In medieval times it was dominated by the clans of O'Donnell and O'Neill. Fiercely Catholic, they bitterly resisted the religious changes imposed by the English in the 16th century. Elizabeth I awarded plantations in Ulster to Scottish Presbyterians loyal to her. Ulster noblemen fled to Spain and other parts of Europe. After this 'flight of the Earls' James I gave more land to English and Scottish landowners.

The oldest city is Derry, which dates from AD 546. In 1609 all the O'Neill property in Derry and Coleraine was given by James I to livery companies in London. Derry's official name was changed to Londonderry, and links between the two cities remain. During the 19th century the small port of Belfast developed its linen and shipbuilding, becoming the largest city of Ulster, and a rival to Dublin.

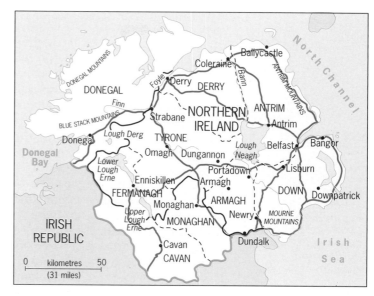

Although most tenant farmers were Catholic, the landowners, larger farmers and a majority of urban voters were Protestant. The decision to divide the province in 1921 and create Northern Ireland was a compromise. The Catholic farmers in the fringe counties feared Protestant domination, while the Protestant politicians were determined to have a built-in majority in the new Northern Ireland Parliament. ◆

▲ Six counties of the province of Ulster are in Northern Ireland (Antrim, Armagh, Down, Fermanagh, Derry, Tyrone) and three in the Republic of Ireland (Cavan, Donegal, Monaghan).

▼ **Find out more**
Celtic myths and legends
Ireland, Republic of
Ireland's history
Northern Ireland

United Arab Emirates

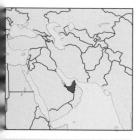

Area 83,600 sq km
Capital Abu Dhabi
Population 2,600,000
Language Arabic, English
Religion Muslim
Government
Federation of sheikhdoms
Currency
1 UAE dirham = 1000 fils

▼ **Find out more**
Arabs
Middle East
Muslims
Oil

The United Arab Emirates (UAE) is a grouping of seven small Gulf states on the northern tip of south-east Arabia under one national flag. They are: Abu Dhabi, Dubai, Sharjah, Ras al-Khaimah, Fujeirah, Umm al-Qaiwain and Ajman. Each is led by a sheikh from a ruling family. Abu Dhabi is a major oil producer and is the leading power within the UAE.

Until the 1960s this remote area of desert and rugged mountains was home for just a small number of fishermen and traders. After the discovery of oil, modern cities sprang up.

Oil and natural gas are the main exports. Dubai is a trading centre, and industries include petroleum products, cement and aluminium smelting. The UAE was created in 1971 after British forces left the Gulf area. ◆

▼ Busy water traffic at Dubai, the chief port of the United Arab Emirates.

United Kingdom

Area
244,046 sq km
Capital
London
Population
58,000,000
Language
English, Welsh, Gaelic
Religion
Christian, Jewish, others
Government
Parliamentary monarchy
Currency
1 pound sterling = 100 pence

The United Kingdom is a country in north-west Europe. It is often called simply the UK, but the full name is the United Kingdom of Great Britain and Northern Ireland. It is made up of the kingdoms of England and Scotland, the Principality of Wales and the Province of Northern Ireland.

The king or queen is Head of State but entrusts the running of the country to the government and its ministers. The government is formed by the political party which is able to command a majority vote in the House of Commons in London. Members of Parliament, often simply called MPs, are elected from areas, or 'constituencies', all over the UK. They make the UK's

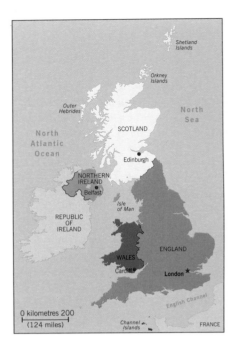

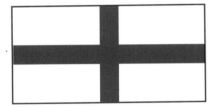

Cross of St George (England)

Cross of St Andrew (Scotland)

Cross of St Patrick (Ireland)

Union Jack

▶ The national flag of the United Kingdom is the Union Jack. It was formed by combining the crosses of the patron saints of its countries: St George (England), St Andrew (Scotland) and St Patrick (Ireland). It was created in 1801, when the Dragon of Wales was not an official national emblem.

laws, but each law also has to be approved by another body, the House of Lords. The House of Lords is also in London, and its members are not elected.

The UK joined the European Community, now known as the European Union, in 1973. It sends 87 elected representatives to sit in the European Parliament and recognizes certain types of laws passed there.

The Channel Islands and the Isle of Man are dependencies of the British Crown but they have their own laws and taxes.

FLASHBACK

The British Isles were invaded by Celts, Romans, Saxons, Vikings and Normans. Each group of settlers brought their own language and culture. Wales resisted Norman rule but was eventually conquered and united with England in 1282. In 1603 James VI of Scotland became James I of England. England and Scotland have had a common parliament since 1707. In 1801, Ireland was united with the rest of Britain to form the United Kingdom of Great Britain and Ireland. After World War I, southern Ireland broke away to form a separate country, the Republic of Ireland. ◆

▼ **Find out more**
British Isles
Commonwealth of Nations
England
European Union
Ireland's history
Northern Ireland
Scotland
Scotland's history
Wales
Wales's history

United Nations

◀ The United Nations headquarters is in New York City. The tall building is where the Secretary-General and his staff have their offices. Flags of all the member states are flown.

UN Secretary-Generals
Trygve Lie 1946–1953
Dag Hammarskjöld
1953–1961
U-Thant 1961–1971
Kurt Waldheim
1972–1982
Javier Pérez de Cuéllar
1982–1992
Boutros Boutros-Ghali
1992–1997
Koffi Annan 1997–

The United Nations (UN) is an international organization whose purpose is to maintain peace and security all over the world. It tries to help countries settle disagreements by getting them to talk to each other instead of going to war. It also provides a place where the representatives of countries can discuss all sorts of problems. Nearly all the countries of the world are now members of the UN. In 1998 there were 185 member countries.

Every member country of the UN has a seat in the *General Assembly*. Representatives discuss problems such as disarmament, environmental pollution and world poverty, and occasionally pass resolutions. At the heart of the UN is the *Security Council*. This is a body of selected member countries which takes decisions on behalf of all the members when there is a crisis. The *Secretary-General* of the UN carries out decisions of the Security Council and promotes the resolutions of the General Assembly. He also takes part in the peace-keeping work of the UN.

Keeping the peace

Since 1945 the UN Security Council has tried to deal with many conflicts. Sometimes it sends a military force, made up of troops from different countries, to keep the peace between warring groups. UN forces have served in Korea, Cyprus, Lebanon, Cambodia and the countries of the former Yugoslavia. While the troops keep the warring groups apart, the Secretary-General and

his staff try to get the groups' representatives round a table to discuss possible solutions to their problems. Unfortunately, these peace-keeping efforts do not always achieve success and the UN is often blamed when peace talks break down and wars continue.

Specialized agencies

Much of the work of the UN is carried out by specialized agencies. These deal with matters such as food aid, agriculture, health, education and finance. Member countries help to pay for the work of these agencies according to how rich they are. Some governments also give extra voluntary contributions to UNICEF and UNHCR for their emergency work with children and refugees.

FLASHBACK

An organization similar to the UN, called the League of Nations, was founded in 1919 after World War I. It was unable to keep the peace, partly because the USA decided not to join, and no action was taken against Japan, Italy and Germany when they invaded other countries in the 1930s, leading to World War II.

The United Nations was founded in 1945 at the end of World War II. The idea arose among the allied nations who fought against Nazi Germany and Japan. At a conference in San Francisco, USA, they drew up a document called the Charter of the United Nations. The UN Charter has become its rule book. ◆

Some UN specialized agencies
FAO Food and Agriculture Organization
IMF International Monetary Fund
ITU International Telecommunication Union
UNESCO UN Educational, Scientific and Cultural Organization
UNHCR UN High Commission for Refugees
UNICEF UN International Children's Emergency Fund
World Bank
WHO World Health Organization
WMO World Meteorological Organization

United Nations' Day is 24 October.

▼ **Find out more**
Twentieth-century history

BIOGRAPHY
Pearson, Lester Bowles

United States of America

Area
9,372,614 sq km
Capital
Washington, DC
Population
257,000,000
Language
English, Spanish, German, Italian, others
Religion
Christian, Jewish, Muslim, others
Government
Federal parliamentary republic
Currency
1 dollar = 100 cents

▶ San Francisco at sunset. The city is built around the largest bay on the Californian coast and it contains a dozen separate ports. Oakland Bay Bridge, shown here, links San Francisco with the city of Oakland, an important industrial and shipping centre.

The Congress of the USA has two houses. The Senate contains two people elected from each state, making 100 in total. The House of Representatives has 435 members. They are divided among the states according to their population size.

During the 20th century the USA has become the richest and most powerful country in the world. It is the fourth largest country by land area and the third largest by population. Russia, Canada and China have more land, and China and India have more people.

The USA is often called just the United States, or more simply 'America', and the people 'Americans'. But this is a mistake, since 'Americans' could be any people living in North, South or Central America, from Canadians to Brazilians.

States and government

Forty-eight of the USA's 50 states make up the main landmass between Canada and Mexico. Alaska, the 49th state, is separated from the rest by Canada. Hawaii was the last state to be made part of the USA. It is in the Pacific Ocean, over 3700 kilometres west of California.

The USA has a federal government that organizes the whole country and conducts the USA's business with other countries, but each state also has its own government. These state governments set their own taxes and make their own laws. Alcoholic drinks are not allowed to be sold in parts of Alabama and Georgia, for example. In the states of California, Florida and Kentucky, the death penalty can be given for very serious crimes, but in Iowa, Maine and Minnesota it cannot.

A huge and varied country

The mainland area of the USA is nearly 40 times the size of the United Kingdom. It is so large that there is a time difference of six hours between its westernmost point in Alaska and the most easterly spot in the state of Maine. The country includes regions with almost every type of landscape and climate on Earth.

In the north, Americans face the possibility of frostbite each winter, while in the south many of their fellow citizens enjoy a subtropical climate where palm trees grow. In Colorado skiing is popular in the Rocky Mountains, while tourists in search of sandy beaches and warm seas head for the holiday resorts of Florida. You can see glaciers in Montana, geysers and hot springs in Wyoming, and white dunes made not of sand but of calcium sulphate (gypsum) in New Mexico. In the state of Arizona you can marvel at petrified forests which are 225 million years old and a meteorite crater 1265 metres in diameter.

In the south-west there are large areas of desert. In the north-west the states of Washington and Oregon have vast forests of beech, chestnut, maple, pine trees and Douglas fir. Some of the southern states, such as Louisiana, have large areas of swamp land, whereas in the states of the north-east, such as Maine, forests of oak, chestnut and yellow poplar trees abound.

Rivers

The Missouri river is the largest river in the USA. It rises in the northern state of Montana and flows into the Mississippi. The Mississippi, in turn, flows south to the Gulf of Mexico. Together, the Mississippi-Missouri make the fourth longest river system in the world. Both rivers have had serious floods in the past, and

CONN.	CONNECTICUT
DEL.	DELAWARE
MARY.	MARYLAND
MASS.	MASSACHUSETTS
MISS.	MISSISSIPPI
N.H.	NEW HAMPSHIRE
N.J.	NEW JERSEY
PENN.	PENNSYLVANIA
R. I.	RHODE ISLAND
VER.	VERMONT
W. VA.	WEST VIRGINIA

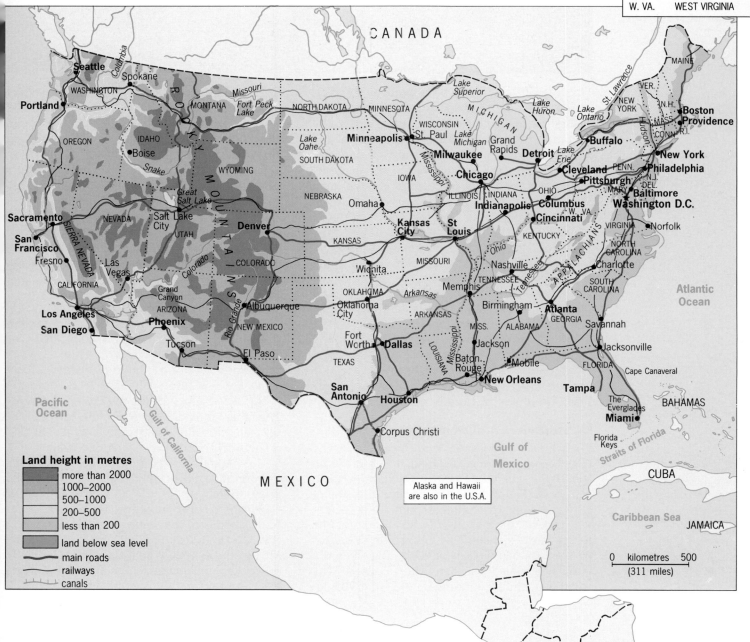

▶ Wheatfields in Montana look like a brown and golden patchwork quilt. Summers are dry and dusty. You can see the dust thrown up by the automobile.

now many dams have been built along their course which helps to control the flow of water.

Another of North America's major rivers, the Colorado, rises in the Rocky Mountains in the state of Colorado and flows south-west to the Gulf of California in Mexico. On the way, the river flows through a spectacular gorge known as the Grand Canyon. Each year nearly 3 million people visit this canyon in the desert to marvel at the mighty work of nature. It is 350 kilometres long and at its deepest point the river is 1870 metres below the surrounding landscape. In some places the gorge is 29 kilometres wide. Downstream of the Grand Canyon the Colorado river is dammed by the Hoover Dam and several others. The waters of the Colorado river are used for many irrigation schemes in south-western USA, and arrangements have been made so that there is enough water left in the river for Mexico to use when it crosses the border.

Earthquakes and volcanoes

The whole west coast of North America is at the edge of two of the great plates which make up the Earth's crust: the Pacific Plate and the North American Plate. This means that the region suffers from earthquakes and, less often, volcanoes. From the air you can see a long line in the landscape stretching from San Francisco all the way to the Gulf of California. This is a fault line called the San Andreas fault. The worst earthquakes happen here. In 1906 an earthquake started a fire in San Francisco which destroyed much of the city and killed 700 people. In 1994 another struck Los Angeles, killing 61 people, destroying 6000 buildings and causing damage costing $20 billion.

There are many extinct volcanoes along the coast. But one exploded unexpectedly in the state of Washington in 1980. This was Mount St Helens. The eruption was very violent and it blew the top 400 metres off the mountain. Sixty-five people were killed and forests were destroyed by the blast up to 20 kilometres away.

Landscapes

Mountains dominate the landscape of the western states but large parts of the middle of the USA are vast, flat plains. Two hundred years ago these huge plains were grasslands where thousands of bison ('buffalo') grazed. Today there are few bison left in the USA. Most of them have been shot for their meat and skins. The grasslands have been ploughed up and planted with crops, especially wheat. The USA is the world's largest exporter of wheat.

The Appalachian mountains have some important coal deposits and are heavily forested. They stretch up to the St Lawrence river in Canada. This river drains into the Atlantic Ocean from a series of five connected lakes known as the Great Lakes. One of these lakes, Lake Michigan, lies totally within the USA, while the other four are shared by the USA and Canada, the border running through their waters.

The south-east of the USA, around the Gulf of Mexico, has a humid and subtropical climate. The peninsula that sticks out from this part of the country forms the state of Florida. In the south of the state is a subtropical wilderness known as the Everglades, an area of wetlands which includes forests, and swamps with alligators and elegant white birds called ibises.

Further west, on the Mexican border, is Texas, the USA's second largest state after Alaska. Cattle graze the dry interior and half the nation's cotton is grown on irrigated fields. In many parts, the landscape is dominated by oil and gas rigs.

People

The people of the USA are descended from peoples who migrated to the USA from all over the world. The USA is young for a country and much of the population has grandparents and other relatives who live in other continents including Europe, South America and Asia.

There are also many black Americans whose ancestors lived in Africa and were brought to what is now the USA as slaves. All these people have migrated to the USA in the last 400 years. But the country was the home of Native Americans ('Indians') for over 25,000 years before people began to arrive from Europe and Africa.

Since people began arriving in the USA, they have continued to move about the country. Every high-school student learns of the migration of people from the east towards the 'Wild West' in the 19th century. Covered wagons, new farmsteads, towns and cowboys have become part of an American legend and the subject of many Hollywood cowboy films. Many Americans are still moving today. As people get older, some who have worked in the colder north choose to retire to the sunny south. Florida, Arizona, New Mexico and California are the most popular destinations. Whole new towns have been founded since the 1950s. The largest of these is Sun City in Arizona. Sixty thousand retired people live here, and there are no children.

Cities

Many of the people arriving in the USA in the last 100 years would have landed in New York, today the USA's biggest city. One of the first sights seen by the people that were crowded onto the ships would have been the Statue of Liberty, a gigantic figure of a woman holding a burning torch to the skies, at the entrance to New York harbour.

Although English is the official language of the country, many other languages are spoken. New York has a number of areas where people have decided to live together because they all originally came from the same country. One part is known as Little Italy. Here people speak Italian. Another area is called Chinatown, where the signs to the shops and restaurants are written in Chinese and the shops sell many

▲ The Statue of Liberty, a symbol of freedom and hope to immigrants arriving by sea from Europe, was a gift from France in 1886.

▶ Central Park becomes a winter playground in the shadow of Manhattan Island skyscrapers in New York.

Chinese products. The person behind the counter is usually of Chinese descent and speaks Chinese as well as English. Similar areas can be found in many cities. Miami, a city in Florida, has a large population from Cuba who speak Spanish and read local newspapers printed in Spanish. These and other Spanish-speakers are called Hispanics, and most are from Mexico, Puerto Rico and other countries in Central America. Large populations of Hispanics live in Los Angeles, San Francisco and other Californian cities. Cleveland, Ohio, has more people of Hungarian descent than any other city, except Hungary's capital, Budapest.

Communications

Communications inside the USA are extremely good. On average there is one telephone for nearly every person. Most families have a car and some have two or even more. In many cities people can drive to a bank and carry out all their business through the window of their automobile. There are drive-in shops and fast-food restaurants selling hamburgers and milk shakes. There is an excellent air transport network in the USA. If you add up the distances flown by all the aeroplanes in the USA, the distance is over 4000 million kilometres each

year. This is more than 10 times as far as the aeroplanes of any other country.

Leisure

Almost every home has at least one television set, and there is a wide variety of channels which can be watched by paying a fee to receive them from a satellite or through a special cable. Some channels present nothing but music. Others show films, and some show news 24 hours a day. Television is one way in which the USA's culture is exported all over the world. Another is cinema. India's film industry is bigger but the USA's films are watched almost everywhere. The movie business is often named after the place where many of the big companies started: Hollywood, part of Los Angeles. In fact the studios have now mostly moved to other parts of the city, but the name has stayed the same. Coca-Cola is another popular American export. The drink was invented in the USA and today it is drunk in nearly every country of the world.

Because American products are so popular around the world, the USA is sometimes accused of weakening other countries' cultures. Canada has a long open border with the USA and France is much further away. But they are

united in their opposition to the rapid spread of American TV and films.

Farming and industry

The USA produces all kinds of agricultural goods. It is a major world producer of maize, soya beans, tomatoes, oranges, peaches, cheese, beef and chickens. The country has deposits of most of the minerals useful to modern society. It mines more coal, copper, gypsum, salt, phosphates and sulphur than any other country. The aluminium, iron and steel, and automobile industries are among the biggest in the world.

Older industries, like steel and automobile manufacture, are mostly found in the north and east of the USA. But since 1970 many factories have closed down. The newer industries, such as electronics and computers, are found more in the west and south. This region is called the Sunbelt. The USA trades a lot with its neighbours, Canada and Mexico. They have signed a pact called the North American Free Trade Agreement (NAFTA) which makes it easier for goods to cross their borders.

Education

At the age of 6, children enter the first grade of elementary schools and stay there up to the age of 12 (sixth grade). Secondary education is usually divided into junior (grades 7–9) and senior (grades 10–12) high schools, but in some communities there is a single high school. After graduating from high school over 60 per cent of students go to college. Every state in the USA has at least one university, and in total there are over 3000 universities and colleges in the country.

The USA has produced some great scientists. They have won more than twice as many Nobel prizes as any other country. Scientists in the USA were the first to build an atom bomb and the first to build a spaceship able to take a man to the Moon and back in 1969.

Politics

In the USA people can vote on lots of issues. They have separate votes for their president and for their parliament, which is called Congress. The president and the Congress choose the Supreme Court judges, who look after the Constitution and important laws. Americans also elect state politicians and city and county officials. Almost all politicians come from one of two parties, called Democrats and Republicans. Also, some states have propositions to be voted on. These may ask for such things as an extra tax to pay for more police officers or a ban on smoking in public places. A voter can spend 20 minutes making all these decisions in the polling place.

The military forces of the USA are the most powerful in the world. The USA often sends its forces to other parts of the world to protect its own interests or those of its allies. Its troops have helped the United Nations in Somalia and in the former Yugoslavia. They removed leaders hostile to the USA in Haiti, Grenada and Panama. From 1965 to 1973 they fought against communists in Vietnam but were unable to defeat them. In 1991 the USA led a coalition of 28 countries which forced Iraq's army out of Kuwait. This was called the Gulf War and many Americans feel that it restored their country's pride. ◆

◀ Minnie Mouse at Disney World, Florida. Since Walt Disney made the first Mickey Mouse short cartoons in the 1920s Disney productions have developed into a multi-million dollar industry including books, music, toys, films, videos, and theme parks. Disney cartoon characters are popular throughout the world.

▼ **Find out more**
Afro-Americans
Alaska
American football
Gulf wars
Hawaiian Islands
Hispanics
Native Americans
North America
Rocky Mountains
United States of America: history

BIOGRAPHY
Clinton, Bill

▼ Cowboys have been the inspiration for many American films. A skilled cowboy can lasso a moving horse or calf with his rope.

United States of America: history

The history of North America goes back over 25,000 years, for the ancestors of the Native Americans have lived there at least as long as that. The history of European exploration and settlement dates back over 400 years. But the history of the United States of America only started in 1776, when the first 13 of the states which had been colonies declared themselves independent of Britain. They soon found that they needed a central government as well as the governments of each state, and so agreed to join together as a 'federal' country. A group of politicians drew up a constitution, and George Washington became the first president.

By 1803 four new states had joined the USA. In that year the size of the USA doubled when the third president, Thomas Jefferson, bought France's Louisiana Territory (the Louisiana Purchase). This extended the western frontier from the Mississippi river to the Rocky Mountains. Sixteen years later the USA bought Florida from Spain. Between 1783 and 1840 pioneer settlers opened up the new territories. The population grew rapidly, as thousands of

Bar graph: Population (millions) vs Year

Population (millions): axis marked 0, 50, 100, 150, 200, 250, 300
Years: 1783, 1820, 1850, 1870, 1920, 1930, 1960, 1970, 1980, 1990, 1994

new immigrants came from Europe, including those who left Ireland to escape the great famine. In 1849 miners from all over the world flocked to California for gold. Men, women and children crossed the ocean in sailing and steam ships. The journey took about 40 days, with one person in 10 dying on the voyage.

The land of opportunity

For most, the USA was a land of opportunity. Some immigrants bought land and started farming. Others looked for work in the cities, where life for the newcomers was often tough,

with unemployment and overcrowding. The development of telegraphs and railways made communications easier. The first railroad to cross the continent was opened in 1869.

For the Native American peoples and for black slaves working on the cotton plantations of the South, life was as harsh as ever. The former were forced westwards and constantly harassed as European settlers took over their ancestral lands. Although slavery was abolished as a result of the Civil War of 1861–1865, black Americans did not have equal rights and opportunities.

US territory continued to expand throughout the 19th century. Texas was absorbed in 1845, and the USA took a vast area in the south-west from Mexico as a result of the war in 1848. The states of California, Arizona and New Mexico were formed from these lands. Britain gave up land claims in the north-west, and the USA bought Alaska from Russia in 1867. This was the period when the West was populated – the time of cowboys, range wars and the gold rushes.

Work and freedom

The 1880s and 1890s brought enormous changes to the USA and its people. Millions of new immigrants arrived from southern and eastern Europe: Italy, Greece, Russia, Poland and Hungary. Many of the eastern Europeans were Jews, escaping persecution. Many had left the poverty of their rural homelands for the dirt of cities such as Chicago and New York, where organized gangs often terrorized

neighbourhoods. There was still plenty of land, where farmers could expand, but few of the new immigrants became farmers.

Meanwhile, the flow of American inventions had become a flood: the sewing machine, the typewriter, barbed wire, the telephone, the gramophone, electric lighting, the combine harvester and dozens more. The development of canning techniques and of refrigeration revolutionized the meat industry.

In 1898, the USA fought against Spain and gained Puerto Rico, Hawaii and the Philippines, as well as control of Cuba. In 1917 it entered World War I, joining Britain, France and Japan against Germany and its allies.

Boom and bust

After World War I the government introduced quotas to slow down the rate of immigration. Meanwhile, many black Americans were moving north from the southern states to find work, particularly in the automobile industry.

From 1919 to 1933 there was an unsuccessful attempt to outlaw the sale of liquor

(Prohibition), but there was also a financial boom. A lot of people made huge fortunes on the stock exchange until this crashed in 1929. Banks closed and, in spite of the growth of new industries such as radio and film-making, millions of people were out of work. To provide jobs, the government financed schemes in forestry, conservation and hydroelectricity, but this 'Great Depression' only ended with World War II, with its demands for armaments.

World superpower

The USA entered World War II in 1941 and played a major part in gaining victory over Germany and Japan, in alliance with Britain and the Soviet Union. It had become a great superpower, but it grew suspicious of the Soviet Union and communist China, and rivalry between these countries developed. This resulted in the Cold War, which led to war in Korea, the development of nuclear weapons, and the space race. During the 1960s US living standards became the highest in the world, and

the black American campaign for equal civil rights seemed to be succeeding. But the decade ended with the Vietnam War and the corrupt presidency of Richard Nixon.

Many people became disillusioned, and there were renewed internal tensions – for example, between the affluent white suburbs and the increasingly poor, racially mixed, inner cities (about six million Spanish-speaking Hispanics illegally entered the country during the 1980s). The ending of the Cold War in 1988 did not bring about the 'peace dividend' that everyone had hoped for. Instead, arms production continued. There were increasing demands for social security benefits to be reduced and for the USA to take less part in international affairs. ◆

▼ **Find out more**
Afro-Americans
American Civil War
American colonial history
American Revolution
American West
Cowboys
Hispanics
Native Americans
Slaves
United States of America
Vietnam War

BIOGRAPHY
Eisenhower, Dwight D.
Kennedy, John Fitzgerald
King, Martin Luther
Nixon, Richard
Reagan, Ronald
Roosevelt, Eleanor
Roosevelt, Franklin. D.
Roosevelt, Theodore
Wilson, Woodrow

SCIENTISTS/TECHNOLOGISTS
Bell, Alexander Graham
Edison, Thomas Alva
Franklin, Benjamin
Lindbergh, Charles
Wright brothers

▲ American troops guard the Haitian presidential palace after the US invasion of Haiti in September 1994. The USA had intervened to force the ruling military regime to hand over power to the elected president, Jean-Bertrand Aristide.

Universe

▶ Earth is a small planet orbiting the Sun. The Sun is just one star among millions in our Galaxy. The Universe is filled with countless galaxies.

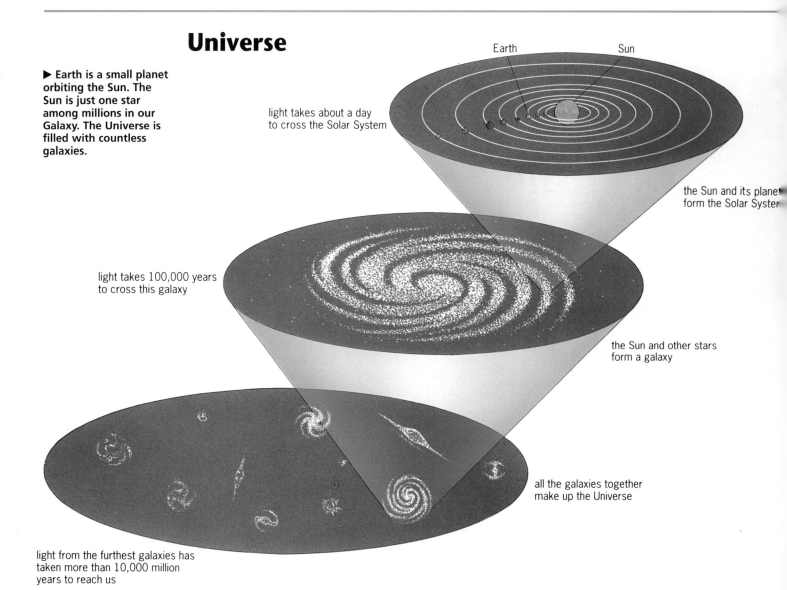

Earth   Sun

light takes about a day to cross the Solar System

the Sun and its planets form the Solar System

light takes 100,000 years to cross this galaxy

the Sun and other stars form a galaxy

all the galaxies together make up the Universe

light from the furthest galaxies has taken more than 10,000 million years to reach us

Light travels at nearly 300,000 km every second. Yet light from the furthest known galaxies has taken more than 10 billion years to reach us.

We use the word 'Universe' to mean everything that exists, from the Earth out to the most distant parts of space that astronomers can possibly see. People used to think that the Earth was the centre of the Universe. Although the Earth is important to us, we know now that it is a little planet going round the Sun, which is just one of millions of ordinary stars in our Galaxy.

The Universe contains countless galaxies of stars. The furthest ones we can see are so distant that their light takes billions of years to reach us. This delay means that we are seeing them now as they actually were long ago. When we look deep into space, we look a long way back in time as well.

We can also tell that the galaxies are rushing apart and that the ones furthest away are going the fastest.

The edge of the Universe

The most distant galaxies we know about are travelling at nine-tenths of the speed of light. Astronomers keep finding more distant ones, but there is a limit to how far we could ever see, even with incredibly powerful telescopes. If there is anything beyond our Universe, we can never know what it is.

Beginning and end

Astronomers have worked out that the Universe we know started about 15 million years ago, with an explosion which they call the 'big bang'. The Universe is changing and getting bigger all the time as the galaxies rush apart. Thousands of millions of years in the future, the stars may stop shining and some theories suggest that the Universe will get smaller again. ◆

Universities

Some of the oldest universities

Bologna	1088
Oxford	about 1150
Paris	about 1150
Cambridge	1209
Vienna	1365
St Andrews	1411
Glasgow	1451
Dublin	1591
Harvard	1636

Some degrees awarded to university students in Britain are:

first degrees
BA Bachelor of Arts
BSc Bachelor of Science

postgraduate degrees
MA Master of Arts
MSc Master of Science
PhD Doctor of Philosophy

Similar degrees, with slightly different names, are awarded in other countries.

▼ **Find out more**
Colleges
Schools

A university is one of the places people can go to if they want to carry on studying after they have completed primary and secondary education. A university has three main purposes. The first is to give its students qualifications which will help them to earn a living. The second is to give them a better understanding of the arts and sciences, and to widen their views of life. The third is to undertake original research.

When students complete their studies and pass their final examinations, they graduate, and are awarded a degree. Until then, students are called under-graduates. They may go on to post-graduate studies and do research which can help to increase our knowledge and understanding of the world.

One of the most ancient European universities is at Bologna, Italy. But the first universities began elsewhere. In ancient Egypt, there was a famous one at Heliopolis. The Roman empire had universities at Rome, Athens, Rhodes and Alexandria. Later, there were Muslim universities at Cairo, Timbuktu and Fez. ◆

Uruguay

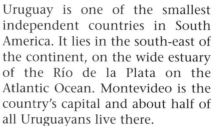

Uruguay is one of the smallest independent countries in South America. It lies in the south-east of the continent, on the wide estuary of the Río de la Plata on the Atlantic Ocean. Montevideo is the country's capital and about half of all Uruguayans live there.

Much of Uruguay is grasslands. Summers are warm and winters mild. Only one-tenth of the land is cultivated. The rest is used for cattle and sheep. Millions of animals are herded by cowboys called *gauchos*.

The nation's main exports are canned and frozen meat, hides, leather goods, and wool. Farmers grow wheat, maize, rice, olives, grapes, and citrus fruits. Uruguay's fine beaches attract thousands of tourists each year.

Uruguay was the first country in South America to provide welfare for its people, and in the first half of the 20th century the standard of living became high. But after World War II there was much violence and lawlessness. The army took control and many terrorists were arrested. Government by civilians returned in 1985. ◆

Area
186,925 sq km
Capital
Montevideo
Population
3,200,000
Language
Spanish
Religion
Christian
Government
Parliamentary republic
Currency
1 new peso = 100 centésimos

Uruguay became an independent republic in 1830, after being controlled first by Argentina and then by Brazil.

▼ **Find out more**
Cowboys
Grasslands
South America
American colonial history

Area
447,000 sq km
Capital Tashkent
Population
21,700,000
Language
Uzbek (Turkic), Russian
Religion
Muslim
Government
Parliamentary republic
Currency
1 rouble = 100 copecks

Uzbekistan

Uzbekistan is a central Asian country stretching from the Aral Sea to the Tien Shan Mountains. Most Uzbeks inhabit oases in the desert and dry plains. Near the Aral Sea, cotton grows on vast irrigated fields, but too much water has been used and the great inland sea is shrinking.

The southern city of Samarkand is at least 2300 years old, one of the oldest in the world. It was a centre of Islamic (Muslim) culture in the 9th century and Tamerlane's capital in the 14th century. It was part of the Russian empire and then of the USSR before becoming independent in 1991. ◆

◀ Melon sellers show their wares in front of a mosque in Uzbekistan.

▼ **Find out more**
Asia
Commonwealth of
   Independent States
Russia's history
Soviet Union

BIOGRAPHY
Tamerlane

Vaccinations

The 'jabs' or 'injections' that doctors give you to prevent you getting diseases are called vaccinations or immunizations.

These contain either harmless, dead germs or substances extracted from them. They work by getting your body's natural defences against germs to behave as if you have been invaded by a disease-causing germ when in fact you have not. Your body starts producing antibodies which kill germs, and protective white blood cells to combat that type of infection. When, later in life, you are infected by some germs of that sort, your body is ready to destroy them immediately, and you do not get sick. ◆

▼ **Find out more**
Blood
Germs
Immunity
BIOGRAPHY
Jenner, Edward
Pasteur, Louis

Vacuums

The first vacuum flask was made by James Dewar in 1892.

The first vacuum cleaner was made by Hubert Booth in 1901. It was pulled by a horse and parked outside the house. A long tube was then passed into the house to clean the carpets.

A vacuum is a completely empty space from which even the air has been removed. Scientists cannot make a complete vacuum; there is always a little air left. The best vacuum we know is in space, though even here there are some particles of gas and dust.

Often when we say vacuum, we mean a partial vacuum, where most, but not all, of the air has been removed. The pressure of the atmosphere will push air or liquid into a vacuum if it can. This happens when you suck a drink up through a straw. The sucking removes air from your mouth and makes a partial vacuum. The atmosphere pushes on your drink, forcing it up the straw and into your mouth.

Vacuums are needed in some electrical equipment. There is a vacuum inside a television tube.

Vacuum flask

A vacuum flask (Thermos flask) uses a vacuum to keep drinks hot or cold, because heat cannot travel very well through a vacuum. The drink is poured into the flask, which has double walls of glass. The air between the walls has been pumped out leaving a partial vacuum. Very little heat can get across the vacuum, and the walls have a shiny coating to reflect the heat back.

So for several hours your drink stays almost as hot or cold as it was to begin with.

Vacuum cleaner

A vacuum cleaner's motor turns a fan, making a partial vacuum inside the cleaner. The air outside rushes in, bringing with it the dust and dirt near the opening. This is all sucked up a tube into a bag, where the dirt is trapped while the air escapes. Some cleaners are pushed across the floor and have a spinning brush which loosens the dirt so it can be picked up easily. Others suck up the dirt with a nozzle or other attachment at the end of a long, bendy tube. ◆

▼ **Find out more**
Air
Atmosphere
Heat
Insulation
Pressure

▼ In a flask there is a partial vacuum between the two glass walls. This, along with the shiny surfaces and the stopper, helps keep heat in or out.

stopper

hot or cold liquid

inner glass wall
partial vacuum
outer glass wall

shiny surfaces

▶ In a vacuum cleaner, a fan creates a partial vacuum. The air rushes in carrying dust and dirt with it.

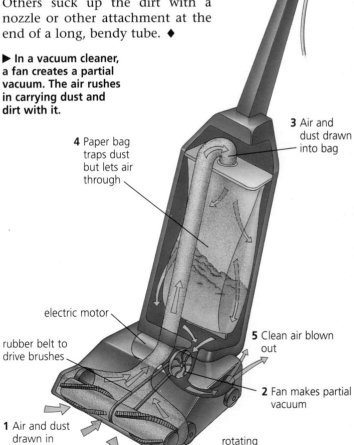

4 Paper bag traps dust but lets air through

3 Air and dust drawn into bag

electric motor

rubber belt to drive brushes

5 Clean air blown out

2 Fan makes partial vacuum

1 Air and dust drawn in

rotating brushes

Valleys

Valleys are formed by the action of rivers or glaciers, wearing away the rocks of the high ground. As the water or ice flows down from the mountain-tops it carves out valleys, leaving ridges of rock in between and giving the mountains their shape.

River valleys

Rivers flowing down steep gradients (slopes) have great cutting power. Rocks and boulders roll down the valley sides into the river and are bounced along its bed, cutting deep into the rocks. River valleys high in the mountains are steep-sided. If you see them in cross-section, they look V-shaped.

Further down the river course, the gradient of the river bed is less, the river flows more slowly and cuts less deeply. It develops a more winding course, flowing around obstacles and cutting a wider valley, like a shallow U.

The river flood-plain has a very slight gradient and may appear almost flat. Some river flood-plains are hundreds of miles wide.

Glaciated valleys

Glaciers can erode valleys much more powerfully than rivers. The ice may be hundreds of feet thick, so a great weight presses down on the valley floor. Rocks and boulders become stuck in the ice on the bottom of the glacier. The ice pushes them along like a giant piece of sandpaper.

Glaciated valleys are U-shaped in cross-section, with very steep sides and flat bottoms. After the ice has melted, the rivers that flow down these valleys look much too small for them. Where tributary glaciers enter the main valley they form 'hanging valleys'. Because these glaciers are smaller, their valleys are not cut so deep. They are seen high up the main valley sides. Picturesque waterfalls often cascade from these hanging valleys after the ice has retreated.

▲ The Colorado River has cut steeply into the rising mountains, forming the spectacular Grand Canyon in the USA. Because of low rainfall the sides of the gorge have weathered little.

◀ A river in Wales is dwarfed by its large valley. The U-shape tells us that a glacier once gouged out its channel along here.

The deepest known canyon is in the Andes mountains in Peru. It is called El Cañón de Colca and is 3223 m deep.

The longest fjord is the Nordvest Fjord of Scoresby Sound, Greenland. It extends 313 km inland.

▶ The slow progress of this river in Germany has allowed time for the valley sides to weather. The result is a wide valley with gently sloping sides.

There are valleys on the sea-bed as well as on land. The deepest underwater canyon is south of Western Australia. It is 1800 m deep and 32 km wide.

Gorges

Where the river follows a line of weakness in the rocks, such as a fault, it may cut a very deep valley with almost vertical sides, called a gorge. Gorges also form in desert areas where rainfall occurs very rarely in the form of heavy thunderstorms. The soil has been baked hard by the Sun and very little water can soak in, so huge volumes of water run off the surrounding land, forming 'flash floods' so powerful that they carry large boulders with them and cut deep gorges called wadis.

Some of the most spectacular gorges are the canyons of the United States. These include the world-famous Grand Canyon, which in places is 1.6 kilometres deep. Here, the mountains were rising as the rivers were cutting down.

Dry valleys and drowned valleys

In some parts of the world, especially where there is limestone or chalk, there are valleys which contain no water. These dry valleys were formed at a time when the climate was much wetter, as at the end of the last ice age. Their rocks are very porous, and water quickly sinks down into them. When there was more rainfall, the water level in the rocks remained above the valley floor, so the rivers flowed. Today, the water is much deeper and only underground rivers occur.

Where coastlines are sinking or sea-levels are rising, valleys may be drowned. When this happens long inlets of the sea called rias are formed. Rias are found on the south-west coast of England. Where deep glaciated valleys are drowned, they form fjords with very steep sides and extremely deep water.

Rift valleys

Some of the widest valleys in the world are the rift valleys. These were formed when huge blocks of rock moved relative to each other; either the blocks on either side of the valley were raised up to form mountains, or the block

in the middle dropped down to form the valley floor. The great Rift Valley of Africa and the Great Glen of Scotland were formed in this way. Other examples include the Baikal rift valley in Russia, and the Rhine rift valley in Germany.

Life in valleys

The climate in a valley is usually much milder than in the hills around it. The valley sides provide shelter from wind, and often the mountains themselves receive much of the rainfall or snowfall, which can even leave the valleys short of rain. Because the valley floor is lower than the hilltops around it, it is warmer. South-facing valley slopes get more light and sun. They are usually warmer than north-facing slopes, and they often have different vegetation.

In some valleys there are special mountain winds which blow down the valley bringing warm or cold air at certain times of year. When frost and fog form, the cold air sinks, and so valleys often have more frost and fog than the mountains above.

In mountain valleys near the sources of rivers the soils are usually thin and not very fertile. Sheep farms are more common than crops. Where the slopes are very steep, farmers may build terraces to prevent the water and soil rushing away down the slope. Where there is no farming, the slopes may be wooded. The trees help to anchor the soil and prevent it being washed away in heavy storms. They also help to prevent avalanches of snow or mud crashing into the valley and onto villages below. There are often trees and shrubs near the river, benefiting from the extra moisture and better soil there.

In many mountain areas, such as the Alps and Himalayas, cattle are moved up to high alpine pastures in spring as the snow melts, and brought back to the shelter of the valley floor in winter to be fed on hay.

In valleys near the river mouth the soil is thicker and the valley floor contains sediments brought down by the river. Good crops can be grown in these fertile sediments.

In lowland valleys flooding may be a problem if the river is suddenly made bigger by seasonal rainfall or melting snow. Settlers have to find the right balance between controlling the damage done by the water by building higher dikes and banks, and benefiting from the rich silt that is left behind by the floods. In many parts of the world today, flooding is being made much worse because forests are being cut down in the hills. With no trees to soak up the water, more of it rushes into the rivers, together with the soil.

Valley settlements

In mountain regions the valleys are the main areas where people live. This is because the climate is sheltered and the soils are thicker. The valleys provide routes for roads and railways, and larger rivers can be used for transport, too. Large settlements often occur where one or more valleys meet, encouraging trading.

Where springs emerge on the valley slopes there may be a line of villages which date back to times when spring water was the main source of water for drinking. In valleys with fair-sized rivers water power may be used to generate electricity for industry.

Communications between valleys may be difficult in mountain country. Roads and railways have to climb winding mountain passes, or pass through tunnels, which are expensive to make. The hills may also interfere with radio and television reception. ◆

Death Valley in California is the deepest valley in the western hemisphere. At the lowest point it is 86 m below sea-level. It is 209 km long and 10–23 km wide.

Transhumance is the word used for the seasonal moving of stock between high and low pastures.

▼ Find out more
Erosion
Fjords
Floods
Glaciers
Mountains
Rivers

Valves

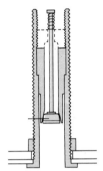

▼ A one-way valve on a bicycle tyre. Air pressure in the tyre normally keeps the valve closed. But pressure from a pump will open the valve so that air flows in.

valve held closed by pressure of air inside tyre

valve opened by pressure of air from pump

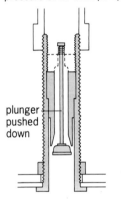

plunger pushed down

One type of valve is a tap, which controls the flow of water into a sink. You use a valve to control the flow of hot water through a radiator. In a car engine, valves open and shut to let gases in and out of the cylinders. All valves control the flow of something, usually a liquid or a gas.

Some valves work automatically. The thermostatic valves fitted to some radiators are like this. Their job is to keep a room at a steady temperature. If the temperature starts to rise, the valve closes and the flow of hot water stops. When the room has cooled a little, the valve opens again.

Some valves allow a flow in one direction only. When you pump up a bicycle tyre, the tyre's valve lets the air in but stops it getting out again. You have one-way valves in your heart so that blood is drawn in and pumped out in the right direction. And there is a one-way valve in the top of a pressure cooker. It lets the steam out if the pressure inside is too great.

Not all valves deal with liquids and gases. Thermionic valves were once used in radios and computers to control the flow of electric currents. Now transistors and microchips do this job. ◆

▼ **Find out more**
Central heating
Electronics
Hearts
Petrol and diesel engines
Plumbing
Pumps
Steam engines
Thermostats

▼ When a tap is closed, a rubber washer blocks the flow of water. Turning the handle raises the washer so that water can flow.

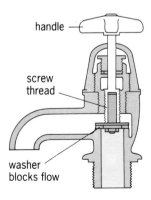

handle

screw thread

washer blocks flow

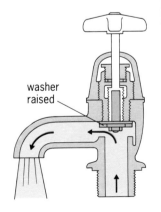

washer raised

Vampires

A vampire is a creature that sucks another animal's blood. Stories about human vampires first appeared in European legends; they were particularly popular in Hungary at the beginning of the 18th century. In the 19th century, the British author Bram Stoker wrote a book called *Dracula*, in which the villain was a vampire. Stories about Dracula and other vampires are even more popular today in films.

Human vampires are supposed to be the tormented spirits of evil people. During daylight they must lie in their coffins. At night they rise, usually as bats, and go off to drink human blood. Mysteriously, they cast no shadow and have no reflection.

Some legends maintain that Dracula was based on a real historical character. Vlad the Impaler was a prince of Wallachia, a real province in Romania, who had his victims put to death with a wooden stake through the heart. Perhaps this was the origin of the legend.

Blood-sucking animals

Vampire bats are real creatures, rather than characters in stories. There are three kinds of vampire bat found in South America. All three feed only on fresh blood. A vampire bat does not take much blood at a single meal, but where there are lots of them, they can cause harm.

Some other animals that live by sucking blood from other living creatures are leeches, lice, ticks, fleas and mosquitoes. ◆

▼ **Find out more**
Bats
Fleas
Leeches
Lice
Mosquitoes

In the novel by Bram Stoker (published in 1897), Count Dracula comes ashore at Whitby on the north-east coast of England. Nowadays there is even a Dracula exhibition in Whitby.

Traditional weapons against vampires:

Garlic

A crucifix

A wooden stake

▼ Bela Lugosi, whose elegant charm and hypnotic eyes made him the perfect vampire, plays Count Dracula in the 1931 film. His victim, Mina Seward, is played by Helen Chandler.

Vatican City

▲ The Swiss Guard wear their brightly coloured ceremonial uniform as they prepare to welcome distinguished visitors to the Vatican.

Area
0.44 sq km
Population
1000
Language
Italian
Religion
Christian
Government
Ecclesiastical state (government of Roman Catholic Church)
Currency
Vatican City lira

Vatican City is so small that you can walk round its boundaries in less than an hour.

Nearly all the citizens of the Vatican are priests or nuns.

▼ Find out more
Christians
Italy's history
Popes

BIOGRAPHY
John Paul II, Pope

The world's smallest independent country is also a palace and a city. It is the Vatican, which occupies 44 hectares in the Italian capital, Rome. It is the headquarters of the Roman Catholic Church, and the home of the Pope.

At the heart of the Vatican is St Peter's Basilica, the world's largest Christian church. Inside the Vatican Palace are the living quarters of the Pope and the offices where the officials work. The palace includes chapels, a library and museums.

As well as being head of the Roman Catholic Church, the Pope is also the head of state of the Vatican. But he leaves the government to a commission, headed by a cardinal.

Vatican City State has its own coins, stamps, postal service, telephone exchange, radio station and daily newspaper. It has its own small 'army' of soldiers called the Swiss Guard, who maintain order and protect the Pope. About 1000 people live in the Vatican.

Vatican City State has been an independent country since 1929. It is all that is left of the Papal States, a large area of central Italy which was ruled by the Popes until 1870. ◆

Vegetables

Vegetables include many hundreds of edible plants. Some vegetables, such as potatoes and aubergines, are always cooked. Others, like lettuce and radishes, are eaten raw. Some can be eaten either way. These include carrots, celery, spinach and green peppers.

The edible part of a plant may be those parts that grow underground, like roots, tubers, bulbs and rhizomes. Or they may be the stems, leaves, flowers and fruit which grow above the ground. The idea of fruit as a vegetable may cause some confusion. Courgettes, tomatoes, peas and aubergines are seen as vegetables by the cook and as fruit by the botanist. A stem vegetable which is used as a fruit and served as a dessert is rhubarb.

leaves lettuce

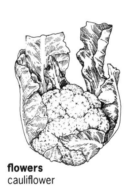
flowers
cauliflower

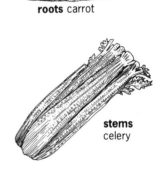
roots carrot

stems
celery

All fresh vegetables contain vitamin C. Dark-green leaves, tomatoes and peppers have the largest amounts. Since vitamin C is gradually lost during storage, preparation and cooking, the sooner the vegetable is eaten after it is picked the better. Green and orange vegetables contain vitamin A. All vegetables are low in energy but high in dietary fibre.

Most of the vegetables we eat today have been cultivated for thousands of years. The onion was probably first introduced into Britain by the Romans. Potatoes were brought to Europe from North America only in the 16th century. ◆

Many vegetables have a very high water content. Lettuces, for example, are 96 per cent water. Potatoes are about 80 per cent water. But vegetables are also a good source of important vitamins and minerals.

▼ Find out more
Food
Fruit
Market gardens
Nutrition
Pulses
Vegetarians
Vitamins

Vegetarians

The vegetarian playwright George Bernard Shaw, who lived to the age of 94, said 'The strongest animals, such as the bull, are vegetarians. Look at me. I have 10 times as much good health and energy as a meat-eater.'

The strictest vegetarians will only eat food which comes from plants, and exclude eggs and dairy products from their diet. These people are called vegans.

Vegetarians have been responsible for the invention of many healthy foods now eaten by meat-eaters as well. These include peanut butter, cornflakes, muesli, and the many high-protein vegetable foods created to look and taste like meat products.

Vegetarians are people who do not eat meat, poultry or fish or any animal products.

People choose to be vegetarians for various reasons. The Buddhists and Jains of India refuse to kill animals for food because their religion teaches that they should not harm other living things. Some believe that killing animals is morally wrong. Many particularly object to the ways in which animals for slaughter are treated and to the conditions in which they are kept. Some people choose a vegetarian diet simply because they think it is healthier to avoid eating meat.

In a world where millions of people are starving, many choose to be vegetarians because they believe that producing meat is actually an inefficient way of feeding a population. They say that it would be easier to feed all the people in the world by growing vegetables rather than using vital land to grow feed for livestock to support the meat-rich diets of wealthier countries. One person could live for five years off just one acre of land growing soya beans, while the same acre could only feed that person for four months if used for growing barley to feed a beef steer.

The healthy vegetarian

Vegetarians obtain the protein they need from nuts, seeds, pulses, cereals, soya products (such as tofu), quorn, and from eggs and milk products. All of the other nutrients they need should be present in their normal diet. Vegans, who do not eat dairy products, require a supplement of vitamin B12, but many foods already contain this vitamin (such as yeast extracts, some soya milks and some cereals). Vegetarians obtain iron from leafy green vegetables, dried fruit, lentils, beans, oats, nuts and brown rice. They get the calcium they need from cheese, nuts, sesame seeds, leafy green vegetables and soya. ◆

▼ **Find out more**
Diets
Food
Nutrition

Venezuela

In 1499 Amerigo Vespucci, an explorer from Venice, saw Native American huts on stilts in a gulf on the Caribbean coast of South America. The waterways between the huts reminded him of Venice, so he named the land Venezuela which in Spanish means 'Little Venice'.

In the north-west, a branch of the Andes mountains forms a string of snow-capped peaks. Further west, lowlands surround Lake Maracaibo. The llanos (grassy plains) cover the central part of the country, where the mighty Orinoco river divides Venezuela in two. Thousands of cattle are raised on the llanos. The densely forested Guiana Highlands rise in the east. There, the Angel Falls, the highest waterfall in the world, plunges 979 metres down into the green wilderness below.

Many Venezuelans have both Native American and European ancestors. Spain ruled Venezuela until the War of Independence, led by Simón Bolívar, finished in 1823.

Venezuela was a poor farming nation until the early 1900s. Then oil was found beneath Lake Maracaibo, and Venezuela quickly became the richest country in South America. But the wealth was not distributed to everyone and many Venezuelans remained very poor. During the 1980s the world price of oil fell and Venezuela faced huge debts. Nevertheless, its large deposits of oil and natural gas, on which the USA depends, remain a great asset. ◆

Area
912,050 sq km
Capital
Caracas
Population
20,700,000
Language
Spanish
Religion
Christian
Government
Parliamentary republic
Currency
1 bolívar = 100 céntimos

▼ **Find out more**
American colonial history
Andes
Native Americans
South America

BIOGRAPHY
Bolívar, Simón
Vespucci, Amerigo

▼ **Some of the 10,000 derricks of Venezuela's rich oilfields are silhouetted against the setting Sun on Lake Maracaibo.**

Venomous animals

Most dangerous jellyfish
Jellyfishes known as sea wasps from the Queensland coast of Australia have poison powerful enough to stop a human heart in 30 seconds.

Most venomous spider
Brazilian wandering spider

Most venomous fishes
Stonefishes from the Indian and Pacific Oceans have 13 spines, sharp enough to go through rubber-soled shoes. A human treading on one usually dies within six hours, unless an antivenin is given.

Most venomous snake
A sea snake called *Hydrophis melanocephalus* has venom 100 times stronger than any other known snake. Fortunately, it feeds only on small eels and is very unaggressive to humans.

▼ When alarmed, the Cape cobra rears up and spreads its hood. Some other cobras are able to spit their venom. They are said to aim for the eyes of an attacker, and can be accurate over a distance of about 3 m. The venom causes immense pain and may cause blindness if it is not washed out quickly.

Venom is the name given to the poisons produced by many kinds of animal. It differs from the poisons in some plants and fungi. These may have a lethal effect if they are swallowed, but the venom of poisonous animals such as snakes and scorpions acts only in the bloodstream and body tissues of the prey. This gives us a clue to how and why it is used.

Venomous animals such as jellyfishes, spiders and rattlesnakes may not look similar, but they have one thing in common: although they are all comparatively slow-moving and helpless creatures, they are all flesh-eaters, usually feeding on animals that are stronger or faster-moving than themselves. They deal with what looks like impossible prey by means of venom. Spiders, snakes and many other venomous creatures, including some prey-seeking wasps, have fangs, spines or stings like hypodermic syringes to inject the venom. Jellyfishes and their relatives have stinging cells that act like tiny knives to cut the skin of their prey and let the poison in.

Each sort of venomous animal has poison that is slightly different from every other kind, but in general it does two things. The first is to subdue the prey, so almost all animal venoms include a nerve poison. This attacks the nervous

system, causing paralysis, so the prey cannot escape or fight its way free. The second thing is that most venoms act as a digestive juice, so that the flesh of the prey is broken down. Many venomous animals, such as poisonous snakes and spiders, cannot chew their food. Snakes swallow their meals whole. Those that have venom are able to digest their food much faster than those without it. Spiders can only feed on liquid. Their prey must be totally broken down before they can suck up their meal.

Poison for protection

Some small and helpless animals, such as ladybirds and toads, are armoured with poisons in their tissues. These are not used to kill prey, but to deter predators. Anything that tries to eat one of these creatures soon finds that it tastes so nasty that it is better left alone. The venomous stings of bees and some wasps are generally used in defence, as are the sharp spines, connected to poison glands, of some slow-moving fishes that live on the sea-bed. Animals that are protected by these internal poisons are often brightly coloured, usually with red or yellow and black stripes or patches. This is called warning coloration. It acts as a signal to predators, telling them not to attack. ◆

▲ The scorpion fish lies on the sea-bed, well camouflaged among the sea anemones. It has venom glands at the base of the sharp spines along its back.

▼ **Find out more**
Fishes
Frogs
Jellyfish
Ladybirds
Salamanders
Snakes
Spiders

Vertebrates

Phylum
Chordata
Subphylum
Vertebrata

The word 'vertebrate' comes from the Latin word for a backbone, so vertebrates are animals with backbones. The bodies of all vertebrates are supported by backbones and the other bones in the skeleton. The ribs and the skull also protect the body's organs.

There are many more kinds of invertebrates (animals without backbones) than vertebrates, but the vertebrates are almost all bigger and more complicated. There are five major groups of vertebrates. ◆

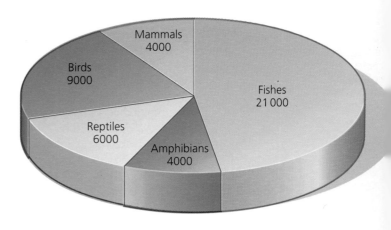

▲ Number of species in each group of vertebrates.

The five vertebrate groups

Fishes are cold-blooded and live in water. They breathe by means of gills, and in most cases the females lay large numbers of eggs, which are not usually cared for. There are several different groups of fishes, including the jawless fishes, the bony fishes and the cartilaginous fishes.

Amphibians are cold-blooded and hatch from eggs as tadpoles. These live in water, later changing into adults that generally live on dry land. They have a soft, moist skin and usually stay near water.

Reptiles are cold-blooded and most spend all their lives on land, though some, like crocodiles, live in water. The females lay shelled eggs, and when the young hatch they look like small adults.

Birds are warm-blooded, feathered animals with wings. Birds lay eggs, and the young are kept warm and cared for.

Mammals are warm-blooded, so they can be active even in cold parts of the world. A few kinds lay eggs, but in most cases the young are born alive and fed on milk.

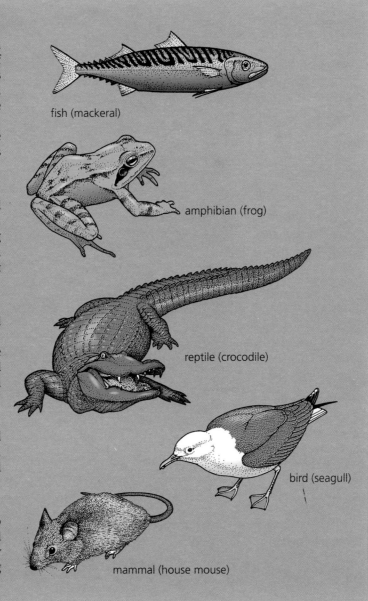

fish (mackeral)

amphibian (frog)

reptile (crocodile)

bird (seagull)

mammal (house mouse)

You can see how the vertebrates fit in with other animal groups in the chart in the article on Animals.

Veterinary surgeons

The word 'veterinary' comes from a Latin word, *veterinae*, meaning 'cattle'.

Veterinary surgeons, or vets, are animal doctors. Human doctors deal only with people, but veterinary surgeons look after many different types of animal. In towns, vets often work in a 'small animal practice'. This means that they care mainly for pets. In the country, vets often have a 'large animal practice' and are concerned with farm animals and horses.

Like human doctors, vets use modern drugs and techniques for curing sick animals. They give many animals injections to protect (immunize) them against illness, just as doctors immunize children against measles and other diseases.

Being a vet is a hard job. An animal that is ill is often frightened and may bite. Also a vet has to be ready day and night to attend a sick or injured animal.

Many people think that they would like to be a vet. But the training is difficult and in Britain takes five years to complete. In spite of this, there is great competition for college courses in vet training.

Another possibility, if you would like to work with animals, is to become a veterinary nurse. This means helping the vet, just as hospital nurses help doctors. ◆

Vibration

'Vibration' is the scientific word for what happens when anything wobbles or shakes. If you 'twang' your ruler over the edge of a table, you make it vibrate. When something that is wobbling makes the air near it vibrate, we may get a sound.

When someone drops a pile of plates, the clatter has irregular vibrations. But if you play a note on a musical instrument, the vibrations are very regular.

Scientists call the number of complete vibrations every second the *frequency*. For example, if you play the note A above middle C on a piano, the piano string will have a frequency of 440 vibrations every second. In scientific language we would say 440 hertz (Hz).

Vibrations do not have to be in solid things. If an electric current oscillates (vibrates), it sets the electric and magnetic fields round the current wobbling too, and the wobbles travel as waves, called *electromagnetic waves*. They could be radio waves that have frequencies of hundreds of thousands of vibrations each second. They could be microwaves in which the frequency might be as high as 2000 million. In a microwave cooker, these vibrations make the atoms in the food wobble at the same frequency so it gets hot very quickly.

If you push a child on a swing at exactly the right frequency, you can easily build up a big swing. Pushing at the right frequency is called *resonance*. If it occurs in a building or a bridge or some other structure, it can cause damage and this is one of the things designers must take into account. ◆

If a delicate wine glass is tapped, it vibrates and produces a lovely, clear note. If a singer can produce a very pure, loud sound, on exactly the same note, resonance can make the glass shatter.

▼ In 1940, the Tacoma Narrows Bridge in the USA was set into resonant vibration by the wind blowing across it (like the reed in a musical instrument) and was destroyed.

▼ **Find out more**
Microwaves
Musical instruments
Radio
Sound
Waves

Victorian Britain

▶ The opening of the Great Exhibition in the huge Crystal Palace built of glass and iron especially for the exhibition in Hyde Park. 'The sight ... was so magical – so vast, so glorious, so touching. The tremendous cheering, the joy expressed on every face, the vastness of the building ... God bless Albert, and my dear country, which has shown itself so great today,' (Queen Victoria's diary, 1 May 1851). On the platform are Queen Victoria and her husband Prince Albert, their eldest children (Bertie and Victoria), and the queen's mother. See Hing, a Chinese sea captain, looked so important that he was included in the front row on the right below the platform, although he had not been invited.

Population of England

1801	8,300,000
1851	16,811,000
1901	32,528,000

Britain in 1851

For many people in Victorian Britain, 1 May 1851 was an exciting day. Queen Victoria, with Prince Albert by her side, opened the first Great Exhibition of industry from countries all over the world. Over half the exhibitors were British, because Britain in 1851 was the leading industrial nation of the world.

▶ Over 6 million people visited the Great Exhibition, many on the new railways. Railway building changed the environment, as motorway building does now. In 1872 Gustave Doré, a Frenchman, drew this London scene of slum houses under a railway bridge, with another railway beyond.

Britain and its empire

The Great Exhibition showed the vast wealth of the British empire. In 1851 Britain ruled over millions of people. Many Victorians worked in India as soldiers, traders and government officials. Victorian explorers were beginning to go deep into Africa. Although most Victorians believed that their empire was good for everyone who lived in it, and were very proud of it, few of them understood the different cultures of the people in the countries they took over.

Sometimes English people did not understand the problems of Scotland, Wales and Ireland either. Ireland in particular was a troubled place. Irish people were the poorest in the British Isles. Most were Catholic. Some already wanted Ireland to be free of Britain. But Ulster in the north was different. More Protestants lived there, and they were more prosperous; they wanted to stay British.

Country life

Landowners had been the richest and most powerful people in Britain for centuries. This was still true in Victorian Britain. The squire who lived in the big house in a village usually

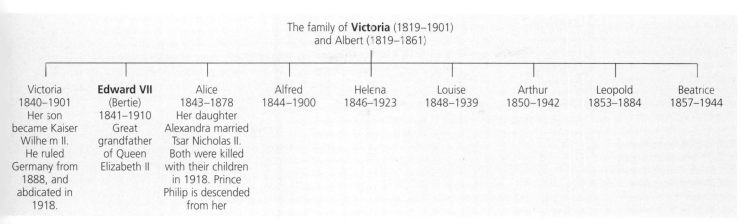

The family of **Victoria** (1819–1901)
and Albert (1819–1861)

Victoria 1840–1901	Edward VII (Bertie) 1841–1910	Alice 1843–1878	Alfred 1844–1900	Helena 1846–1923	Louise 1848–1939	Arthur 1850–1942	Leopold 1853–1884	Beatrice 1857–1944
Her son became Kaiser Wilhelm II. He ruled Germany from 1888, and abdicated in 1918.	Great grandfather of Queen Elizabeth II	Her daughter Alexandra married Tsar Nicholas II. Both were killed with their children in 1918. Prince Philip is descended from her						

owned the villagers' homes, and employed most of them to work on his land. A good squire who looked after the villagers and helped them in hard times could be like a kind father, but even so he would have been a figure who had to be obeyed. Owners of small farms were often prosperous and quite independent. Ordinary villagers lived in damp, cold houses with no indoor water supply, and could be very poor.

Things began to change in about 1880. Cheap wheat poured in from the USA and Canada; meat could now be frozen, so that could be imported too. Margarine was invented, and was cheaper than butter. All this competition hit British farming badly. Landowners did less well, wages fell, and there was more unemployment. This contributed to the increase in the number of people who left their villages to find jobs in the growing towns.

Town life

In 1801, 20 per cent of Britain's people lived in towns. By 1901, the number had increased to 75 per cent. London especially was like a great octopus with its tentacles reaching out into the surrounding country. Life in the big city slums was grim. Although the population as a whole was increasing, more babies died young in the cities than anywhere else. Rail travel made it easier for the better-off to get to work, and so suburbs grew up on the edge of towns, with bigger houses, trees and gardens. By 1901 people could shop in the new department stores in city centres. Big cities like Birmingham and Manchester had fine new town halls, libraries, art galleries and parks.

Factories and cities

More industry meant more cotton mills, bigger coal mines and more factories all over the country. Existing and new cities grew quickly. By 1880 the industrial town of Middlesbrough with 50,000 people had grown up on the River Tees. In 1830 there had been only one farmhouse on the site. This huge change in people's lives brought problems. Employers did not often fence off machinery, and factories and mines were unhealthy places to work. There were no rules about hours of work or wages. Workers' houses were built as cheaply as possible, huddled together with no taps or toilets indoors. They soon became slums. Filthy drains were often close to pumps providing drinking-water.

Cholera, spread by infected water supplies, first appeared in Britain in 1831 and became known as the 'Victorian Plague'. Not only the poor suffered. Prince Albert died of typhoid in 1861, which he caught from water contaminated by the drains in Windsor Castle.

1837	Victoria becomes Queen
1840	Victoria and Albert marry
1851	Great Exhibition
1854	Crimean War
1857	Indian 'Mutiny'
1865	First woman doctor begins work
1867	Workers in towns get the vote
1870	Education Act Trade unions legal
1875	Public Health Act
1884	Workers in country get vote Irish demand Home Rule
1892	Keir Hardie elected first Labour MP
1899	Boer War
1901	Death of Victoria

◀ In many Victorian homes, Sunday was kept as a special day, and the family often went to church more than once. This picture, accompanied by the verse below, 'Preparing for Sunday', appeared in a children's magazine in 1868:

Haste! Put your
  playthings all away,
Tomorrow is the
  Sabbath Day.
Come bring to me your
  Noah's Ark,
Your pretty tinkling
  music cart;
Because, my love, you
  must not play,
But holy keep the
  Sabbath Day.

Struggle for change

The 1830s were bad years for working people, with low wages and much unemployment. Many workers believed they could not change their lives for the better until they could vote and have a say in making laws in Parliament.

In 1836 a group of skilled workers in London, led by Francis Place and William Lovett, decided to draw up a Charter. This demanded several reforms by Parliament, in particular the vote for all adult males (though not for women), and payment for MPs so that working people could be elected to Parliament. The Charter caught on, and workers all over the country campaigned to get it accepted.

Some 'Chartists' believed in violence, and in 1839 there was a serious riot in Newport, Monmouthshire, when Parliament rejected a huge Chartist petition. By 1848 two more petitions had come to nothing. The Chartists did not get the reforms they wanted, but many working people had learnt how to organize meetings, run newspapers and sort out their own ideas. Employers and politicians also became more aware of the problems of the working classes.

Strikes

The failure of the Chartists showed how hard it was for ordinary people to change their lives for the better. Gradually workers realized that if they joined a trade union, they could help each other, and perhaps force their employers to improve wages and working conditions. In the late 1880s, strikes by the women making matchboxes (match girls) and the dockers were both successful, partly because newspapers reported their terrible problems, gaining them public sympathy and support. But strikes were very risky. Employers tried hard to make strikes illegal, and often 'locked out' strikers, so they lost their jobs. Then their families could starve.

Reforms

Many Victorians worked hard for reform, and most of the changes the Chartists wanted came about in the end. By 1884 most men over 21 could vote, so MPs had to win ordinary men's votes if they wanted to be elected. By 1900 there were even a few working-class MPs, though MPs were not paid until 1911.

Many people began to realize that rules were needed to make towns healthy, and workplaces safe. By 1875 Parliament had passed laws enforcing clean water supplies, proper drains and dustbin collections. Cholera gradually disappeared. There were laws which stopped children working in mines and factories.

▼ This picture appeared in 1866 and was called *The Black Country round Wolverhampton*. The reason for the name is obvious. Coal was the fuel for furnaces and the steam engines which drove factory machines. Its smutty smoke caused air pollution. Thick greenish fogs, nicknamed 'pea-soupers', were quite common in Victorian cities.

◀ In the hot summer of 1858 the River Thames, London's chief sewer and main source of drinking-water, became so smelly that people called it 'the Great Stink'. This photograph shows the modern sewage system being built in 1862. It carried London's sewage right away from the city, and was complete by 1865.

y 1878 a factory worker's day was limited to
0 hours, and there were rules about safety at
ork. Married women gained some rights by
882. They could keep their own property, and
usbands had to pay for their keep if there was
divorce. The first Act of Parliament to give
omen the vote was defeated in 1886. Things
nproved, but poverty and disease did not
isappear.

chools for rich and poor

ich boys usually went to 'public' schools which
ere not public but fee-paying. Dr Arnold's
eforms at Rugby School in the 1830s
ncouraged better standards, and other public
chools copied his ideas. The North London
ollegiate School founded in 1850 was one of
he first to provide a good education for middle-
lass girls. The Church provided some primary
chools, but Britain was slow to provide enough
chools for all its children (though there were
nore schools in Scotland). After 1870 there
ere 'elementary' schools for all 5- to 10-year-
lds. By 1901 these schools were free for
veryone up to 12. But the difference between
chools for rich and poor remained.

Women's lives

Women did not have the vote and had few
ights. A working-class woman lived a hard life.
he usually had a large family and lived in a
mall, cramped house. Everyday jobs like
vashing clothes were very hard work. She often
ad to earn money as well to make ends meet,
erhaps by sewing shirts or making matchboxes
or very low pay. Some women left home to
vork. In 1871 1.5 million people worked as
lomestic servants, and this number went on
ising. Over two-thirds of them were women.
They lived with their employers, usually in an
ttic or basement, and had very little free time.
'ay might be £20 a year.

Richer women had different problems. Most
vere just educated to get them a better husband.
When they did marry, they became dependent
on their husbands. Married women could not
own property. Anything they possessed, and any
noney that had been theirs before their
narriage, belonged legally to their husbands.
This situation changed during the Victorian
period, after pressure from women. And in spite
of the difficulties, some women began to find
new opportunities. Better schools gave girls the
chance to do more. The first woman doctor,
Elizabeth Garrett Anderson, began work in 1865.
About 10 years later, the first women studied at

"Sweet Sixteen"

◀ These advertisements
show two of the new
devices available to
households at the end of
the 19th century. These
made housework easier,
but any family who could
afford it still employed
servants to clean, cook
and look after children.

Oxford and Cambridge universities. Some began
to work for 'Votes for Women', even though
Queen Victoria called it 'mad, wicked folly'.

Emigration and immigration

Some people left the crowded cities of Victorian
Britain to make a new life elsewhere. They went
mainly to Canada, Australia and New Zealand.
Emigrants from poverty-stricken Ireland went
to the USA with bitter memories of British rule.
Some Irish became 'immigrants' in British cities
like Liverpool and Manchester. Russian and
Polish Jews arrived in London in the 1890s,
escaping from persecution at home.

Fun and games

The rich enjoyed the London 'season', a time of
the year for lots of socializing, when people went
to balls, banquets and theatres. Music halls were
much cheaper and provided the popular music
of the time. At home, magic lanterns (simple
slide projectors) were exciting new inventions.
The first cinemas in the 1890s showed short
silent films and were called bioscopes. Rail travel
made outings to the seaside or to London Zoo
easy. People went to football matches, and to
horse races. County cricket began, and W. G.
Grace was a national hero. Lawn tennis was
becoming popular by 1901. ◆

Video

▶ **Cutaway picture of a compact video camera. Such cameras are slim and light enough to be held steady with one hand.**

*V*ideo is Latin for 'I see'.

Digital recordings code signals as numbers (digits). Digital signals made from a video can then be moved to a different medium, say to a computer, converted back into signals for pictures or sounds, and called up onto the screen.

The word 'video' is used to describe the various devices which record and produce moving pictures electronically. A video camera records moving pictures. A video recorder plays video tapes on a television, and records television programmes so that you can watch them later. Video pictures can also be recorded digitally, and played on a computer screen.

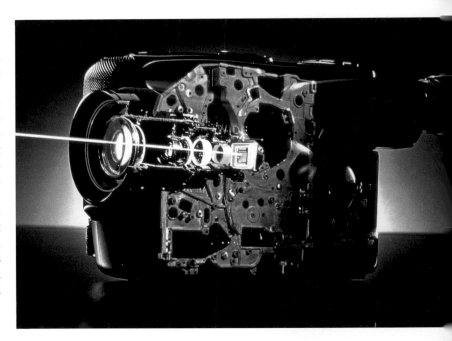

Video recorders

Video recorders record pictures on video tape in the same way as cassette recorders record sound on cassette tape – as a magnetic pattern. The electric signals which are recorded are the signals which a television needs to create pictures on its screen. Many more signals are needed for recording pictures than are needed for recording sound, so a video tape is much wider than a cassette tape, and the signals are recorded in diagonal stripes.

Video tape is stored inside a cassette on two reels. When you load a cassette into a video recorder, levers inside the machine pull a loop of tape out of the machine and wrap it around a metal drum. The drum is set at an angle to the tape, and there are two recording and playback heads set in it. When the machine is recording or playing, the drum spins as the tape moves past it, making the heads move across it in diagonal lines.

Video cameras

A video camera takes pictures of a scene, and turns them into electrical signals. The camera lens focuses light from the scene on to a special light-sensitive microchip. The signal can be recorded on video tape to be played later. A *camcorder* records pictures on a mini video tape.

Using video

Many people have video recorders at home for recording and watching programmes and feature films. They might also have a camcorder for recording family events and holidays. Television companies use video for news reporting. Video is also used for pop videos and for making adverts. Security video cameras in shops and banks record all the time but only take a picture every second or so. If a robbery is attempted, the criminals can be identified on the video.

Video editing

Pop videos, advertising videos and video clips for news programmes are carefully edited. They often start as many small video clips lasting just a few seconds. The editor cuts out unwanted bits and joins other bits together to make the final video. Video clips are often digitized and then edited on computer. Special effects, such as mixing bits from each clip, can also be done easily on computer. ◆

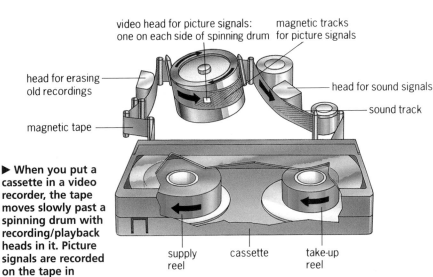

video head for picture signals: one on each side of spinning drum

magnetic tracks for picture signals

head for erasing old recordings

head for sound signals

sound track

magnetic tape

▶ **When you put a cassette in a video recorder, the tape moves slowly past a spinning drum with recording/playback heads in it. Picture signals are recorded on the tape in diagonal stripes.**

supply reel

cassette

take-up reel

Vietnam

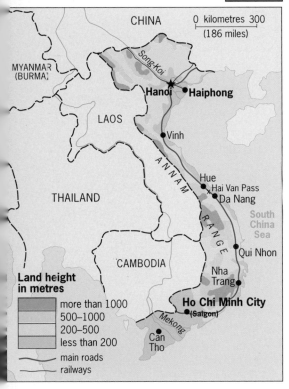

Land height
in metres

more than 1000
500–1000
200–500
less than 200
— main roads
- railways

Vietnam, in South-east Asia, is a long, narrow country shaped like a tall letter S. The widest part is in the north, bordering China, and includes the delta of the Red River (Song-Koi), so called because it carries away so much red soil. From there to the Mekong river delta in the far south is about 1600 kilometres. A beautiful coastline with sandy beaches stretches the length of the eastern side of the country, while to the west a mountain range climbs up into neighbouring Laos.

Vietnam generally is damp and humid. The north has four seasons, with cool winters and hot summers. Travelling south, over the Hai Van Pass you are in a sunny land, warm to very hot all year round. In the mountains it rains a lot, but near the coast it can be very dry. Yet almost every year typhoons roar in from the east, with wild seas and flooding causing havoc.

It is a typical sight to see Vietnamese people in their large, round, conical straw hats working hard in the paddy fields. Less than a third of the country can be used for agriculture, because of the mountains and the coastal sands. But nearly three-quarters of the population work on the land. Rice, maize and sweet potatoes are the most important crops. Peanuts grow well, especially in the central provinces. Fishing and forestry are also

important. Many trees are being planted to replace 70,000 square kilometres of forest destroyed by war and wood-cutting for fires.

FLASHBACK

Temples, pagodas and stone sculptures from an ancient Buddhist kingdom called Champa are evidence of the great antiquity of civilization in the area now known as Vietnam. For many centuries the Chinese controlled the country, until an independent Vietnamese kingdom, Annam, arose. For just over 60 years this land was part of Indo-China under French control. A war of independence resulted in 1954 in the formation of two separate countries, North Vietnam and South Vietnam. North Vietnam had a communist government led by Ho Chi Minh. Elections had been promised at the 1954 Geneva Conference. Almost certainly the communists would have been voted into power in the south, too, but elections were never held.

From the early 1960s the USA sent troops to defend the south from communism. American forces fought against communist guerrillas, the Vietcong. American bombers attacked the north and neighbouring Cambodia and Laos. Millions of tonnes of bombs were dropped; people were burnt by napalm; forests and crops were destroyed by chemicals which caused trees to lose their leaves. Eventually the Americans realized that they could not win, and by 1973 had withdrawn. Three years later North and South Vietnam joined as one nation under a communist government. ◆

Area
329,556 sq km
Capital
Hanoi
Population
70,400,000
Language
Vietnamese, Chinese, French, English, others
Religion
Buddhist, Christian
Government
Republic
Currency
1 dong = 10 hao = 100 xu

Following a Chinese invasion of Vietnam in 1979, thousands of Vietnamese people of Chinese origin were forced to flee the country. In the mid-1990s over 20,000 of these Vietnamese 'boat people' were still held in camps in Hong Kong.

Half the forests and one-fifth of farm lands were devastated by US bombing in the 1960s and 1970s.

◀ Fishing boats in north Vietnam. The refugee 'boat people' fled the country in boats similar to these.

▼ **Find out more**
Asia
Refugees
Twentieth-century history
Vietnam War

BIOGRAPHY
Ho Chi Minh

Vietnam War

The success of North Vietnam in the Vietnam War of 1964–1975 owed a good deal to the skills of Ho Chi Minh (1890–1969). He was born into a peasant family and spent some of his early life in Paris. After that, he devoted his time to the advance of communism. Known as 'Uncle Ho', he was an able general, a wise politician and an inspiring leader. In 1975 the capital of South Vietnam, Saigon, was renamed Ho Chi Minh City in his honour.

Vietnam War deaths 1964–1975

1 million North Vietnamese soldiers.

500,000 civilians.

200,000 South Vietnamese soldiers.

1 million Cambodians killed and wounded by US bombing.

56,555 US troops.

One-fifth of US soldiers who died were killed by other US troops.

▶ **In the Vietnam War napalm bombs were used. These children were running to save their lives after being burnt by napalm in 1972. The naked girl recovered after several skin grafts but suffered pain for years afterwards.**

▼ **Find out more**
Cold war
Twentieth-century history
United States of America: history
Vietnam

BIOGRAPHY
Ho Chi Minh

During the 19th and early 20th centuries, Vietnam was part of France's empire in Indo-China. The country was occupied by Japan in World War II, then returned to France in 1945. The Vietnamese immediately declared their country independent and began a long struggle to drive the French out. France managed to hang on to South Vietnam, but could not defeat the communists in the north. The North Vietnamese, led by President Ho Chi Minh, were aided by Communist China. In 1954 the French finally left and the country was divided along the 17th parallel. The communists controlled North Vietnam, where they improved industry and agriculture and built up a large army. A shaky pro-western government tried to rule South Vietnam. In 1960 the National Liberation Front (NLF) was formed to unite North and South into a single communist state, and South Vietnam dissolved into civil war.

Enter the Americans

This was the time of the cold war between communist countries (mainly the USSR and China) and capitalist countries (mainly the USA and Western Europe). The Americans promised to help 'free peoples' stand up to communism. They also believed in the

'domino theory'. This said that if one country fell to the communists, the one next door would fall, then the one next to that, and so on. To stop this happening, the Americans decided to resist communists everywhere. By 1960 they had military advisers helping the South Vietnamese fight the NLF army, known as the Vietcong. Then, in 1964, the Americans said one of their warships had been attacked by NLF boats. The Americans were furious, and President Johnson got permission to send US forces into Vietnam. Marines arrived in 1965. By the summer of 1967 there were 2 million US soldiers in bases in South Vietnam. Troops also

arrived from Australia, New Zealand, South Korea and Thailand.

The Americans had made a serious mistake. Their men were not trained to fight in the jungles and swamps of Vietnam, where their superior technology, such as tanks and heavy artillery, was useless. The Vietcong, on the other hand, were fighting on home territory against a foreign invader. Time and again their skilful and brave troops outwitted their enemies. The Americans turned to massive air raids on North Vietnam and, later, on neighbouring countries. Civilian and military targets were attacked. Huge areas of the jungle were destroyed with fire bombs and chemical weapons. But nothing stopped the Vietcong advance.

The end of the war

Young men were forced to join the US army, and the war became very unpopular. By 1968 the Americans realized they could not win. The following year they began to pull out of Vietnam and peace talks started in Paris. By 1973, when a cease-fire was agreed, all American forces had been withdrawn. The cease-fire broke down in 1974 and a year later South Vietnam fell to the communists and the country was united. ◆

Vikings

In the Middle Ages the word Viking meant a robber who came by sea, a pirate. Today we use Viking as the name of Norse peoples who lived in the Scandinavian countries of Norway, Denmark and Sweden. In their own countries they were farmers. In the 8th century AD they began to look for more land. They made raids across the seas and settled in other countries. They were great traders, too, reaching as far east as Byzantium (Istanbul) and westwards across the Atlantic to Newfoundland.

Everyday life

Most Vikings were farmers and they built the same sort of farmhouse wherever they settled. The most important part was the great hall. In earlier times this was where the family lived, ate and slept. Later the hall was divided into eating and sleeping rooms. The house would often be smoky inside because the cooking was done over an open fire in the middle of the room.

Viking farmers grew all sorts of crops to eat, such as wheat, oats, barley and vegetables like cabbages, beans and carrots. They kept cattle, sheep, pigs and chickens but they also hunted animals, birds and fish. Some of this food would be smoked in the roof of the hall or dried or salted to eat during the winter.

Viking men and women liked bright clothes and decoration and jewellery. Women often wore headscarves, an ankle-length dress of wool or linen, with an overdress held on by great brooches. They might also wear necklaces, bracelets and rings. Men wore woollen trousers with a tunic or shirt on top.

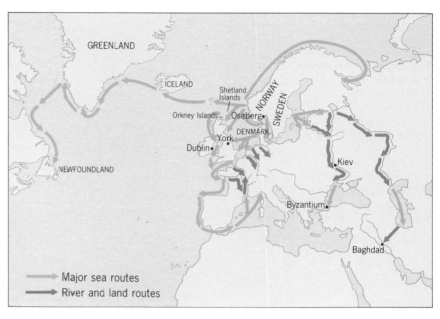

Jorvik, a Viking town

In AD 866 some of the Vikings who had settled in East Anglia marched north and took over the Anglo-Saxon capital of Northumbria, then called *Eoforwic* (previously the Roman city of *Eburacum*). The Vikings called it *Jorvik*. Recently archaeologists have discovered some of the houses of Viking Jorvik in modern York. They were not as big as the farmhouses, just one-room wooden houses. It was a rich town, though, full of merchants and craftspeople. The Vikings ruled Jorvik for nearly 90 years. Their last king, Eric Bloodaxe, was thrown out by the English in the year 954.

Merchants and traders

One writer said that Jorvik was 'filled with treasures of merchants from many lands'. The Vikings were famous for the goods they made themselves and for their trade with far-off countries. They traded as far north as Iceland and with the Lapps (for ivory and furs), as far south as Baghdad (for silk and spices) and into Russia (for slaves and furs). In towns, craftspeople made a variety of products; for example, pots and pans for the kitchen, clothes and jewellery, tools and weapons of bronze and iron. They exchanged goods but they also minted their own coins.

◀ Archaeologists found the remains of Viking houses at Jorvik still standing over a metre high. From these remains, and all the other evidence, they have been able to rebuild part of Coppergate in York: 'the street of the wooden-cup makers'.

▲ The Vikings made their journeys between the years 780 and 1100.

▼ These 10th century Viking combs were made out of bone and antlers. The round objects are spindle whorls used for spinning. Remains of textiles have survived too.

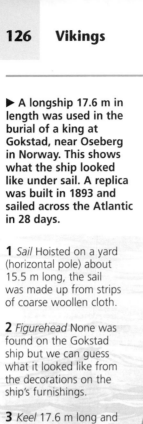

▶ A longship 17.6 m in length was used in the burial of a king at Gokstad, near Oseberg in Norway. This shows what the ship looked like under sail. A replica was built in 1893 and sailed across the Atlantic in 28 days.

1 *Sail* Hoisted on a yard (horizontal pole) about 15.5 m long, the sail was made up from strips of coarse woollen cloth.

2 *Figurehead* None was found on the Gokstad ship but we can guess what it looked like from the decorations on the ship's furnishings.

3 *Keel* 17.6 m long and 45 cm deep, it gave strength and stability to the ship.

4 *Side rudder* Attached to a block on the hull, it could be hauled upwards in seconds.

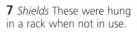

7 *Shields* These were hung in a rack when not in use.

8 *Mastfish* The mast was slotted into this, and could be lowered or raised without being taken out of its socket.

9 *Mast* About 10 m tall.

10 *Crutches* These carried the yard and mast when the ship was being rowed.

5 *Deck* Made of loose planks with storage room.

6 *Hull* 16 rows of overlapping planks reinforced with ribs and cross-beams.

Raiders

The Vikings are probably best known as fierce raiders of other peoples' lands. They first invaded Britain in AD 793 when they attacked the island of Lindisfarne off the Northumbrian coast. Raiders would be looking for rich plunder, but also for slaves.

Slaves, called *thralls*, worked on the farms for freemen, called *karls*. More important than freemen were the rich landowners who were also chieftains. They were called *jarls*. Warriors on raiding parties were heavily armed with swords, shields, spears and axes. They wore helmets and chain mail.

Viking ships

The key to the success of the Vikings in trading and raiding was the ship. Shipbuilding was a very skilled craft. Of course, other peoples, such as the Anglo-Saxons, had ships. The Vikings, however, built fast, strong ships that could withstand even an Atlantic crossing. In about AD 1000 the Viking explorer Leif Ericsson journeyed all the way to Newfoundland in North America.

The Vikings built not only 'longships' for raiding (one was known to have held 200 fighting men), but also wider, deeper ships called *knarrs* for trade, and little rowing boats called *faerings*. Ships had both oars and sails. ◆

Villages

Villages are settlements in the country. They are smaller than towns or cities. Fewer people live in a village and there are fewer roads and buildings. Villages are traditionally places where farmers live so that they are close to the land they work on. Not all the people living in villages are farmers. Others provide services to farmers and their families, such as a few shopkeepers and a doctor.

Villages in India

In India, three out of every four people live in villages. Most of these people work in agriculture. Many farmers have a small piece of land, perhaps two hectares. Others do not own land, but rent it from a landlord. The rent they pay may be cash or some part of their harvest. Other agricultural workers in Indian villages get work from day to day, on a landlord's land. Their payment may be food and a place to sleep.

Agricultural workers usually live in a small hut, often with just one room where the family lives, eats and sleeps. Some farmers keep a cow, if they can find enough fodder to feed it. The cow's dung is collected, dried in the sun and used as fuel for a fire where meals are cooked. Otherwise women and children spend time searching for firewood.

▲ In the village of Dogon, in Mali in West Africa, people live in flat-roofed houses. They keep their grain in buildings with thatched, cone-shaped roofs.

◄ A small village lies just below the high mountains of the Himalayas in Nepal.

Commuting

In Europe some villages have changed from places where the main work is farming. Village houses have been bought by people who work in cities and each day travel into the city by car or train. These *commuters* have decided that they would like to live in the country, away from the noise and dirt of the city. This often means that they spend a longer time each day getting to their place of work, but they consider this extra time to be worthwhile because of the benefits of living in the peace of the countryside.

FLASHBACK

Many villages in Europe are hundreds of years old. If you look on a map at the distribution of buildings that make up a European village, you may notice some interesting patterns. Many villages are built in a line stretched out along a road or a river. Others are very compact, where all the houses have been built close together because in times gone by they were more easily defended against attack. In hilly areas villages were often built on hill slopes, so leaving the level land for farming. Most villages had a number of farms, each with the piece of land where the farmer worked, and usually a bigger manor house where the landowner lived. Also there was a church and sometimes an open space or village green. Most of these parts of the old village survive in the villages of today. In England the village green is the traditional spot where the village cricket teams play their matches. ◆

▼ **Find out more**
Cities and towns
Population: human

Virtual reality

In some virtual reality systems you can actually feel the objects as well as see them. This is done with gloves with tiny inflatable bladders inside, or by small motors which push or pull your hand.

A virtual reality system that makes you feel as though you are really in the world is called an 'immersive system'. There are also non-immersive systems and augmented systems, where you see a virtual world mixed with the real world.

Virtual reality (or VR for short) is a way of simulating a world using pictures and sounds generated by a computer. The world is called a 'virtual world'. You can enter a virtual world by wearing a special headset that is connected to the computer. This shows three-dimensional pictures in tiny television screens, and creates sounds through headphones. This fools your brain into thinking that you are really part of this artificial environment. You can touch and move things in the virtual world with a hand-held controller.

You can meet other people in a virtual world. They can be virtual people generated by the computer (called virtual actors), or representations of real people.

What is it used for?

Virtual reality already has many uses, and it will have many more as the technology it uses improves and becomes cheaper.

Used in training and education, virtual reality can simulate almost any situation in the real world. For example, a virtual aircraft can be used for pilot training and a virtual car for driver training. Virtual training is cheaper and safer than the real thing.

In the future, children will be able to learn with virtual reality. Imagine being able to learn about the ancient Romans by visiting a virtual Roman world.

Objects in a virtual world do not have to be the same size as they are in the real world. Scientists have designed chemicals by joining huge virtual atoms which seem to float in mid-air.

For entertainment and leisure, amazing virtual worlds can be invented to play computer games in. Virtual reality games and rides can be found in some theme parks.

Manufacturers can construct virtual objects, such as cars, to test them before they make them for real. Architects can build virtual buildings and walk through them before construction begins.

Creating a virtual world

At the heart of every virtual reality system is a powerful computer. It needs to be quick at drawing the three-dimensional pictures needed. The computer is often called the 'reality engine'. Plugged into the computer are a headset, containing television screens and headphone, and a hand-held controller. An electronic tracking system works out which way the headset and the controller are pointing. The information that tells the computer what the world is like is held in a database in the computer's memory. It describes the shape, size, colour and position of all the objects in the world. The computer looks at the database so that it can draw the world. Finally, a computer program (called the application software) decides exactly what happens in the world. ♦

▼ This doctor is learning about anatomy by using virtual reality. The leg, shown here, does not exist in real life. It is an image generated by a computer. The doctor sees this image and by wearing special gloves, linked to the computer, can touch it in the same way that he would touch a real leg.

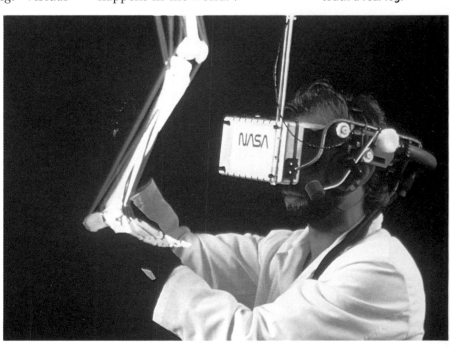

Viruses

Diseases such as flu, colds and cold sores are caused by viruses, and so is AIDS. Distemper in dogs and seals is a viral disease, and so are a number of plant diseases, including tobacco mosaic disease.

Viruses cause diseases in animals or plants. They are so small that scientists measure them in millionths of a millimetre. Viruses are either rods or spheres in shape.

Viruses are not cells and scientists are uncertain whether they are living things. They consist of a coat of protective protein which surrounds the material they need to reproduce (DNA or RNA). They can only reproduce inside the cells of the living things they infect. They take over these cells and turn them into virus factories which produce hundreds of new viruses before the cells are killed. ♦

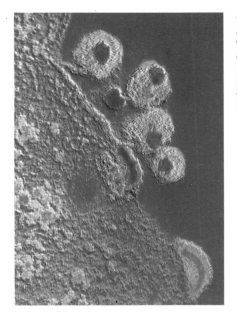

◄ The virus which causes AIDS, magnified many thousands of times. The colours in the photo are used to enhance the image – they are not the true colours of the virus in nature.

▼ Find out more
AIDS
Cells
Colds and coughs
Diseases
DNA
Germs

Vitamins

The word vitamin comes from the Latin word *vita* meaning 'life'.

Vitamins are chemical substances that are essential for life and health. They exist naturally in a wide variety of foods. The body uses these vitamins to perform important chemical processes. The amounts needed to keep a person alive and well are extremely small and can be obtained from a normal, balanced diet. There are 13 major vitamins: A, C, D, E, K and 8 different B vitamins. ♦

▼ Find out more
Food
Nutrition
Vegetables

Vitamin	Found in	Used for
A	Carrots, milk, butter, eggs, fish-liver oils, liver, green vegetables	Keeping skin and bones healthy, fighting disease and infection
B	Yeast, wholemeal bread, nuts, peas, beans, fish, meat, eggs, milk, cheese, green vegetables	Helping the body to release energy from food for growth, keeping skin and nerves healthy
C	Oranges, lemons, limes, tomatoes, blackcurrants, green vegetables	Helping wounds to heal, keeping blood, gums and teeth healthy, protection against colds
D	Liver, butter, cheese, eggs, fish. Also made in the body by the effects of sunlight on the skin	Keeping bones and teeth strong and healthy. Important in childhood
E	Wholemeal bread, brown rice, butter, green vegetables	Believed to help cell growth and wound healing
K	Green vegetables, liver	Clotting blood

Voice

Many animals use special sounds to communicate with each other. These sounds are called the animal's voice.

Our voice is much more complex than that of any other animal, because of the use we make of speech in communication. We make sound with a group of organs based in the throat and mouth. The *larynx* (voice box) is a thickened part of the windpipe. It contains flaps called *vocal cords*. Air forced out over the vocal cords produces the basic sound of our voice. We change that basic sound by changing the shape of our mouth and, most importantly, by moving our tongue very quickly and precisely. Our spoken languages would be impossible without our thick, quick-moving tongues.

In other animals different sound-producing organs may be used. Crickets 'sing' by rubbing their wings together rapidly, and frogs have special air sacs in their throats to amplify their croaks.

The voice of an animal may be used to attract mates, warn off rivals and defend territory boundaries. The song of a songbird may perform all these functions. ♦

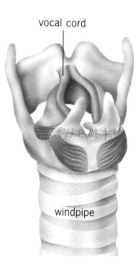

vocal cord

windpipe

▲ The location of the vocal cords in the larynx.

▼ Find out more
Communication
Frogs
Grasshoppers
Singing and songs
Sound

Volcanoes

Vulcano is an Italian island which has given its name to all other volcanoes.

Mauna Loa is the world's largest volcano. It reaches 4170 m above sea-level, but its base is on the Pacific Ocean floor, 5180 m below sea-level.

▶ Kilauea is a small volcano on the slopes of the much larger Mauna Loa in Hawaii. Most of the time the lava swirls and seethes in the fire pit, but occasionally it erupts explosively.

▼ Cross-section through an erupting volcano. Lava bursts through the main vent, and also through side passages called dykes. Sills are lava-filled passages running between rock layers.

A volcano is a mountain or hill made of lava which comes from deep beneath the Earth's surface. When a volcano erupts, lava and ash build up to make a cone. Some volcanoes give off clouds of ash and gas when they erupt. Others have streams of red-hot lava pouring down their side. Volcanoes can form on land or on the ocean floor. Some undersea volcanoes grow high enough to reach above sea-level and become islands.

The birth of a volcano

It is not often anyone can see a volcano begin and then grow. In Mexico, in 1943, some villagers were worried by earthquakes. Then a crack appeared across a cornfield and smoke gushed out. The crack widened, and ash and rocks were hurled high into the air. Soon, red-hot lava poured out. After a week, a volcano 150 metres high stood where the cornfield had been, and the villagers had to leave. Mount Paricutin grew to 275 metres in a year, and to 410 metres after nine years.

How a volcano grows

The molten rock deep beneath the Earth's crust is called magma. It forces its way up through cracks and weak spots in the Earth's crust and spills out of vents as lava. As magma rises, gases separate out from the molten rock. These gases may collect near the surface and cause a great explosion. On Martinique, in the Caribbean, 20,000 people were killed by an explosion of hot gases and ash when Mont Pelée erupted during 1902.

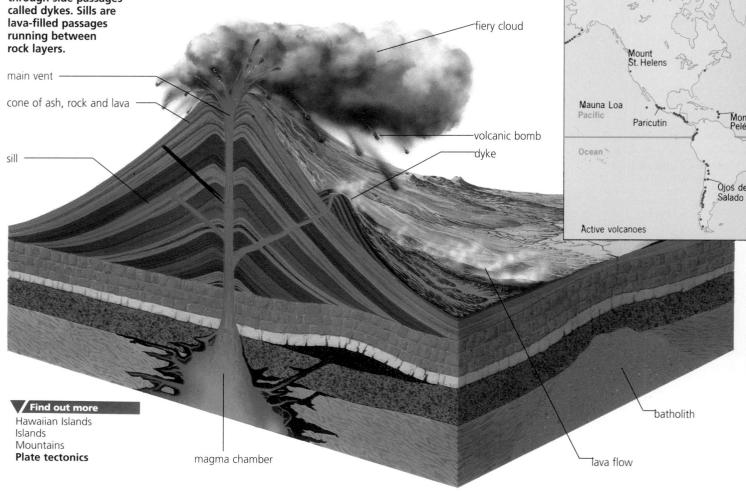

main vent

cone of ash, rock and lava

sill

fiery cloud

volcanic bomb

dyke

magma chamber

lava flow

batholith

Mount St. Helens

Mauna Loa
Pacific

Paricutin

Mont Pelée

Ocean

Ojos del Salado

Active volcanoes

▼ **Find out more**
Hawaiian Islands
Islands
Mountains
Plate tectonics

When a volcano erupts, pieces of broken rock and ash are often thrown out with the lava. Large lumps are called 'volcanic bombs'. As the rock and ash cool, they make layers of solid rock. When Vesuvius, in southern Italy, erupted in the year AD 79, the town of Pompeii was completely buried under volcanic ash. Further round the Bay of Naples, Herculaneum was buried by mud which swept down the side of the volcano. Today, the remains of both towns have been dug out for all to see.

Dormant and extinct volcanoes

Volcanoes eventually die. A volcano that has not erupted for a long time is said to be dormant. There is always the danger that a dormant volcano may suddenly erupt. When people think a volcano has finally died, then it is called extinct. Gradually, the volcano will be eroded. The softer rocks are worn away first, and in some places the only part left is the hard plug which filled the vent of the volcano.

There are about 700 active volcanoes in the world today, including some that are under the sea. The map below shows that most of them

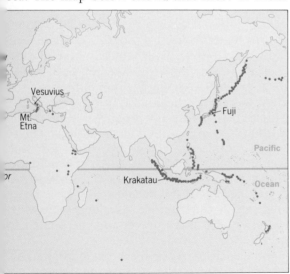

are arranged like beads on a string. Notice how many volcanoes surround the Pacific Ocean. The areas with volcanoes are also the areas which suffer from earthquakes.

This fact has helped scientists to come up with the theory of plate tectonics. They believe that the Earth's crust is broken into huge slabs, called 'plates'. Most of the world's volcanoes occur where plates meet, which is where magma can rise to the surface. A few, such as the volcanoes in Hawaii and the Canary Islands, occur above 'hot spots', where there is a hole or weakness in a plate and magma can pierce through. ◆

Voles

Voles may be mistaken for mice, but differ in having short tails and legs, and blunt faces with small eyes and ears. They often feed on very tough plants. To deal with this, most voles have teeth which continue to grow throughout their lives, keeping pace with the wear caused by such a harsh diet. Voles rarely live for more than one year, but most females produce several litters of young in this time. Most are eaten by foxes, owls or other predators but sometimes enough survive to cause a huge increase in numbers. They live in northern parts of the world.

Some northern voles are known as lemmings. These animals often have huge increases in population, which then drops suddenly when many migrate to find new food sources. ◆

◀ The bank vole is a common species over most of Europe and Asia. Like most voles it is often active during the daytime. It lives among rough vegetation or burrows in the surface of the soil. It makes stores of food, sometimes hiding its larder in an old bird's nest.

Distribution
North and Central America, Europe and Asia
Largest
Musk-rat, head and body length up to 32.5 cm
Smallest
Head and body length less than 8 cm
Number of young
Up to 12
Lifespan
Between 1 and 2 years
Subphylum
Vertebrata
Class
Mammalia
Order
Rodentia
Number of species
110

▼ **Find out more**
Lemmings
Rodents
Teeth

Volleyball

This is an indoor and outdoor game played between two teams with six players a side. Each team tries to hit or knock the ball with hand or arm (or any part of the body above the waist) over a net across the centre of the court so that the opposing team is unable to return it or prevent it from hitting the ground.

Each team can hit the ball a maximum of three times before sending it back across the net, but they cannot catch or hold the ball.

The game was invented in 1895 in America by a games instructor called William Morgan. He wanted a game for people who did not want to play basketball. ◆

A leather ball is used, similar to a soccer ball but lighter.

▼ **Find out more**
Basketball

Wading birds

Subphylum
Vertebrata
Class
Aves
Order
Charadriiformes
Number of species
Over 200

Wading birds are found along coasts worldwide, and on shallow inland waters, estuaries, marshes and mud flats. Birds that feed in wet places need to be specially equipped. Long legs allow them to wade into water, and long bills help them to pick up small creatures, even those that are hiding in mud.

In Britain most 'waders' are sandpipers and their relatives. In North America these are called 'shorebirds', and 'waders' means herons and egrets.

The long and the short

Herons are large with long necks, legs and toes for climbing in trees and among waterside plants. They eat animals, often fish, which they grasp in their dagger-like bills.

Wading birds spend much of the year near water. Many are at home in open spaces and breed on the northern tundra.

Size and feeding methods vary. Snipe have extremely long, straight bills and probe deep into the mud for worms. Oystercatchers have long, strong bills for prising open mussels, clams and other shellfish.

Avocets have long up-swept bills which they sweep from side to side as they search for tiny creatures to eat. Plovers have short, stubby bills. They run, stop, bend and seize their prey from the surface.

Flight for survival

Many wading birds live in the far north where food is plentiful in summer. The summer is short, but there is very little darkness and the young grow fast. Before the Arctic winter returns the birds must fly south. For some, like the ringed plover, which breeds over a wide area, the most northerly breeding birds make the longest journeys and winter farthest south. They 'leap-frog' the southerly breeding birds, which move hardly any distance.

Family groups do not migrate together. Often one parent leaves when the chicks are still young. If food is short this action may help the young survive. With some species, such as the spotted redshank, the female leaves the male to look after the young. On migration the juveniles will often travel together in their own flocks.

Some waders make remarkable journeys. The lesser golden plover flies from Siberia to Australia and New Zealand. Others near by in Arctic Canada winter in South America and fly the shortest route, which is mostly over sea, a continuous journey of 3800 kilometres.

Safety in numbers

Outside the breeding season many of these species form large flocks. They feed on estuaries where food is plentiful, and numbers may build up to thousands. As they search for food they all spread out over the mud. As the tide comes in they are driven off their feeding grounds and onto high-tide roosts where they wait, saving their energy, until the tide starts to fall again. ◆

▲ **Marbled godwit with the typically long legs and long beak of the wading birds.**

curlew probing deep into the mud

pratincole feeding in the air

▶ **Wading birds find food in many different ways.**

turnstone searching under stones

phalarope feeding from the surface water

avocet filtering food from water

▼ **Find out more**
Birds
Bird-watching
Migration
Water birds

Wales

Wales is a principality of the United Kingdom, in north-west Europe. Much of Wales is mountainous and the highest peak is Yr Wyddfa (Snowdon). A narrow gauge railway runs to the top. Beneath the peaks of Snowdonia are great caverns and slate quarries. Welsh slate was used to tile roofs all over the United Kingdom. The trains which once took the slate to the coast now carry 750,000 tourist passengers a year. Snowdonia's deep valleys and sharp peaks were shaped by glaciers in the last Ice Age. To protect the landscape it was made a national park. This means that no development is allowed that would spoil the area's appearance.

There are many lakes and rivers in Wales. Fast-flowing mountain rivers are used to turn turbines to make hydroelectricity. The power station at Maentwrog uses water from an artificial lake at Trawsfynydd. The lake water is also used to cool the reactors of a nuclear power station. Water from Llyn Brenig and other lakes in mid-Wales goes by pipeline to Birkenhead, Liverpool, Birmingham and other English cities.

Industries

North Wales has a small population which lives mainly from farming, tourism and some industry. Sheep-farming is common. South Wales is industrial and it is where most Welsh people live. Inland there is a landscape of long streets, terraced houses, and hillside chapels built around the coal mines in narrow valleys. There are far fewer working coal mines now than there were in the first half of the 20th century and many new factories. On the low-lying coastal strip the tradition of metal-working and engineering continues. Factories make cars, refrigerators and televisions. Foreign companies from Japan and elsewhere have invested in the region. There are offices, too. The government department that issues licences for drivers and vehicles is at Swansea.

People and languages

North and South Wales have different cultures. Traditions such as rugby football and choral singing are more common in the south. The northern and central areas are where most of the people who can speak Cymraeg (Welsh) live. About half a million people speak Cymraeg and English. A few speak only Cymraeg. Once it was feared that the language would die out. Efforts were made to keep it alive by the government and the people. A political party called Plaid Cymru was formed to protect the culture and press for Welsh independence. Road signs and official documents are now in both languages. An annual festival of Welsh culture the Eisteddfod, gives prizes for poetry and music. In a vote in 1997, the Welsh voted for greater self-government. The majority in favour came from the Cymraeg-speaking counties. Many from the eastern, more English counties, were less keen. ◆

Area
20,761 sq km
Capital
Cardiff
Population
2,835,073
Language
Cymraeg (Welsh) and English
Religion
Christian
Highest peak
Yr Wyddfa (Snowdon) 1085 m
Largest lake
Llyn Tegid (Bala) 4.38 sq km
Longest river
Usk

▲ A bilingual sign with a harp, the symbol of Wales.

◀ The Clywedog dam on the River Severn in central Wales. For 30 years slightly under half the water collected in Wales for public supply has been consumed in England.

Key to county names

BG Blaneau Gwent
BR Bridgend
CAE Caerphilly
CAR Cardiff
MT Merthyr Tydfil
NPT Neath & Port Talbot
NW Newport
RCT Rhondda Cynon Taff
SW Swansea
TO Torfaen

— main roads
--- county boundaries
— railways

Wales's history

Burial chambers thousands of years old have been found by archaeologists in Wales, but little is known about life there until the coming of the Celts from Europe some time after 700 BC. The Celts built hillforts such as Dinorben (in north-east Wales) for protection just as they did in the rest of Britain. When the Romans invaded after AD 54, they found it very hard to crush the Celts of Wales. The mountains always made Wales a very difficult place to conquer.

The Romans built a huge fortress at Isca (Caerleon) in south Wales and smaller forts dotted around the country. At first the Celts fought back fiercely, but in time those in the south were attracted to Roman ways of living. Here Romans built villas and a large town named Venta Silurum (Caerwent). But they never totally conquered the mountainous areas. By the time the Romans left Wales around AD 390, Celtic and Roman ways had merged together in some inland parts of Wales and people had been converted to Christianity.

A Christian and independent country

In Wales 1 March is a special day. It is St David's Day and it reminds the Welsh people of the period 1400 years ago when David, a Christian monk, struggled to keep Wales a Christian country at a time when the rest of Britain had been overrun by pagan Angle and Saxon tribes. Although some of these invaders attacked the coasts, they too found the mountains of Wales too difficult an enemy to conquer.

After the Romans left, Wales remained independent for over 800 years, but it was not a united country. There were many local rulers who fought one another and often tried to take each other's land. Sometimes a strong ruler like Hywel Dda (died 950) forced other leaders to obey him, but usually fighting started again once the strong ruler died. One of the problems was the custom of dividing land between all the sons when the father died, which meant that the land was split up into ever smaller pieces. Yet there were many things which kept Wales together. There was the love of the Welsh language and poetry, and the laws which had been gathered at the time of Hywel Dda.

When the Normans reached Wales in 1076, they succeeded in conquering only the flat areas of the south and parts of the borders. They could not defeat the rulers or princes in the mountains. At times, usually when the Normans quarrelled among themselves, Welsh princes such as Owain Gwynedd (1100–1170) and Llywelyn the Great (1172–1240) gained control of large parts of Wales.

Loss of independence

The greatest struggle was between Llywelyn ap Gruffudd and King Edward I of England. After a long war Llywelyn was killed in 1282 and Edward began to rule the lands of the Welsh princes himself. He built a series of vast castles and proclaimed his eldest son the Prince of Wales. The lands he seized became known as the Principality of Wales (a title which is still used to this day).

For years afterwards the Welsh people dreamt of freedom from English rule. Owain Glyndwr fought the English between 1400 and 1413, but was finally defeated. Harsh laws were passed and the Welsh had to pay even heavier taxes.

Union with England

Still the Welsh dreamt of freedom, and many thought that day had arrived when a Welshman, Henry Tudor, became king of England in 1485. But Henry VII showed little interest in the land of his birth. Even so, things were beginning to change.

Some of the richer Welsh landowners wanted to follow English customs and they begged Henry Tudor's son, Henry VIII, to change the way Wales was ruled. So in 1536 the English parliament passed the Act of Union. From then on Wales was divided into 13 counties, had the same laws as England, and elected members to the parliament at Westminster. The Act said that the Welsh language was not to be used for official business, and soon many of the landowners began to forget the Welsh language and customs.

The Welsh language

The Bible shown here was the first Bible translated into Welsh (Cymraeg) by Bishop William Morgan in 1588. The fact that the Bible could be read in Welsh did more than anything else to keep the Welsh language alive.

Welsh, one of the oldest languages in Europe, might have disappeared if people had not grown to love the language of the Welsh Bible. Today, over 500,000 people still speak Welsh and many more want to learn it.

Chapels

From the 16th century onwards, Welsh people increasingly took an interest in religion. Over 80 per cent of all the Welsh books published were about Christianity.

Many of the Welsh people were Nonconformists, that is Protestants who did not agree with the teachings of the Church of England. By 1900 there were more than 5000 chapels in Wales. Most of these chapels used Welsh in their services, and this greatly helped to preserve the Welsh language.

▲ In 1910 these women and girls at Aberdare carried coal home from the tips to use while their menfolk were on strike.

Coal mines and industry

Up until the year 1800 most of Wales was a country of small farms and villages. But this too was changing. Ironworks opened around Merthyr Tydfil in the south, and thousands of people migrated from rural Wales and from Ireland and England looking for work. Later, after 1850, even larger numbers of people moved to the coal-mining valleys to find work. Although mining was very dangerous, people could earn higher wages than in the country, and some found town life more exciting. By 1913 Cardiff, Barry, Newport and Swansea had grown into large ports sending coal all over the world. In north Wales too, the slate quarries employed many people. Life was also getting better in the countryside. New roads and railways meant that farmers could get their goods to market.

Unemployment and new industry

After World War I, demand for coal, steel and slate fell sharply. Many people who worked in these industries became unemployed and were forced to leave Wales. This was especially so in the 1930s, when over 250,000 people left Wales to find work. In 1914 there were 250,000 miners in Wales. In 1990 there were fewer than 4000.

But things in Wales are changing. A number of foreign firms have moved into Wales, bringing new jobs to replace those lost in the coal mines. Great efforts are also being made to strengthen the Welsh language (Cymraeg), with more people attending language classes, more schools teaching in the language, and a growing popularity of the Cymraeg television channel. In 1997 the Welsh narrowly voted for greater self-government, through a Welsh Assembly. ◆

In Welsh, the principality of Wales is called Cymru. This comes from a Celtic word meaning 'fellow countrymen', whereas Wales comes from an Anglo-Saxon word meaning 'foreigners'.

▼ **Find out more**
Castles
Celtic history
Eisteddfod
Hillforts
Normans
Protestants
Roman Britain
Wales

BIOGRAPHY
David, Saint
Edward I
Glyndwr, Owain
Henry VII
Henry VIII
Lloyd George, David
Llywelyn the Great

Warm- and cold-bloodedness

The terms warm- and cold-bloodedness are not very appropriate for describing the difference between the animals concerned. A 'cold-blooded' snake may sometimes have a higher body temperature than a 'warm-blooded' rat living in the same environment. The crucial difference is that the rat maintains its temperature at a constant level by internal means, while the snake controls its temperature through its behaviour – for instance, by moving in or out of the shade.

Human beings, like all other mammals and like birds, are warm-blooded. This does not mean that we never feel cold, but that we have a kind of thermostat in our brains, which keeps our bodies at a temperature of about 37 °C all of the time. In general, small mammals have a higher body temperature than large mammals, and birds tend to have a still higher body temperature. By maintaining a constant temperature, our bodies can go on working at a steady rate, digesting food and giving the same amount of energy, whether our surroundings are cold or hot.

What happens in winter

Most mammals and birds keep going with their normal life, even in winter, though a few hibernate. Cold-blooded animals such as reptiles and amphibians have body temperatures that go up and down much more with the temperature of their surroundings. Lizards and snakes, for example, are sluggish in the cold and bask in the Sun to increase their body temperature. During cold weather, many cold-blooded animals hibernate.

Warm-blooded animals are protected against weather and climate in a number of ways. Human beings, whales and seals have an insulating jacket of fat under their skin. Mammals usually have hair or fur, which insulates them against heat and cold, while birds have feathers for the same purpose. Warm-blooded animals also shiver, which produces extra heat in the muscles.

If we get too hot, our blood flows close to the surface of our skin and we cool off as we lose heat, like a radiator. Many other mammals, such as dogs and rabbits, have very thin fur on their ears and they lose heat from these areas in the same way. Panting and sweating also increase heat loss. ♦

The mammal with the highest body temperature is the dromedary, or Arabian camel, with a body temperature of 41 °C.

Find out more
Fur
Hair
Hibernation

Washing machines

Just putting dirty clothes in water will not get them clean. They need to have water forced through the fibres of the cloth. Most washing machines work by swirling the clothes in water in a revolving metal drum. Detergent is used to get the water more deeply into the fabric. It also removes the grease.

Most washing machines are automatic. They can be left to do the whole wash by themselves. Often, these machines can be controlled electronically. You choose from a range of different programs so that the machine hot-washes cotton clothes or cool-washes woollens. It mixes hot and cold water to the right temperature, gives the clothes a long or short wash, rinses them, then spins out most of the water. Some washing machines tumble-dry as well. ♦

Washing machines were once equipped with a mangle. This had two rollers which squeezed the water out of wet clothes. Later, twin-tub machines were made, with one tub for washing and another for spin-drying.

The first electric washing machine was made in 1906.

Find out more
Detergents
Household equipment

▼ In this machine, the dirty washing goes in the revolving drum. Here it is washed, rinsed and spun almost dry.

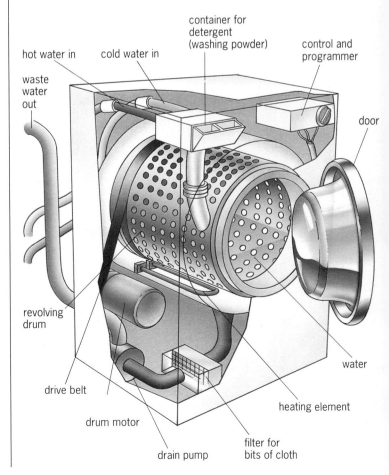

container for detergent (washing powder)

hot water in

cold water in

control and programmer

waste water out

door

water

revolving drum

heating element

drive belt

drum motor

drain pump

filter for bits of cloth

Wasps

Distribution
Worldwide
Largest social wasp
The hornet *Vespa crabro* grows up to 3.5 cm
Smallest wasp
Some adult parasitic wasps are less than 0.2 mm long
Phylum
Arthropoda
Class
Insecta
Order
Hymenoptera
Number of species
About 800 social wasps, 3000 potter wasps, 7700 digger wasps, 37,700 parasitic species, 2000 gall wasps

Most people think of wasps as insects with yellow and black stripes that protect themselves with a sting. But these are social wasps, which are only a small part of a huge group of insects. They are all closely related, but lead very different lives.

Social wasps

The wasps that make themselves a nuisance to us in the late summer are workers (sterile females) that are part of large family groups. All members of a family are the offspring of one female, called the queen. By the end of the summer the family might contain 50,000 wasps, nearly all workers.

The grubs that hatch from the eggs laid by the queen are flesh-eaters. The worker wasps feed them mainly on other insects. Early in the summer, when the family is growing fast, wasps kill huge numbers of pests. The workers themselves need only sugars to keep them going. They take nectar from flowers and in some cases act as pollinators. At the end of the summer, fewer young are born. The workers no longer need to hunt, but find easy food in the sugars made by ripe fruits.

Fully sexed males and females are produced late in the season. These fly from the nest and mate.

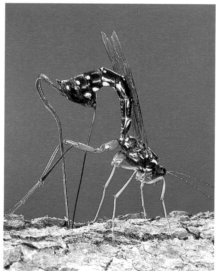

► An ichneumon wasp lays her eggs on the larva or pupa of another insect lying in a burrow under the bark of a tree. When it hatches, the ichneumon larva will parasitize the host.

With the arrival of cold weather the colony dies. Only the young mated females will survive, in hibernation. They emerge as queens next spring and found new colonies.

Diggers and potters

Many other kinds of wasps are solitary hunters. Each female produces a very small family, without workers. Once a female has caught her prey, which is usually a spider or a caterpillar, it is stung and paralysed, but not killed. Digger wasps make holes in sandy ground and lay their eggs on the helpless creatures. Potter wasps make small clay nests, like pots, which they stock in a similar way. In both cases their grubs have plenty of fresh food.

Parasites and gall makers

Almost all other relatives of the true wasps are parasites, feeding on other insects. The females lay their eggs through a tube, called an ovipositor, which they usually stick into the body of the host that will feed their grubs.

Gall wasps lay their eggs into a fast-growing part of a plant. When the grub hatches, the plant swells up to form a protective wall round it. The inner part of the wall is food for the grub. Many gall wasps have strange life histories. In some, only females are known. In others, two quite different generations succeed each other. Oak trees carry more galls than most other plants. You may find oak apples, oak marbles and at least four kinds of oak spangle gall. ◆

◄ This large wasp is called a paper wasp. These wasps live in smaller groups than most other social wasps. One of them lays an egg in each hexagonal cell. The other builders of the nest will probably go on to make nests and lay eggs of their own.

Social wasps build their nests of paper. To do this, they scrape tiny bits of dead wood from tree stumps or fence posts and mix it with their saliva. The cells in which the eggs are laid and the grubs grow are hexagonal. This allows the best use of available space.

Normally each species of parasitic wasp uses the same type of insect host for its grubs. If they eat insects that harm cultivated plants, they are often used by fruit growers and farmers to control pests. This form of 'biological control' is a very good way of dealing with pests, for unlike insecticides, it causes no pollution.

▼ **Find out more**
Bees
Insects
Parasites

Waste disposal

Every home produces vast quantities of tin cans, packaging, waste paper, glass and other rubbish. Britain alone throws out about 70 million tonnes of waste a year, which is more than 1 tonne for each person in the country. If this rubbish is not disposed of carefully, it can become a health hazard. Rotting rubbish not only looks and smells unpleasant, it also acts as a breeding ground for flies, rats and other carriers of disease. In addition, waste can pollute the air, water and soil.

▼ An incinerator or waste-burning plant in Bielefeld, Germany. Heat from incinerator furnaces can be used to produce steam for generating electricity.

Tipping

The easiest and cheapest method of disposing of rubbish is to tip it into a hole in the ground. In some areas there are many large holes caused by quarrying and open-cast mining, and these are often used for waste disposal.

During tipping, each layer of rubbish is covered with soil, so that in cross-section the tip looks like a giant layer cake. Care has to be taken to see that rainwater running off the tip does not enter rivers, since such water often contains poisonous substances.

Reclaiming land

Tipping can be used to reclaim waste land or marsh land. Once the hole is filled to the desired level, it can be capped with soil and used for planting crops or trees. It takes a long time, though, before the reclaimed land can be used for building. This is because the land may sink as the buried rubbish rots.

▶ A typical British family puts over 2 tonnes of rubbish into its wastebin every year. Here, you can see the percentages of different materials in household waste.

▼ **Find out more**
Pollution
Recycling

Almost 80 per cent of Britain's rubbish is disposed of by tipping. However, in many places there is now a shortage of suitable places where tipping can occur.

Burning rubbish

In some areas, waste is disposed of by incineration (burning). This has the advantage that it greatly reduces the volume of the waste material. Nine cubic metres of household waste are reduced to one cubic metre of ash, which can be tipped. The ash is also clean and germ-free.

In some towns the heat produced by burning waste is used to generate electricity. A massive incinerator in the London suburb of Edmonton, for example, burns some 400,000 tonnes of rubbish a year and uses the heat to generate electricity. In other places, waste is ground up and turned into solid fuel pellets. These can be used in boilers instead of coal or coke.

Making compost

The incinerators used to burn rubbish are large and expensive, and they produce smoke that can pollute the air. One alternative is to grind up the rubbish and turn it into compost for use by farmers and gardeners. Great care has to be taken, though, to see that the compost does not contain poisonous materials.

Recycling materials

It has been estimated that 60 per cent of the materials we throw away could be sorted and recycled (used again). New glass, for example, can be made from old, while new paper can be made from waste paper. Recycling waste saves raw materials and fuel, and causes less pollution. ◆

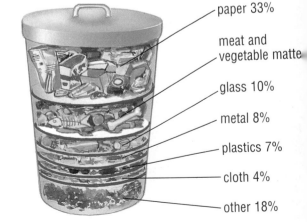

paper 33%
meat and vegetable matter
glass 10%
metal 8%
plastics 7%
cloth 4%
other 18%

Wastelands

If there is land which we cannot farm, or find any obvious productive use for, we label it wasteland. But such land is not really 'wasted'. The frozen 'wasteland' of the polar regions provides a home for specially adapted wildlife; for example, polar bears in the Arctic, and penguins in the Antarctic. The hot, dry 'wasteland' of the Sahara Desert is home to a whole range of plants and animals too, and there are groups of people who have found a way of living in these hostile places. The Inuit people can build shelters from blocks of snow, and hunt through the ice for fish. The Bushmen of the Kalahari know just which spot in the dry sand to dig a hole and find water.

Industrial wasteland

In the less remote parts of the world, most so-called 'wasteland' has been made unproductive by the actions of people. Mining and quarrying have left great scars in the landscape. All kinds of waste materials have been dumped to form mountainous waste tips, and land has been poisoned, too, with chemicals from industry.

A great deal of new wasteland was created in Europe and North America during the 19th and early 20th centuries. Now mining, dumping and chemical pollution are creating new wasteland in the Third World countries.

Wasteland within towns is usually land which has been used in the past, often for buildings, and where these are no longer needed, and get knocked down, the land is abandoned.

Wasteland wildlife

There are special plants and animals that can make their home on this kind of wasteland. Most of the plants have seeds which will blow in on the wind, the fluffy down of willows, dandelions and thistles for example; the superlight seeds of silver birch, and the winged 'helicopter' fruits of sycamore and ash trees. The dust-like spores of fungi and mosses are often the first to colonize when new wasteland is created. Many of the wasteland flowers are very colourful. They need to attract insects to the new habitat, and urban wastelands are very good places to see butterflies, bees and moths. Flocks of small birds fly from site to site, feeding on the masses of seed they find there, and many wild creatures such as foxes and hedgehogs often use the shelter of wasteland to hide from people during the daytime.

Uses for wasteland

People have found all kinds of 'unofficial' uses for wasteland in towns. Lots of children play on them. When local people are short of land, they often use wasteland to make temporary gardens, or even set up city farms.

Very often, urban wasteland is used for dumping rubbish, but if the edges are kept clean and tidy, people will respect the wasteland, and nature will quickly take over and create a new green space where children can play, wildlife can live, and where the trees and bushes can help clean up the air, slow down the wind, and make the city a pleasanter place to be. ◆

▼ **Find out more**
Antarctica
Deserts
Pollution

▼ Wastelands in London: flourishing great bindweed (left) and home for a red fox cub (right).

Water

Almost three-quarters of the Earth's surface is covered with water, and in places the oceans are kilometres deep. Frozen water forms the ice-caps at the North and South Poles, and snow covers the highest mountain ranges the whole year round. In the sky, massive clouds of water vapour bring rain to us, and where the rain falls and the rivers flow, plants and animals thrive. Without water there would be no life on our planet.

H₂O

Like many other substances, water is made up of molecules. These are so small that even the smallest raindrop contains billions. Every molecule of water consists of two atoms of hydrogen stuck to a single atom of oxygen. Scientists say that the chemical formula for water is H_2O.

Water and you

Two-thirds of your body is water. Most of your blood is water. Every organ of your body, your brain, heart, liver and muscles, contains water. Press your skin and feel how bouncy it is compared to pressing a sheet of paper. Skin is like a layer of tiny water-filled balloons.

Every day your body loses lots of water. About a litre goes down the toilet. Another half a litre disappears as sweat and in the air you breathe out. On a cold day you can see this water vapour in your warm breath. On hot days sweating helps keep you cool. The moisture (sweat) that seeps through pores (small holes) in the skin then evaporates into the air, taking with it some heat from the body.

Unlike camels, which can store many gallons of water in their tissues, we have no store of water and must replace what we lose each day. We need a litre and a half of water every day to stay alive. Much of that water can come from the food we eat. Many vegetables and fruit are three-quarters water, and even a slice of bread is one-third water.

Plants and water

Plants need water to grow. They use water and other chemicals to make the substances needed for new plant growth. They use water to carry substances between their roots and leaves. And they use the pressure of water in their cells to stay firm and rigid. Without water, plants wilt and eventually die.

Plants usually take in water through their roots and lose it through pores in their leaves. Plants which must survive in deserts have a waxy coating on their leaves to stop water escaping.

Different kinds of water

There is not just one kind of drinking water. It can taste completely different depending upon where you live.

The water that comes out of the tap has had a long journey that begins as rain falling through the air, washing over rocks and flowing along rivers. On its travels, the rain-water dissolves gases from the air and many different substances from the rocks. The kind of drinking water we end up with depends very much on what is in the local rocks.

Where there are chalk and limestone rocks, these dissolve in the rain and join with the dissolved gas, carbon dioxide, to form a substance called calcium bicarbonate. This and other similar chemicals produce 'hard' water which leaves a hard, yellowish deposit in the bottom of kettles called 'limescale'. It is difficult to make a good lather with soap in hard water. Water that does not have these particular substances is called 'soft'. But it still contains lots of different chemicals. Really pure water has no trace of anything. It is called distilled water and it is tasteless and unpleasant to drink.

Water at home

You use 10 litres of water every time you flush a lavatory, and more than seven times that amount to have a bath. Using a washing machine needs at least 100 litres. If a house catches fire the fire brigade might pump thousands of litres on the flames. ◆

Water expands when it freezes, and can break pipes.

The freezing point of water was taken as zero on the Celsius (centigrade) scale of temperature, so that water freezes at 0°C. The boiling point of water was taken as 100°C.

▼ **Find out more**
Atoms
Heat
Ice
Liquids
Molecules
Water cycle
Water power
Water supplies

▶ **In Europe, a family of four uses about 3500 litres of water every week. The bar graph shows how much water can be used each time in washing and other activities.**

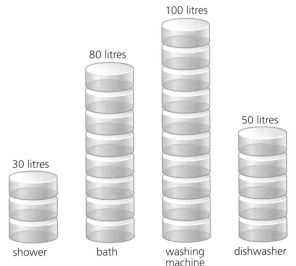

100 litres

80 litres

50 litres

30 litres

10 litres

toilet flushing   shower   bath   washing machine   dishwasher

Water birds

Many birds live on or near water. Here we look more closely at those which are not sea birds, waders, or ducks, geese or swans, but nevertheless feed in lakes and rivers.

Birds which find food regularly in water need to use special methods. A heron will use its long legs to wade into the water and wait patiently until a fish comes within reach. An osprey dives into the water, talons first, to seize its prey. Wagtails run along river banks or flit from stone to stone to catch flies.

Colourful fishers

There are over 80 kinds of kingfishers but many do not catch fish at all. They are all large-headed birds, with strong bills, short necks and short tails. Most are found in tropical forests, where they feed on ground-living creatures as well as fish.

The brilliantly coloured kingfisher of Europe and Asia nests in river banks at the end of 50 centimetre tunnels which it digs with its bill and feet. It catches fish by hovering or diving into water from an overhanging perch. Fish are swallowed whole, generally head first so the scales and fins slip down the throat easily.

A secret life

Members of the rail family are often very secretive and some are nocturnal. Although a few live in dry places, most are water or swamp birds and prefer to remain hidden than to fly.

Perhaps the least shy rail is the coot. It is black with a white bill and forehead. It swims and dives to pull up water plants. Its feet are 'lobed', which means that the toes have round flaps of skin which help it to swim.

Masters of the deep

Fish-hunting under water is highly specialized, but the divers (called 'loons' in North America) and grebes have mastered the art.

Divers have long, straight, pointed bills and long bodies with rather small wings. The legs are set so far back on the body that the bird is awkward on land. A diver's normal hunting time under water is between 30 and 60 seconds.

Many of the grebes have crests or tufts on their heads. They have many of the same features as the divers, but the smaller species are more likely to hunt insects. Grebes are known for their elaborate courtship displays. The males and females preen themselves, shake their heads, dive, and tread water rapidly with their bodies upright.

◀ This heavy-billed, colourful kingfisher is the only European species.

◀ Dipper diving in stream to feed on insect larvae and other water-living invertebrates.

Walking under water

Dippers are rather like large wrens, except that they are never found far from water. They have developed the most unusual feeding method.

Their food consists of many kinds of water creatures living in fast-flowing rivers and streams. To feed, the dipper will wade into shallow water. In deeper water it will first wade and then dive to the bottom. To stay submerged the bird flies against the current and the pressure of water helps to keep it under the surface of the water. ◆

Of all the fishing birds, only the darters spear their prey. Most use their beaks like forceps to grasp the fish.

Water cycle

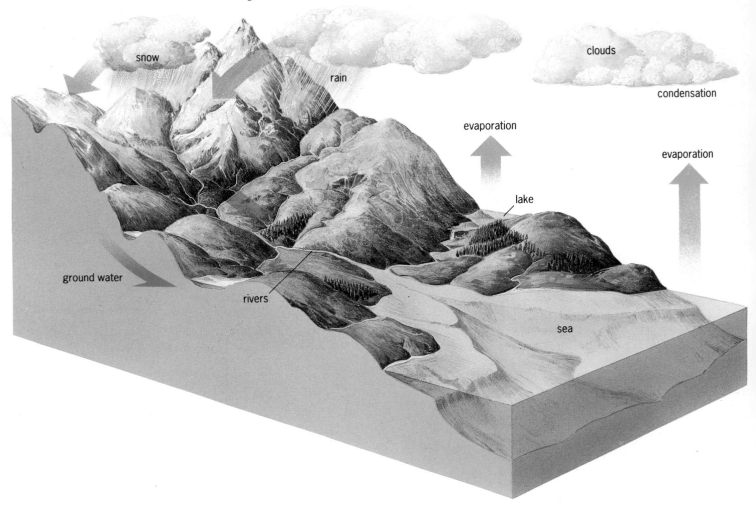

snow

rain

clouds

condensation

evaporation

evaporation

lake

ground water

rivers

sea

▲ Water is never used up, it just goes round and round this cycle. It is a remarkable fact that the oceans hold about 97 per cent of the world's water. A further 2 per cent is frozen in the polar ice-caps. This means that only about 1 per cent of the world's water is going round the water cycle at any one time.

You may sometimes wonder what happens to all the water that falls on the land. Much of it flows down to the sea in streams and rivers. Some soaks into the ground, but will eventually come to the surface as a spring, or seep back into rivers or the sea. Some stays as ice for a long time, but eventually melts and also flows to the sea.

But where does the rain and snow come from in the first place? The warmth of the Sun evaporates water from the sea, from rivers and lakes, and also from the soil and plants on the land. The water is turned into water vapour, which is one of the invisible gases that make up the air we breathe. Air is moving about all the time. If it rises high up into the atmosphere, or if it comes into contact with a cold area, it will cool down. Cool air cannot hold as much water vapour as warm air, so some of the water vapour will turn into tiny droplets of water. When this happens on the cold window of a room at home, we call it condensation. In the

sky, the tiny water droplets form clouds; near the ground we call them fog, mist or dew. If the tiny water droplets combine to form larger droplets, they will fall to Earth as rain, or as hail or snow if they are frozen. The land is watered again.

Pollution

Water is constantly being recycled in a process called the water cycle. The cycle is kept going by the Sun's energy. In some parts of the cycle the water is a liquid (rain), in other parts it is a gas (water vapour) or a solid (ice). Each part of the cycle depends on the other parts, which is why any interference by people, such as pollution, is a danger.

Polluting gases that are added to the air in one place join the water vapour and are carried to another place. Then the rain becomes acid, making the water of streams and rivers acid. This in turn affects rocks and soil, plants and fish and other animals. ◆

Waterfalls

Spectacular waterfalls occur when a large river plunges into a gorge or falls from a high plateau. The world's highest falls are the Angel Falls in Venezuela. Here the Carao River falls 979 metres over the edge of a high plateau of hard rock.

What makes a waterfall?

The rocks in the bed of a river are worn down slowly by stones and grit that are rolled along in the water. Large rivers will flow across many different kinds of rock. Some rocks are tougher than others so do not erode quickly. Others will be worn away quite easily. When a river flows over bands of hard then softer rock, there will probably be one or more waterfalls or rapids where the different types of rock meet. The river will plunge off the resistant rock, and wear away the softer rock underneath even faster. The river will undercut the hard rock on top of the falls. Sometimes there is a hollow with a ledge wide enough for people to walk behind the waterfall.

At the Niagara Falls, on the boundary of Canada and the USA, there is a flat layer of resistant limestone on top of a much weaker rock called shale. The river erodes the shale more quickly, and big blocks of undercut limestone crash down from the edge of the falls. This happens most often in the centre of the river where the water flows most powerfully. This erosion has caused the marvellous Horseshoe Falls, the Canadian part of Niagara.

The highest waterfall in Europe is in Norway. The Utigard Falls are 800 metres high. Water from the Josterdal Glacier falls in Nesdal which is far below. The sides of Nesdal were worn away by a glacier and are very steep.

Mountain rivers often have lots of waterfalls. The water rushes down steep hillsides, tumbling over boulders and rocky ledges in a series of small falls. Waterfalls are not so common at the coast, though they do happen when a river falls over a cliff into the sea. ◆

▲ The Niagara Falls on the USA side. Behind the thundering curtain of water lies a cavern, the Cave of the Winds.

In Africa the spectacular Victoria Falls flow through a gorge 80 km long.

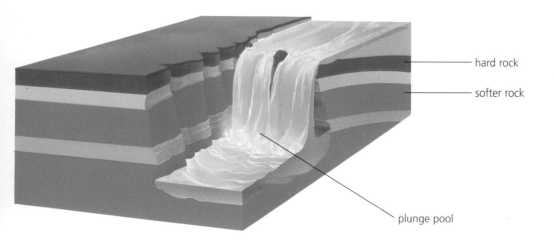

hard rock

softer rock

plunge pool

◀ Waterfalls form in river valleys where there are bands of hard and soft rocks. The hard rock resists erosion while the softer rock beneath is eroded away.

▼ **Find out more**
Erosion
Rivers
Water power

Water power history

100 BC Water wheels first used, in Greece.

1827 Fourneyron produces the first water turbine, in France.

1881 The world's first electric power station opens, in Godalming, UK. It is driven by the flow of water in a local river.

1990s Itaipú hydroelectric project, in Brazil and Paraguay, designed to provide over 12 million kilowatts of power.

▶ A water wheel near Murcia in south-east Spain. Water wheels are one of the oldest forms of water power, believed to have been developed in about 100 BC.

Water power

Water naturally flows downhill under the force of gravity. This movement can be used as a source of energy. It can be the flow of a river, or water falling from a great height as in a waterfall or dam. It is one source of energy that will never run out. There will always be a supply of moving water on Earth.

The earliest water wheels, invented by the ancient Greeks, were placed horizontally in the water flow. The Romans used vertical water wheels for milling grain. The millstone was turned by wooden gearwheels linked to the water wheel. Vertical wheels were of two main types. The *undershot* wheel was placed in a fast-flowing stream. The *overshot* wheel turned when water fell onto it from above.

During the Industrial Revolution, large water wheels provided power for many factories. The water turbine, an improvement on the water wheel, was first developed in the 1820s.

Today, water power is used to generate electricity. In a hydroelectric scheme, water flowing from a dam turns turbines which drive generators. In a tidal power station, turbines are turned when the tide flows in or out. Scientists are also exploring ways of using the up-and-down motion of waves to drive generators. ◆

Water sports

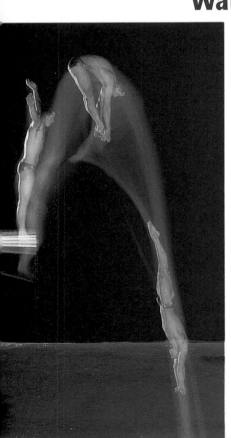

Most people live near water, whether it is a river, a canal, a reservoir, a lake or the sea. Water provides all sorts of opportunities for recreation, but it is vital to learn to swim before you take up any water sport. It could save your life one day.

In sports that take place on the sea or perhaps on fast-moving rivers, life-jackets should be worn, even by good swimmers.

Indoor water sports

A swimming pool is where most children have their first experience of water sport. Many pools run 'parent and toddler' sessions where infants can

◀ Special-effects photography illustrates this dive from the springboard. It is a forward dive, and the diver takes up a 'pike' position before hitting the water with arms and legs stretched out to make a perfectly straight entry.

get used to the water even before they can walk. Once they have learnt to swim, children may want to compete in swimming galas – competitions with all types of races, usually split into age groups. Competitive swimming calls for concentrated training. Top swimmers might spend several hours a day in the pool. But it is a sport where teenagers tend to excel.

There are races for four different strokes: *freestyle* (front crawl is always used), *breaststroke*, *backstroke* and *butterfly*. In major championships, freestyle events range from 50 to 1500 metres, and the other strokes each have 100-metre and 200-metre events. There are also medley races, in which a swimmer uses a different stroke for each leg, over 200 and 400 metres, and relays.

Another major pool sport is diving, which has more in common with gymnastics than swimming. Springboard diving is done from a flexible board 3 metres above the water, while highboard diving is done from a fixed platform 10 metres above the pool, which must be at least 4.5 metres deep. Divers perform dives of varying difficulty from a programme of more

...an 80 standard dives, and are marked by a ...anel of judges.

Other pool sports include synchronized ...wimming, in which women competitors ...erform ballet routines in the water in time to ...usic, and water polo, in which two teams of ...even players try to score by throwing a ball ...nto their opponents' goal.

...utdoor water sports

...lany people prefer to enjoy water sports out in ...e open, in a boat or on a board. Some, like ...anoeists and rowers, use only their own ...uscle power to get along. Others, like sailors ...nd surfers, rely on wind or wave power.

Windsurfers combine the ideas of surfing and ...ailing to steer their sailboards at high speed ...cross the water. A relatively new sport, ...indsurfing, or boardsailing as it is properly ...nown, was pioneered in the USA in the 1960s,

In windsurfing, the sailor holds on to a boom ...round the mast and sail, and uses it to steer the craft.

...nd gained rapidly in popularity to such an ...xtent that it was accepted as an Olympic event ...n 1984. The sail rig is attached to the board by ... device called a *universal joint*. The boardsailor ...teers without a rudder by moving the sail, ...vhich is controlled by a 'wishbone' boom ...ncircling it. In addition to racing, there are ...reestyle events, in which the boardsailors ...perform routines and tricks. 'Funboarding' is ...nother branch of the sport, with boards and ...igs designed for sailing in strong winds.

Competitors perform spectacular stunts such as somersaulting their sailboard from the waves.

Yacht racing goes back to 17th-century England, when it first became a royal pastime. Racing yachts range from simple one-person dinghies. which most people can afford, to ocean-going vessels that cost millions of pounds to design and build and require a crew of 20 or more. Racing takes place both inshore and offshore. In major regattas and competitions, such as the Olympic Games, one-design events are raced over a triangular course marked by buoys, with competitors earning points according to their finishing positions in as many as seven races.

Powerboat racing is another outdoor water sport in which various classes of boat compete. Motor boats are also used in water-skiing, to tow the skier by means of a long rope. Water-skiers compete in three main events: 'slalom', in which they ski in and out of a line of buoys; 'jumping' for distance over a ramp; and 'tricks', performing routines and stunts while being towed. ♦

▲ Water-skiers are pulled across water on a ski or skis by a rope attached to a speedboat.

▼ **Find out more**
Canoeing
Divers
Rowing
Sailing
Sport
Surfing
Swimming

▼ Close racing between dinghies of the same type. The 470 class is an Olympic event in both men's and women's yacht racing. The helmsman controls the mainsail and rudder, while the crew controls the jib sail and hangs on to a trapeze to balance the boat.

Water supplies

In our homes, we need water for drinking, cooking, washing, cleaning, and flushing the lavatory. In factories, huge amounts of water are needed for manufacturing things.

Where our water comes from

All our water comes from rain (or snow in the winter). Most of this rain falls in hilly areas. Some evaporates, some sinks into the ground, and some runs into streams and rivers. The water can be collected in various ways. A stream or river can be dammed to make an artificial lake called a reservoir. A well can be dug and underground water pumped up. Or water can be taken straight from a river.

Before the water leaves the waterworks, chlorine gas is bubbled through it. This kills any bacteria not removed by filtering. In some areas, fluoride is also added to the water to help prevent tooth decay. The water is now clean but not quite pure. For example, in some areas it may have tiny amounts of rock dissolved in it. This is harmless, but you can see it slowly building up as scale ('fur') in a kettle.

Pumping and storing

Water from the waterworks is pumped through pipes to storage tanks. The tank supplying your area may be on a hill or at the top of a tall tower. The height of the tank gives the water the steady pressure which pushes it along the pipes to your taps.

Recycling water

Used water from homes and factories usually passes to a sewage works for cleaning. It may then be pumped into the sea or returned to a river. The water from some large rivers is taken out and used several times on its journey towards the sea. For example, a glass of water from a tap in London may already have passed through six or seven people. ♦

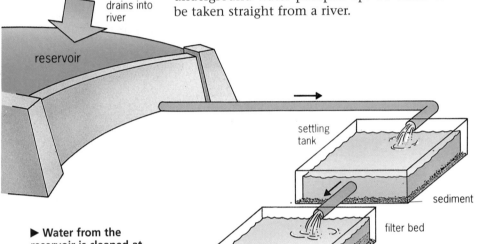

rain-water drains into river

reservoir

▶ Water from the reservoir is cleaned at the waterworks. It is pumped to a storage tank which supplies homes, factories and other buildings in the area.

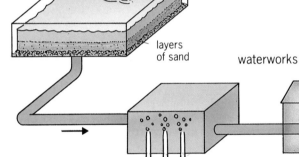

settling tank

sediment

filter bed

layers of sand

chlorine added to water

waterworks

pump

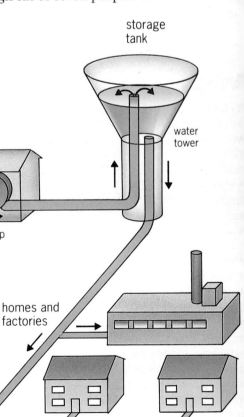

storage tank

water tower

homes and factories

Cleaning the water

Before water from a reservoir, river or well can be pumped to your home, it must be cleaned. This job is done at the waterworks. First, the water is left to stand in large tanks so that particles of sand, mud and grit settle out. Next, the water passes to filter beds where it soaks through layers of coarse and fine sand. This removes any dirt remaining and also some of the bacteria. Some waterworks use a faster method of filtering. They clean the water in large, closed metal drums filled with sand and a chemical jelly.

Waves

The word 'waves' might first call to mind the sea, but there are waves in all kinds of things. Suppose a line of children is waiting for a bus. Ian is late and dashes up and crashes into Julie who is at the end of the line. Julie bumps Ben, who bumps Michelle and so on down the line. The 'bump' is a wave travelling along the line. When it has passed by, all the children are back in the position where they started.

If you drop a stone into a pond, waves spread out in circles and you can see the movement outwards. A toy boat floating on the surface may go up and down, but it does not move outwards with the wave.

If the wave is started by something that is wobbling in a regular way, the scientific name for the wave is 'periodic'. For example, the sound wave made by a tuning fork is periodic. The air is alternately squashed and expanded, and the squashes travel out as a wave. We can measure three things about such a wave. Its speed is the speed at which any one squash is travelling along. Its frequency is the number of wave crests that pass a particular point every second. Its wavelength is the distance between two crests.

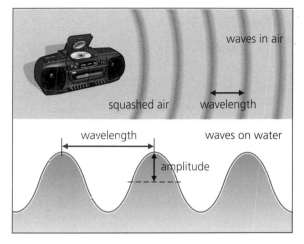

waves in air

squashed air   wavelength

wavelength   waves on water

amplitude

◄ With some waves, the wobbles make squashes which travel along. With other waves, the wobbles make up-and-down movements which travel along.

Scientists measure frequency in hertz (Hz). If 10 waves are passing every second, the frequency is 10 Hz.

▼ Some typical measurements of common waves.

	frequency	wavelength	speed
sound	30–20,000 Hz	10 m–15 mm	300 m/sec
medium-wave radio	1 million Hz	300 m	300 million m/sec
light	600 million million Hz	1/2000 mm	300 million m/sec
X-rays	2,400,000 million million Hz	1/8,000,000 mm	300 million m/sec

A magnet or an electric current has a field round it. You can see the lines of the field if you scatter iron filings on a piece of paper. If the current wobbles, waves travel along these lines. They are called electromagnetic waves. Light, radio, ultraviolet and X-ray waves are all electromagnetic waves. ◆

▼ Find out more

Colour   Vibration
Light   X-rays
Magnets
Microwaves   **BIOGRAPHY**
Radiation   Maxwell,
Radio   James Clerk

Wax

Waxes are naturally white or yellow fatty substances. There are many different kinds of wax. Some are made by plants or animals, and others are made from minerals. All waxes soften and melt when heated and burn with a sooty yellow flame. Waxes do not dissolve in water, and they form a waterproof layer when spread on a smooth surface. This quality also makes wax useful in polishes.

Mineral waxes

Candle wax (paraffin wax) is a mineral wax. It is made from crude oil or shale. It melts at quite a low temperature: about 50 °C. When liquid, it can be coloured and poured into moulds to make candles and waxwork figures. Paper is sometimes coated with this wax to make airtight bags for foods, such as cornflakes, which must be kept crisp. Most ordinary polishing waxes contain paraffin wax.

Animal waxes

Beeswax is the best-known animal wax. It is formed in flakes on the abdomens of honey bees. The bees scrape it off and use it to make the comb of their nests. Eggs are laid and grubs grow in the hexagonal cells of the comb. Honey is stored in other cells. When a cell is full, it is sealed with a wax cap to protect the honey or pupa.

Many other kinds of animals make waxes. We, and other mammals, make a waxy substance in our ears. This helps to stop dust and dirt from entering them. Sheep make lanolin, which contains wax, to waterproof their wool, and other creatures use a waxy material to help protect their skin or fur. Birds have preen glands that give a waxy water-proofing to their feathers. Insects' bodies are coated with wax, which prevents them from drying out in hot climates.

Vegetable waxes

Vegetable wax is formed in the bark of some trees. One kind, called carnauba wax, comes from the leaves of a Brazilian palm tree. Carnauba wax is sometimes used for making candles and waterproof polish. ◆

The larvae of some relatives of the ladybirds grow a coat of fine, sticky, wax threads that deter ants, which are their main enemies.

The sperm whale has in its head up to 1900 litres of waxy oil. Sperm oil and wax used to have many industrial uses. Wax from the jojoba desert plant now replaces them, saving the lives of sperm whales.

▼ Find out more

Bees
Candles

Weapons

▶ A catapult used by Roman soldiers to throw stones of about 12 kg. Larger catapults could throw stones of up to 50 kg. The slider (A) was pulled back along the stock (B) bringing the bowstring with it. A trigger (C) released the bowstring.

Gunpowder was discovered in China nearly 1000 years ago.

Hands and feet were the first weapons, but these were not much use against sabre-tooth tigers or mammoths. So prehistoric people learnt to use sticks and stones as weapons, then pointed sticks as spears and sharpened stones as knives and axes. Bows were used as much as 20,000 years ago to fire arrows further and more accurately than a man could throw a spear. When metal-working developed, bronze daggers replaced flint ones, but arrowheads of flint or bone continued to be used even in the Iron Age. Swords were made of bronze and later of iron.

The Greeks and Romans used large catapult-like weapons to throw huge rocks at enemy castles. The chariot was one of the earliest *weapon delivery systems* – vehicles by which weapons can be carried to the place where they may be used. Chariots were first used by the Sumerians, and by the ancient Egyptians at least 3000 years ago.

▶ *Firearms* were and are weapons which can be used by a single soldier. *Artillery* is the term used for military weapons which are too big to be managed by an individual. The cannon, like modern artillery, works in much the same way as firearms, but fires bigger projectiles over much longer distances.

The longbow was the main weapon for English soldiers from the time of William the Conqueror to the reign of Elizabeth I. It had a range of 180 metres.

Muskets were used by infantrymen in Europe from the 16th to the 19th centuries. The musketeer fired from a rest stuck in the ground. Gunpowder and padding were poured down the barrel, together with a bullet. The fuse was lit with a glowing match, rather like a firework.

Cannons like this were used in the 18th century, drawn by horses. A powder charge with cannon balls was rammed down the barrel, then lit.

Gunpowder

Until gunpowder was discovered, weapons could only cut or hit. Cannons, guns and bombs all use the explosive power of gunpowder. Cannons and guns appeared in Europe in the 14th century, but they were inaccurate, took a long time to load and had the unfortunate habit of blowing up in your face. The English longbow was still better than the early guns.

The cannon was improved in the 16th century, but even so was still not very effective. The development of the musket in the 16th century greatly improved the gun. The musket's bullet could penetrate a soldier's armour, but muskets took a long time to load. Knives, called bayonets, were added to the gun's barrel so that they could be used as spears as well.

The rifled barrel

In the 19th century a new development, the rifled barrel, made the gun much more accurate. This made bullets spin in flight, so they could travel in a straighter line and further than those fired by older guns. Round bullets were replaced by longer, pointed ones, which also improved accuracy. A musketeer would be lucky to hit a target at 100 metres. But marksmen using the new rifles could easily hit such a target over 1000 metres away. Unlike the original muzzle-loader, breech-loaded rifles, which became widely used in the mid-19th century, can be loaded more quickly because they have the charge and shot loaded at the rear.

Modern weapons

Modern weapons are very powerful and complicated. Although guns carried by soldiers today are very similar to those used in World War I, most other weapons have changed a lot. In World War I aircraft and tanks were first used to carry weapons. By the end of World War II the invention of the long-range rocket and the nuclear bomb changed the face of warfare. Guided missiles can hit aircraft travelling at over 1800 kilometres per hour. They can even hit other missiles. Large rockets can carry nuclear bombs half-way around the world to their targets. Tanks can travel at over 60 kilometres per hour across rough ground, firing as they go.

Many different weapons are carried by ships and aircraft. A modern warship has large and small guns, guided missiles, torpedoes and depth charges to defend it. This use of many weapons together is called a *weapons system*. The tank, ship and aircraft are all weapon delivery systems. Most modern weapons have several parts; for example, a guided missile usually needs a launcher with radar and a computer to guide it to its target. ◆

Modern 'smart' missiles are programmable and can be guided to their targets with pinpoint accuracy.

◀ The Apache helicopter reveals the massive firepower it carries as a 'weapon delivery system'.

Weasels

Largest Sea otter, which may weigh up to 45 kg
Smallest Weasel (least weasel) females may have a head-and-body length of as little as 11.5 cm and weigh as little as 25 g
Subphylum Vertebrata
Class Mammalia
Order Carnivora
Family Mustelidae (weasels)
Number of species 64

▼ **Find out more**
Badgers
Mammals
Otters
Skunks

▼ **One of the smallest of the carnivores, the European weasel has a reputation for fierceness.**

Members of the weasel family are generally long-bodied, short-legged hunters. They live in many ways: the martens, for instance, are tree climbers, the otters are swimmers, and the badgers are diggers. In Europe the animal known as the weasel is the smallest of all the family. The tiny females are said to be able to squeeze through a wedding ring! They are often active during the daytime, for though they hunt mainly by scent, they have good senses of hearing and sight.

Weasels feed mainly on small rodents, and in the northern part of their range they are tiny enough to be able to chase mice and voles down their tunnels. Further south they tend to be larger and rely on catching bigger animals.

The prey is killed with a bite to the base of the skull. When food is plentiful, it is sometimes stored. Young weasels may remain with their mother after they are weaned, and can sometimes be seen hunting together. ◆

Weather

Rain, clouds, sunshine, wind: the conditions in the atmosphere and their day-to-day changes make up the weather. Knowing what the weather will be like saves money and can also save lives. Will it be safe to climb the mountain tomorrow? Do we need to grit the roads tonight? Will it be dry enough to harvest the crop this week?

Weather recording

Weather stations on land need to be on open sites, away from buildings and trees which can influence the accuracy of readings. Observations must be precise and presented in a standard way so they can be compared with those taken at other sites and times. Most observations are made at ground level, but instruments can be carried into the atmosphere by balloons which transmit readings back to Earth by radio.

Weather forecasting

Accurate weather forecasting depends on an accurate supply of information about weather conditions all over the Earth. Forecasters have to know what is happening over the whole planet, because today's weather in America could affect the weather in Europe a week later.

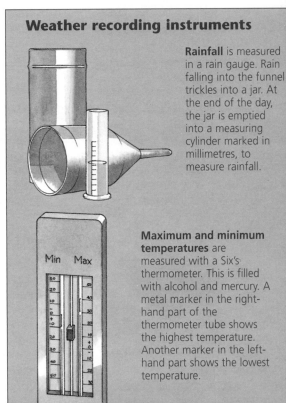

Weather recording instruments

Rainfall is measured in a rain gauge. Rain falling into the funnel trickles into a jar. At the end of the day, the jar is emptied into a measuring cylinder marked in millimetres, to measure rainfall.

Maximum and minimum temperatures are measured with a Six's thermometer. This is filled with alcohol and mercury. A metal marker in the right-hand part of the thermometer tube shows the highest temperature. Another marker in the left-hand part shows the lowest temperature.

Thousands of separate pieces of weather information are collected several times a day from weather stations on land, from ships and from aeroplanes. This data is fed into a giant communications network called the Global Telecommunications System. The information is sent round the world at great speed by satellite, radio and cable. Weather forecasters in every country take from the system the data they need to make their own local forecast.

The information is first mapped on a 'synoptic chart', which shows the overall weather situation. Using their knowledge of how the atmosphere behaves and with the help of computers which show what happened the last time when there were similar conditions, meteorologists make their forecasts. These must then be turned into maps and descriptions of what the weather will be like for the next 24 hours, for newspapers, television and radio.

Forecasts are becoming more accurate as time goes by, especially for short periods ahead. However, long-range forecasting is still difficult.

Weather and people

People have always made up sayings about the weather. Some are nonsense, but others are based on good observations. Many sayings are based on what the sky looks like. 'Red sky at

◀ This meteorological balloon is being launched in New Mexico, USA, to study a developing thunderstorm. The balloon carries instruments to measure temperatures, pressures and wind speeds.

night, shepherds' delight' is not always true, but 'Red sky in the morning, shepherds' warning' is usually reliable.

Many weather rhymes relate to farmers or sailors, because they are usually more aware of the sky and winds than people who live in towns. If it rains on St Swithin's day (15 July), there is supposed to be rain for the next 40 days. Keep a record to see if this is true! ◆

Scientists who study the weather are called *meteorologists*. Meteorology comes from two Greek words meaning 'study of what is high in the air'. (The word meteor originally meant anything unusual that appeared in the sky.)

It is likely that the weather affects people's moods. The warm, dusty sirocco wind of the Mediterranean or the Mistral wind which blows down the Rhône Valley in France are famous for making people irritable.

A **sunshine recorder** uses a strip of heat-sensitive card to measure the amount of sun a place receives each day. The glass ball of the recorder acts like a lens, focusing the sun onto the card and burning it. The length of the burn shows the amount of sunshine.

Wind direction is measured by a weather vane. The vane points to the direction from which the wind is blowing. (The north wind blows *from* the north, not towards it.)
Wind speed is measured with an anemometer (below). It records wind speed in metres per second.

Air pressure can be measured using a barograph. In the centre of this instrument is a metal box with very little air in it. When the air pressure changes, the top of the box bends. A pen records the movement on a rotating drum. Measuring air pressure is important in weather forecasting because low pressure often brings rain or snow, while high pressure brings more settled weather.

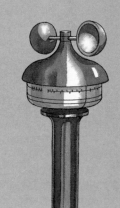

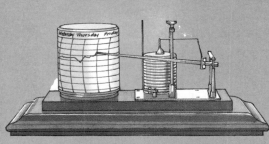

▼ Find out more
Barometers
Climate
Clouds
Cyclones and
    anticyclones
Depressions
Fog
Frost
Rain
Snow
Sun
Thermometers
Thunderstorms
Tornadoes
Wind

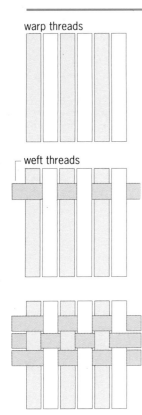

warp threads

weft threads

Weaving

Threads are woven together to make cloth. You can see how weaving is done by using strips of paper. Cut out thin strips of paper about 1 centimetre wide and 10 centimetres long. You will need three white strips and three coloured strips.

Lay them alternately on a sheet of paper. Fix them together across the top with sticky tape. These are the *warp* threads. Now cut 10 more strips in another colour, 1 centimetre wide and 8 centimetres long. Lift up all the white strips. Slide in a strip of paper. Lift up all the coloured strips. Slide in a strip of paper. Keep going to the end. These are the *weft* threads.

To weave with threads you need a loom. This is a frame which will hold a set of threads, the warp, so tightly that you can weave a second set of threads, the weft, across and through them. To make it easier to weave the weft threads through the warp, the end of the weft is tied onto a short stick called the shuttle.

Types of loom

Weaving is a very ancient craft. It was developed by people who lived before about 6000 BC. Early weaving frames were made of wood. The warp was weighed down with heavy wooden bars and large pebbles.

A *ground loom* is pegged into the ground. The weaver often sits on top of the finished weaving and uses a forked beater to force the threads down tightly. Looms like these are still used by nomads in Iran and Jordan. When they move camp, the loom can be rolled up and carried on camels or mules.

The *frame loom* is used for small weavings, especially tapestry pictures. The warp threads can be picked up with the fingers, and the weft threads are passed under two threads at a time. The length of the weaving cannot be greater than the length of the loom.

▲ This Mayan woman in Guatemala is weaving using a backstrap loom.

Backstrap looms are used all over the world. The weaver ties one end of the loom around the waist. The other end can be tied to a tree or a door knob. The weaver leans backwards to keep the warp threads tight and raises alternate warp threads by using a heddle.

Mechanical looms

Today most fabric is woven in factories using mechanical looms. These power-driven looms can make thousands of metres of fabric a day. Many different kinds of cloth can be made. Some is flat weave, like tweed and sheeting. Another method is called pile weaving. Little tufts or loops are woven into the fabric. Towelling and velvet are made like this, and so are some carpets. ◆

▼ To use this handloom, the warp threads are first attached to the heddle shafts. By pressing down on a treadle, the warp is parted, producing a gap through which the shuttle carrying the weft is passed. This process is repeated many times on different warp threads to form the woven fabric.

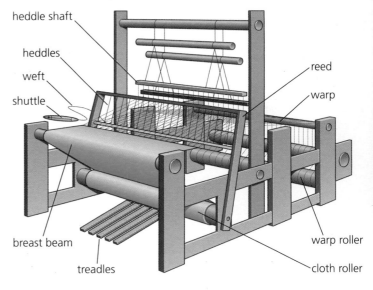

heddle shaft

heddles

weft

shuttle

reed

warp

breast beam

treadles

warp roller

cloth roller

▼ **Find out more**
Tapestries
Textiles
Wool

Weddings

▲ This Roman Catholic couple make their marriage vows at the church altar with the blessing of the priest. The bride wears white as a symbol of purity.

▶ At a Sikh wedding the bride wears red. Red is also the colour worn by Hindu brides when they get married. Here a Sikh couple walk together round the Holy Book, which will help them in their lives together.

A wedding is the rite or ceremony that takes place when a woman (the bride) and a man (the bridegroom) get married. Because it is a celebration, people like to wear their best clothes, and over the last century it has become common in western countries for brides to wear elaborate white dresses. After the ceremony there is often a feast for families and friends.

A wedding may take place in a registrar's office, or in a place of worship such as a church or a temple. A registry office wedding is a legal, not a religious event. Also, for a marriage to be legally valid in Britain, couples must sign a civil register even if they have a religious wedding ceremony. Since 1995, the law in Britain allows weddings to take place anywhere that is considered to be sufficiently dignified.

Wedding customs

People of different religions have different customs to show the importance of what is happening. Eastern Orthodox Christians crown the bride and groom, who are like a king and queen on their wedding day. Protestant and Catholic couples exchange wedding rings and make marriage vows in front of a vicar or priest, and guests. Hindu couples walk seven times round a sacred fire to show their unity, and the Sikh bridegroom leads his bride round the Sikh holy book, which will be at the centre of their lives together. The Jewish bridegroom crushes a glass under his foot to show that love is finely made and easily destroyed. ◆

▼ Find out more
Marriage
Rites and rituals

Weeds

▲ Although they are very attractive, these poppies and sow thistles at the edge of a cornfield are looked upon as weeds by farmers.

Weeds are any plants growing where they are not wanted. Even a rose bush might be considered a weed if it is growing in the middle of a vegetable patch. Most weeds are quick-growing plants able to produce a large quantity of seeds in a very short time. Usually the seeds are easily spread, like the dandelion clock on which each fruit has its own tiny parachute to carry it away on the slightest breeze. Some weed flowers will go on setting seed even after they have been pulled up, like the common garden weed groundsel. Its flowers will make a mass of hairy seeds if put on the compost heap. Other weeds, such as creeping buttercup, produce shoots which root wherever they touch the ground. With these runners the plant spreads very quickly. Some weeds, such as convolvulus, have to be removed from the soil completely. Any remaining fragments of stem will grow into whole new plants.

Control of weeds

The best way to control weeds is to dig them up and kill them before they have time to spread. This is why a gardener hoes the ground between plants. Any weeds are uprooted or sliced off at ground level by the sharp edge of the hoe. In the past children were paid to pull wild oats in corn fields. More recently weeds have been killed by chemicals called herbicides. Selective weedkillers will kill only weeds and not crops. There is now concern about the harmful effects these chemicals might have on wild plants and animals. ◆

▼ **Find out more**
Flowering plants
Gardens

Weight

Astronauts floating around in space are weightless because they cannot feel the effects of gravity. Here on Earth, we can measure the force of gravity pulling us towards our planet. Scientists call this force weight. They measure all forces in newtons, so they measure weight in newtons as well. Our weight depends on where we are because the pull of gravity gets less if we move further away from the centre of the Earth. The Earth bulges out slightly at the Equator. A girl weighing 200 newtons at the North Pole would weigh about one newton less if she moved to the Equator, and less again if she then climbed a high mountain.

In shops, the 'weight' of things is usually shown in kilograms or pounds, though these really measure mass. Mass is the amount of matter contained in something. It stays the same wherever it is. There is a connection between mass and weight because the more matter there is in something, the more strongly it is pulled to the Earth by gravity. ◆

On Earth, every kilogram of mass weighs about 10 newtons. The weight of an apple is about 1 newton. The weight of an average 10-year-old is about 300 newtons.

▼ **Find out more**
Forces
Gravity
Mass
Measurement

Welfare State

A Welfare State is a country where the government takes responsibility for the well-being of its citizens, in such matters as old-age pensions, unemployment pay and health care. This is known as social security.

The term came into use in Britain in the 1940s, when a plan for care 'from the cradle to the grave' was carried out by the Labour Government of 1945–1951. The scheme was drawn up by the social reformer William Beveridge (later Lord Beveridge) in 1942, during World War II. It is funded partly by National Insurance contributions and partly through taxes. Most developed countries now have some form of social security. ◆

The Welfare State has its origins in the accident, sickness and old age insurance introduced by the German chancellor Otto von Bismarck in the 1880s. In Germany the term used is 'Welfare Society'.

National Insurance contributions are paid by employers and their employees to cover the cost of social security schemes such as pensions and unemployment benefits.

▼ **Find out more**
British history since 1919
Employment
German history
Pensions
Poverty

Wells and springs

A well is a deep hole dug or drilled in the ground to obtain water or oil. This article deals with water wells. Oil wells are described in the article on oil. A spring is the name given to any natural flow of water out of the ground.

Permeable and impermeable rocks

Some of the rain that falls on the land finds its way into rivers and streams and flows down to the sea, and some evaporates back into the atmosphere, but a lot sinks into the ground. The water soaks easily through rocks such as sandstone or chalk. These rocks are said to be permeable. But some materials, such as clay, stop the water sinking any further, and are said to be impermeable. The water that goes into the ground sinks until it reaches either a layer of clay or some other impermeable rock, or a rock that cannot soak up any more water. The level in the ground below which water collects is called the water table.

Springs

Springs are often found where permeable rocks lie above impermeable ones, particularly at the foot of steep slopes. Long ago, villages frequently grew up around large springs, and many of our largest rivers begin their lives as springs.

Wells and the water table

If a hole is dug deep enough to reach below the water table, water will seep from the surrounding rocks into the well. The water table is not always at the same level. In dry weather it may fall, and a well may empty, while in wet weather the water table will be much nearer the surface and the well will be full. Before water pipes were invented, every village had its own well.

Artesian wells

Sometimes a layer of water-holding rock is sandwiched between two layers of impermeable rock. London is built in a giant saucer-shaped hollow over rocks like this. At one time, if a well was dug down to the water table under London, water was squeezed so hard that it came out of the well like a fountain. A well like this is called an artesian well. In London, so many artesian wells have been bored to provide water for all the people that the water table has fallen and its pressure has decreased. Now the water has to be helped to the surface by pumps. Underground water is particularly important in

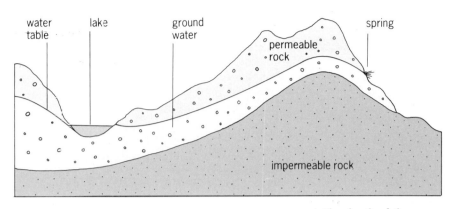

▲ The depth of the water table depends on the climate and the rocks underground.

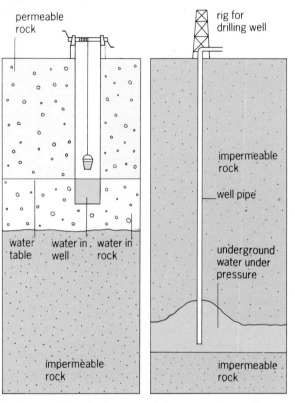

▲ Water collects in the bottom of the well and has to be drawn or pumped up to the surface.

▲ In an artesian well, the pressure underground forces water up a pipe to the surface.

At many points in the Sahara Desert, water-bearing rocks come to the surface. These places are called oases.

dry areas where rain is infrequent. Water from artesian wells has made it possible for cattle and sheep farms to be set up in the dry interior of Australia.

Holy and wishing wells

Many years ago, people used to think that the way water rose to the surface in wells and springs was miraculous or magic. Many wells were thought to be holy or lucky. The Celts of western Europe frequently built altars and made sacrifices at wells, while the Romans dedicated their wells to goddesses. ◆

The practice of dropping a coin into a well and making a wish probably began with the belief that wells are holy.

West Indies

Since 1995 much of the tiny island of Montserrat has been devastated by the activity of the South Soufrière Hills Volcano. Most people have either been relocated on the island or have fled abroad.

Antigua and Barbuda
Area 442 sq km
Capital St John's
Population 80,000

Dominica
Area 750 sq km
Capital Roseau
Population 88,000

Grenada
Area 344 sq km
Capital St George's
Population 112,000

St Kitts and Nevis
Area 261 sq km
Capital Basseterre
Population 45,100

St Vincent and the Grenadines
Area 344 sq km
Capital Kingstown
Population 104,000

The chain of islands to the north and east of the Caribbean Sea is often called the West Indies. This is because Christopher Columbus thought he had found an Atlantic route to the 'Indies' in Asia when he reached the Caribbean in 1492. But many people today call them the Caribbean Islands.

The islands stretch for over 3000 kilometres from the coast of Mexico, past the southern tip of the USA, to Venezuela. The largest island, Cuba, is over 1100 kilometres long, and has a population of 10 million. There are more than 20 other independent or self-governing countries in the region, and hundreds of other smaller islands, many of which are uninhabited.

Cuba, the Dominican Republic and Puerto Rico are Spanish-speaking. They have more inhabitants than all the other Caribbean countries put together.

People in Haiti, Martinique and Guadeloupe speak French or a local language called Creole. Haiti has been independent since 1804. The other French-speaking islands are Overseas Departments of France. They are governed in much the same way as the French mainland and are part of the European Union, but the way of life is distinctively Caribbean.

The Netherlands Antilles consist of three islands off the coast of Venezuela – Curaçao, Aruba, and Bonaire – where people speak Dutch or a language called Papiamento, and three smaller islands, Saba, Statia and part of St Martin, where Dutch is the official language but most people speak English. These islands are self-governing, but are linked to the kingdom of the Netherlands.

Most of the other islands are independent English-speaking countries, which were once ruled by Britain and are now members of the Commonwealth of Nations. These islands are grouped together in the Caribbean Community (Caricom). The most important Caricom island countries are Jamaica, Trinidad and Tobago, and Barbados. Belize and Guyana on the mainland of South America are also part of Caricom. Many of the Caricom islands are very small, but some have well-established democratic governments. In the past, most people in these islands were very poor. Today, more of the islands are becoming prosperous. Many people still earn their living from farming, but tourism, manufacturing, mining and banking are increasingly important.

Windward Islands

Grenada, St Vincent, St Lucia and Dominica are known as the Windward Islands. They are mountainous, volcanic islands. Much of the land is covered with forests, and there are beautiful, fast-flowing rivers and streams. There are many small farmers, and bananas have long been an important export crop. They all have a thriving tourist industry. Many people on St Lucia and Dominica speak Haitian Creole, a Creole language (a pidgin language that has become established in its own right) derived from French.

Leeward Islands

To the north of the Windwards are the Leeward Islands – Antigua, St Kitts, Nevis, Montserrat and Barbuda. Antigua is a drier island. The land is not so good for farming, but there are beautiful sandy beaches. More than 100,000 tourists visit the island every year. Nearby is a twin island country – St Christopher (known as St Kitts) and Nevis. St Kitts is the smallest independent country in the Caribbean.

Some of the smaller islands – Montserrat, Anguilla, the British Virgin Islands, the Turks and Caicos Islands, and the Caymans – are still British Dependent Territories. The United States Virgin Islands and Puerto Rico are linked to the USA. ◆

▲ Postage stamps often tell us something about the history or geography of a country. These stamps show us that bananas are one of Grenada's most important export crops and that Dominica has mangrove swamps along the Indian River. The third shows us an example of the sort of building you might see on St Kitts.

Wetlands

Wetlands are damp, boggy areas where water may lie on the surface, forming lakes or pools, or where plants have grown out into open water to form a marshy cover. Generally, wetlands are formed wherever water is trapped by rocks or impermeable (water-resistant) soil. There are many different kinds of wetlands. Some are formed naturally, while others result from human activities.

Wetlands are some of the richest places on Earth, supporting huge numbers of plants and animals. Eight times as much plant matter grows on some wetlands as in an average wheat field. The value of wetlands to humans is enormous. For example, two-thirds of the fish caught around the world began their life in wetlands.

Wetland wildlife

Wetland ground is soft, so many small *invertebrates* (animals without backbones) live in it. These are food for shrews, frogs, toads and wading (shore) birds, such as sandpipers and curlews, which probe in the mud with their slender bills. Other birds, such as herons, feed on fish, frogs and toads in shallow waters.

Insects thrive in wetlands. Mosquitoes and dragonflies lay their eggs in the water and hunt for food over the surrounding land. Insect-eating warblers and flycatchers nest nearby, and seed-eating birds are attracted by the seed heads of the reeds and rushes. Wetlands also attract large mammals to drink. On the African plains, lions, antelope, zebras and even elephants visit wetlands at dawn and dusk to drink.

Because of the rich feeding available, wetlands around the world are important stopover places for millions of migrating birds. The birds stop to feed and rest, roosting safely on the water out of reach of hunters. Other birds stay to breed on wetlands, especially in the tundra of the far North where birds find plentiful food in the brief Arctic summer.

Flood-plains and estuaries

Where rivers meander slowly over large flat flood-plains, river bends sometimes get separated off, forming pools and lakes. As the river slows down, it drops the fine particles of soil and rock (sediment) it has been carrying, forming banks of mud or gravel. Mud builds up on the shores of estuaries, where rivers meet the sea, as the tide slows the running water. At the mouth of the largest rivers, this mud forms vast, fan-shaped deltas. Plants which can cope with occasional flooding by salty sea water grow here, forming salt-marshes which are home to many invertebrates and wading birds.

Mangrove swamps

The coasts of some tropical seas are fringed with mangrove swamps. Mangroves are trees adapted to live in wet, salty places. Their roots stick up into the air from the mud. These help the plants take in the oxygen gas from the air which they need to live, because there is very little oxygen in the wet mud.

Mangrove swamps are home to many different animals. Fiddler crabs scuttle about

Wetlands cover about 6 per cent of the Earth's land surface.

▼ Lake Nakuru in East Africa supports a huge population of water birds, including pelicans and the spoonbill in the foreground.

▶ Egrets and other waders live in the swamps of Florida, USA. This is a habitat rich in wildlife.

The value of fish and shellfish caught in wetlands around the world is estimated at £450 million a year.

▼ The Okavango Swamps are a vast area of marshland in the north-west of Botswana in southern Africa. This is natural wetland formed where the Okavango river divides into small streams.

the mud, scavenging the dead remains of plants and animals. Mudskippers skitter over the mud on their front fins. These small fish can stay out of water for long periods, breathing a mixture of air and water stored in their gill chambers.

Millions of invertebrates live in the mud, which is enriched by dead mangrove leaves. The warm, shallow waters are a nursery for the young of many ocean fish, which are hunted by crocodiles, alligators and birds such as storks, ibises and herons.

Peatlands

Vast areas of the cooler areas of the world are covered in peatlands, which make up 3 per cent of the land surface. These are formed by remarkable plants called bog mosses, which are able to grow in waterlogged areas. As they grow, bog mosses trap water amongst their leaves, like a natural sponge. When they die, their remains scarcely decay, because the bacteria that normally break up dead plants are inactive in these cold, waterlogged areas. New bog mosses grow on top of the dead remains below. Peat is this partially decayed mass of dead bog moss. In places, over many thousands of years, it has built up to depths of 12 metres.

Peatlands are important areas for many breeding birds, and for humans. For hundreds of years, people have cut peat for fuel, but now large peat-fired power stations in some countries are taking peat from vast areas, much faster than the bog mosses can replace it. Peat is also used by gardeners, but this is wasteful and leads to destruction of wild peatlands. Peat-free alternatives are now available for gardeners.

As bog mosses grow, they take in carbon dioxide from the atmosphere to make food by photosynthesis. In doing so, they help to lock up some of the excess carbon dioxide that humans are producing from factories, cars and power stations. Carbon dioxide is the main cause of global warming, so peat bogs have a vital role in helping to stop the threat of climate change.

Artificial wetlands

Some wetlands are made by human activity. Disused gravel pits fill with water, and marshes develop around the edges of reservoirs, and many of these make valuable nature reserves. In warm countries, flooded paddy fields, made for growing rice, are home to fish, egrets and herons.

Ever-changing wetlands

The margins of wetlands are always changing. Where rivers drop their sediment into lakes or the sea, mud banks gradually build up. Wetland plants can begin to grow here, building up the mud further, until plants of dry land can move in. In the same way, salt-marshes along coasts gradually extend out to sea. Some wetlands disappear naturally as they become silted up, but new ones form where rivers change course or become blocked by landslides or dams.

Destruction of wetlands

In recent years, people have been destroying wetlands at an alarming rate. Many have been drained so that the land can be built on or farmed. Others have been filled in as rubbish dumps. Many have become polluted as the rivers that feed them have picked up pesticides and other chemicals washed off farmland or from factories.

Today it is estimated that half the wetlands which once existed have been destroyed by people. Many more remain under threat, with plans to flood some wetlands to make hydro-electric dams, to build canals for shipping, or to dig irrigation channels to carry water to dry areas where crops could never be grown in the

past. All too often, these plans are aimed at short-term gain for a few people and ignore the long-term value of wetlands in protecting our environment.

The loss of wetlands destroys the habitats of plants and animals, but it can be disastrous for humans too. Wetlands soak up water during storms and let it drain out gradually. This lessens the effect of floods downstream. Where wetlands have been drained or ploughed, villages and farms further down river are much more at risk from flooding and crop damage. Wetlands also act like a water filter, removing impurities from the water that passes through them. In some places loss of wetlands has led to poor-quality drinking water for local cities.

Wetlands protect the coast

At the coast, the loss of wetlands can be even more serious. In many parts of the tropics, mangroves have been cut down for timber or to make fish farms. This has resulted in severe damage to villages further inland during tropical storms and hurricanes. Expensive barriers have had to be built to stop the damage that mangroves once prevented. The loss of mangroves can also reduce fish catches, since many commercially caught fish breed in mangrove swamps.

Wetland reserves

In many parts of the world, conservationists are persuading governments to set aside wetlands for wildlife, for people to visit, and to maintain their valuable role in protecting the environment. But simply leaving wetlands alone is not enough. Many would gradually silt up and disappear. Their water supply must be carefully controlled, and, if surrounding areas continue to be drained, the water in the reserve will soon drain away.

Extra funds can sometimes be produced for conservation by allowing tourists into wetland reserves to enjoy their wildlife and scenery. In the Everglades in Florida, USA, many kilometres of wooden walkways direct people along tracks without damaging the habitat. ◆

The marshes at Bharatpur in India were originally created by people to attract ducks for them to shoot. Today they are a famous bird reserve, home to large numbers of birds, including the rare Siberian crane, and even a species of fishing cat.

People are slowly learning the usefulness of wetlands. In some places, beds of reeds are being planted to act as a natural filter for sewage, instead of building expensive treatment works.

▼ **A drainage ditch in the Somerset Levels in the west of England. For centuries, farmers living in this low-lying area have experienced flooding. Recently, peat has been cut so extensively that the habitat for birds and other wildlife has been destroyed, although attempts are now being made to restore some of these wetlands as nature reserves.**

Whales

▲ Pilot whales usually swim in large groups, or schools.

Distribution
All of the oceans of the world; most stay in deep water and rarely come close to land
Largest
Blue whale: 25–33 m, females slightly larger than males; weight 100–120 tonnes, record about 180 tonnes
Number of young
1 suckled for several months at least; females produce a baby every other year or every third year
Lifespan
Fin and blue whale thought to live for over 110 years
Subphylum
Vertebrata
Class
Mammalia
Order
Cetacea
Number of species
38 (not including dolphins)

▶ Toothed and baleen whales: the sperm whale (top) and the bowhead whale.

Whales are mammals. They are intelligent, warm-blooded, air-breathing creatures, which produce live young and feed them on milk. Yet they live all their lives in water and die if they are forced onto dry land, because out of the water their weight crushes their lungs. The term 'whale' is generally used for creatures more than 10 metres long, but porpoises and dolphins are also members of the same order, the Cetacea.

All whales have streamlined bodies. They swim using a horizontal tail fin called a fluke. A pair of large flippers near the front of the body is used mainly for steering. Inside the flippers are bones similar to those of your arms and hands. Whales have no hind limbs at all. Their skin is very smooth. Unlike most mammals, which have hair or fur, whales have at most a few short, bristly hairs around their jaws. They are kept warm by a layer of blubber beneath the skin. In a big whale, this can be 60 centimetres thick in places.

Breathing

A whale's nostrils are placed together on top of its head. They are called its blow-hole. Air

breathed in goes down to the lungs; from there oxygen is carried to the muscles. When it comes to the surface, a whale breathes deeply. As it does so, it squirts out of its blow-hole an oily stuff from its air passages. This contains nitrogen, trapped from the air, and is most of what can be seen when a whale 'blows'. A whale does not breathe water out of its blow-hole, as a whale with water in its lungs would drown, just like any other mammal. Because it can remove the nitrogen from the air it breathes, a whale can dive deep and come to the surface quickly. This would kill human divers.

Sight and sound

Whales' eyes are not large, and since they close their nostrils when they submerge, a sense of smell would be of little use to them. Their smooth bodies have no visible ears, but they do actually hear very well indeed. They use sounds we call whale songs to communicate with each other. Some whale songs carry many hundreds of kilometres underwater. They use sound to locate obstacles and food (echolocation). Loud bursts of sound are also used to disable prey.

Hunting and conservation

Whales have always been an important source of food and oil to Arctic peoples, but commercial whaling, particularly in the 19th and 20th centuries, has brought most whale species near to extinction. The International Whaling Commission now monitors numbers. As a result of its work, most whales are now protected, though a few countries continue to catch whales and dolphins, against its advice. Whale conservation has been helped by the revulsion that most people feel at the cruelty involved in harpooning the animals. Some species are not beginning to increase in numbers as a result of conservation. It has been suggested that all Antarctic seas should be a whale conservation area.

Toothed and baleen whales

Toothed whales catch and hold fishes and squid with sharp pointed teeth, though, strangely, many have very few teeth. The largest whales feed on shrimp-like krill. They have no teeth, but triangular plates of baleen hang down from the roof of their mouth. This is made of stuff very much like fingernails and the inner edges of baleen are fringed, like thick hairs. Huge mouthfuls of water are strained through the baleen, and the krill are caught in it. ◆

Wheels

Wheels make it much easier to move or turn things. Without wheels, everything would have to be dragged or carried around. At one time, most wheels were made of wood. Nowadays, they can be made of steel, aluminium light alloy, or plastic.

Most of the wheels you see are on vehicles, but almost every machine or instrument with moving parts has wheels in it. Grinding wheels are used for sharpening tools. Potters' wheels are used for turning soft clay so that it can be moulded into round pots. Ferris wheels carry you high above the ground at a fair.

Wheels have a rod through the middle called an axle. If the wheel rubs against the axle, there is friction. This makes the wheel more difficult to turn and wears out the materials. Oil or grease helps to reduce friction. But most wheels also have bearings to reduce friction even more. Usually, the bearings are very small metal balls or rollers which fit between the wheel and the axle.

FLASHBACK

The idea of the wheel may have come from the use of tree trunks as rollers to carry heavy loads. Instead of having to put the rollers under the load, it might have seemed a good idea to fit slices of tree trunk to rods sticking out of a platform. By about 3200 BC, solid wooden cartwheels were being used in Mesopotamia. By about 2000 BC, wheels with wooden spokes had been developed. ◆

Find out more
Machines
Pottery
Pulleys
Stone circles
Turbines
Water power

The wheels on furniture and supermarket trolleys are called castors. They swivel so that they always point in the direction you are pushing.

◄ Main wheels on the undercarriage of an airliner. Each wheel may have to support a load of over 20 tonnes.

The development of the wheel

Before the wheel was invented, heavy loads were moved using tree trunks as rollers. But someone had to pick up the rollers at the back and move them to the front.

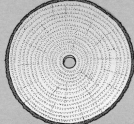

The first wheels were probably slices of tree trunk. If a hole was made in the middle, a rod, called an axle, could be pushed through.

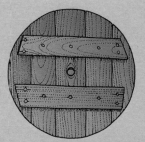

Bigger wheels were made by cutting short planks of wood and fixing them together. A knot-hole in the middle made an ideal place for the axle to go.

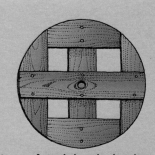

It was found that, by leaving out some of the middle pieces, wheels could be made lighter but just as strong.

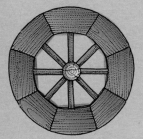

A rim (edge) for the wheel was made with shaped pieces. These were connected to the centre by thin wooden strips called spokes.

During the Industrial Revolution, iron became plentiful and wheels could be cast in iron. They were hard-wearing but brittle.

A strong, less brittle wheel could be made of wood with a thin strip of iron fixed all the way round the rim.

Tight wire spokes helped to make wheels lighter and stronger. Rubber round the rim gave a softer ride. Later, air-filled rubber tyres were made.

Wildlife

The word 'wildlife' means all of the plants and animals in the world which are not tame or domesticated. Nobody knows how many different kinds (species) there are, but many will have become extinct before we are even aware of their existence.

If you were to travel about the world, you would notice a change in the kinds of plants and animals as you went from one area to another. This is partly because of climate and environment and partly because the big landmasses of the continents are separated from each other by water. The plants and animals in each one have evolved over millions of years and adapted to their separate environments.

The world can be divided into six *biogeographical zones*. Each zone tends to have many plants and animals not shared by the others, although they often have related species. Even when the same kind of habitat exists in different zones, there are different animals occupying the same niche or way of life. For example, the prairies of North America and the steppes of eastern Europe and Asia are both grasslands with hot summers and cold winters. In the steppes, susliks and marmots live in basically the same way as the related prairie dogs of North America.

In a few cases the same animals may be present. This happens in northern North America, northern Asia and Europe. If you were to take a trip round these cold regions, you would find reindeer (caribou), wolverines and brown bears in the whole area, although many of the small animals are different. The reason for this is that until about 10,000 years ago there was a land bridge between north-east Asia and Alaska. Animals were able to move from one great landmass to the other. Now the sea has broken through that bridge, and the American and Asiatic animals have been separated. But they have not been apart from each other for long enough to have changed very much.

It is easiest to see the biggest differences in wildlife among the mammals. Birds, which can fly, often move between two or more zones during migration, and some kinds, such as the swallow and the peregrine falcon, are found in almost all regions. Even plants can travel between zones, as their seeds can be carried by birds (stuck to their feet, beaks or feathers and in their droppings) or by wind or water.

The Greek word *bios* means 'life' and so biogeography is the geography of living things.

The main animal and plant zones of the world

The world can be divided into six biogeographical regions (zones). Each zone contains wildlife not found anywhere else.

☐ **The northern Old World area (Palaearctic zone)** includes the whole of Europe, North Africa as far as the Sahara, and Asia to the southern edge of the Himalayas. Animals found in no other zones include camels, yaks and Asiatic asses such as onagers. Some, such as Przewalski's wild horse, are now found only in zoos.

☐ **The northern New World area (Nearctic zone)** includes all of North America and its nearby islands. The animals are in many cases like those of Europe and Asia, but those found nowhere else include pronghorns (deer-like animals), skunks, racoons and the strange, rare mountain beavers (true beavers live in both the northern zones).

☐ **South America and its nearby islands (Neotropical zone).** South America was a separate landmass until about 10 million years ago. It has many animals which are not found anywhere else, including sloths, armadillos, New World monkeys and unique rodents such as guinea pigs. Many other creatures which once lived in South America died out when it became joined to North America. Animals moved in both directions across the land bridge.

Very few South American animals succeeded in their new habitat, although the Virginia opossum and the nine-banded armadillo managed to survive in the north. Some North American animals, such as the jaguar, moved south, and these invaders took over from similar original inhabitants. South America has some of the strangest living and fossil mammals to be found anywhere in the world.

☐ **Africa south of the Sahara (African or Ethiopian zone)** is a great landmass which is the home of many animals that have become extinct in Europe and Asia. They include hippopotamuses, giraffes and many species of antelope. In the past, relatives of these animals lived in Europe, but were forced southwards as the climate changed.

Nearctic		African (Ethiopian)
Neotropical		Oriental
Palaearctic		Australasian

1	mountain beaver	**9**	giraffe	**17**	gibbon
2	pronghorn	**10**	hippopotamus	**18**	siamang
3	racoon	**11**	aardvark	**19**	orang-utan
4	armadillo	**12**	Bactrian camel	**20**	wild horse
5	capuchin monkey	**13**	onager	**21**	echidna
6	tree sloth	**14**	Asian elephant		(spiny anteater)
7	giant anteater	**15**	yak	**22**	duck-billed platypus
8	roan antelope	**16**	giant panda	**23**	kangaroo

☐ **Southern Asia (Oriental zone)** contains some animals related to other creatures found in warm climates. These include various monkeys, which are similar to those found in Africa, and the orang-utan, which is an ape related to the gorilla and chimpanzee. Animals found nowhere else include giant and red pandas, gibbons and their close relatives the siamangs.

☐ **Australia and nearby islands (Australasian zone).** Australia is sometimes called the island continent, because it is separated by sea from all of the other great landmasses. As a result, the animals that were there about 100 million years ago, when it first became isolated from the rest of the world, have evolved without any competition from other species. They include animals which scientists think must be like the very earliest of all mammals: the platypus and the echidnas (spiny anteaters). These lay eggs, like reptiles, instead of producing living young as all other mammals do. But the babies are still fed on milk, like those of all other mammals.

Almost all of the rest of the native mammals of Australia are marsupials. They include kangaroos and wallabies, wombats, possums, and koalas. The only exceptions are a few small rodents, bats, the dog-like dingoes and humans. Australasia includes New Guinea and some other islands which stretch towards South-east Asia. The line separating them from the Oriental zone islands was first charted by an explorer and naturalist called Alfred Russel Wallace, and is called Wallace's Line.

Island animals

The isolated islands of the world are mostly formed by volcanoes which have erupted in the middle of the oceans. They include the Galapagos Islands, the Hawaiian Islands, the Seychelles and many others. They do not make a single biogeographical zone, but they are of great interest to biologists because the animals found there usually got there by accident. Once there, they were usually unable to escape and evolved over thousands of years into strange forms that are unknown elsewhere.

There are very few mammals on isolated islands because – unlike birds – they cannot be blown off course, nor are they likely to survive long spells at sea. On some islands there are no mammals at all, but there may be reptiles, some of which are very large as they have less competition than there would be on the mainland. Giant tortoises were at one time found on many islands. Birds and insects may get blown to islands. Those that stay may change, and often the survivors become large and flightless, such as the dodo or the Gough Island rail. Such animals are at risk when their island homes are discovered by humans. Like the dodo, they may become extinct because they are attacked and their habitat destroyed.

Animal globe-trotters

In the past, when human beings explored the world, they often took animals from home with them. Sometimes this was to make sure that they had food in their new lands, sometimes they wanted beasts of burden, or maybe they just wanted to have something which reminded them of home. Horses were taken to South America by the Spanish conquistadores, and rabbits and foxes were taken to Australia. Goats, pigs and camels have all become wild in many places far from their original homes. Often the newcomers do a great deal of damage to the environment, sometimes causing the original animals to become very rare or even extinct.

Biological control

Sometimes animals are introduced into new lands as a natural solution to biological problems, such as pests on crops. This usually involves introducing a natural predator or parasite to the pest, and it is called *biological control*.

If your greenhouse is full of greenfly and you do not wish to spray your plants with insecticide, you can gather as many ladybirds as you can find and put them in the greenhouse. The ladybirds will eat the greenfly.

Myxomatosis is a very infectious disease that occurs naturally in some South American rabbit species, usually causing death. The disease is caused by a virus and was deliberately introduced into Australia and western Europe to reduce the numbers of wild rabbits.

Biological control has not only been used to kill pests. In Australia local dung beetles were unable to cope with disposing of all the dung produced by newly introduced cows. Dung beetles from Africa were introduced to help with the problem.

However, the use of predators and parasites to control pests can have unforeseen consequences. For instance, the large American cane toad was brought to Australia to combat insect pests in sugar-cane plantations. Unfortunately, it settled in so well that its numbers escalated out of control and it rapidly became a pest itself.

Conservation

Today humankind controls almost all of the Earth. Too often this control results in harm to the environment, as a result of pollution, or the destruction of habitats such as forests and wetlands. Often the harm is unintentional. But habitats have evolved over thousands or millions of years; once they are destroyed and their plant and animal inhabitants become extinct, they cannot be replaced. We should think before we destroy, for only by conservation of wildlife can we keep the variety and richness of the world. ♦

▼ A marine iguana from the Galapagos Islands. This species of reptile has evolved in isolation in its island home and is different from all other iguanas. Most iguanas are agile and live in trees or on the ground, but the marine iguana is a heavy animal that lives on the coast and feeds by diving for seaweed.

Wind

Wind is air moving. If you pick up a magazine and move it back and forth in front of you then you will feel the air on your face in the form of a slight wind. Flapping the magazine needs energy. If you flapped for an hour your arms would get very tired. Wind also needs energy and this energy comes from the Sun.

Sunshine warms and cools different parts of the air. When the Sun warms the ground, the air above it rises up and cooler air flows in to take the place of the air which has risen. This flowing air is the wind.

You can feel wind on the ground and high up in the air. Weather forecasters use the scale of winds shown below, called the Beaufort scale. It was expanded from 12 to 17 wind speeds in 1955.

Special winds

Many winds have names. Among the most constant winds are the 'trade winds'. These blow towards the tropics most of the year round. They were named the trade winds in the times when much world trade was done by sailing ships. Ships always tried to avoid other areas in tropical oceans where winds hardly ever blow. These are called the 'doldrums'.

A breeze is a light wind. Where the land and the sea meet, for example, you get land and sea breezes in summer. This is because the air is hotter over the land than the sea by day and cooler over land than sea at night. So the winds blow from the sea to land during the day and from land to sea at night.

In southern France a wind called the 'Mistral' often blows in March and April. It is a cold, northerly wind, which can blow for several days. In the USA a wind called the 'Chinook' is a warm, dry wind that blows down the eastern slopes of the Rocky Mountains. When the Chinook starts to blow, the temperature rises quickly, sometimes by as much as 22 °C (40 °F) in 5 minutes. These winds often make snow thaw rapidly. The word Chinook means 'snow eater' in a local Indian language. Winds of a similar kind occur in other parts of the world and are called *foehns*. ◆

▼ **Find out more**

Cyclones and
    anticyclones
Depressions
Hurricanes
Monsoon
Tornadoes
Weather

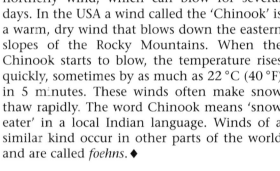

◄ **The original Beaufort scale, including calm (with no wind) and 12 different wind speeds.**

Beaufort scale

number	km/h	mph
0	below 1	below 1
1	1–5	1–3
2	6–11	4–7
3	12–19	8–12
4	20–28	13–18
5	29–38	19–24
6	39–49	25–31
7	50–61	32–38
8	62–74	39–46
9	75–88	47–54
10	89–102	55–63
11	103–117	64–73
12–17	over 117	over 74

Calm

Light air

Light breeze

Gentle breeze

Moderate breeze

Fresh breeze

Strong breeze

Moderate gale

Gale

Strong gale

Storm

Violent storm

Hurricane

Wind power

In 1840 there were around 10,000 working windmills in England and 8000 in Holland.

By the year 2010, more than 10% of Denmark's energy is expected to come from wind power.

The wind can be very destructive. Gales can uproot trees and lift tiles off roofs. But the wind can also be put to work. Sailing ships and yachts have sailed round the world on wind power alone. And for centuries windmills have used the power of the wind for grinding corn and pumping water. Today, aerogenerators are using the wind's energy to generate electricity. Unlike oil and gas, the wind is one source of energy which will never run out.

Aerogenerators

Most aerogenerators have a tall, slim tower with huge blades like an aircraft's propeller mounted on top. The blades can be over 20 metres long. As they spin in the wind, they turn a generator which produces electricity. Aerogenerators are placed on exposed, windy sites, often in large groups called wind farms. Unlike fuel-burning power stations, they do not pollute the atmosphere, but the force of the wind is unpredictable and few sites in the world are suitable.

Windmills

A hundred and fifty years ago, there were thousands of windmills across the Netherlands and the fens of eastern England. Many were used to drain water from low-lying land. Very few remain today, but some have been kept in working condition. They have vanes (sails) which turn a shaft. This is connected by gearwheels and another shaft to a pump, or a stone for grinding corn, or some other machinery. When the wind changes direction, the sails must be turned so that they face into the wind. In post mills, the whole building turns on a vertical post. In later designs, called tower mills, only the top part of the tower turns. The main tower, made of wood or bricks, is fixed.

Windmills around the world

Windmills are still used in many parts of the world for pumping water from wells and drainage ditches. Some have fabric or slatted wooden sails. Others are made by cutting an old oil drum in two and attaching the two halves to a rotor arm on top of a vertical shaft. In Australia and America, one common type of windmill has a tall, framework tower. The rotating part has lots of steel blades with a tail vane to turn it into the wind. ◆

▶ Tower mills like this were once used to pump water from low-lying land. They were also used to drive grinding stones, saws and other machinery.

▼ Find out more
Greenhouse effect
Pollution
Turbines

▼ These aerogenerators are positioned on high ground in California, USA, to catch the maximum wind force. Many hundreds of aerogenerators are needed to produce as much power as a single power station.

Wine

Grape vines are grown and wine is made in the temperate and Mediterranean climates of the world. In the northern hemisphere, this includes most of central and southern Europe, and California and Oregon in the United States. In the southern hemisphere, wine is made in Australia and New Zealand, South Africa, Chile and Argentina.

Wine is an alcoholic drink usually made by fermenting grape juice with yeast so that it is chemically changed. The yeast grows on the sugar in the grape juice and produces alcohol, and carbon dioxide gas which is lost to the air. Country wines may also be made with other fruits, vegetables, herbs and flowers, such as red currants, cherries, beetroot, cowslips, dandelions and elder flowers.

Wine-making

Red wine comes from black grapes. White wine comes from white grapes or from black grapes with the juice extracted before the skins can stain it.

The grapes are crushed, and in the case of red wine the juice (called must) is left in contact with the skins. Yeast is added and the juice ferments. The wine is then filtered and stored in vats or barrels to mature it. Finally it goes into bottles. Wine labels may show the *vintage*, (the year the grapes were harvested).

▲ After the grapes have ripened in the summer sun they are picked by hand.

FLASHBACK

Wine-making may have first started in ancient Sumeria, but the wine and its secrets were soon transported along the Mediterranean coast. The Greeks and Romans both made wine, and the Romans established some of the earliest vineyards in France and Germany. ◆

▼ **Find out more**
Alcohol
Farming
France
Yeasts

Winter sports

The main competition for winter sports is held every four years as the Winter Olympic Games. The events include the biathlon (skiing and shooting), bobsleigh, luge, ice hockey, ice skating and skiing.

Winter sports take place on ice or snow. Skating, skiing and ice hockey are the most popular of winter sports. Tobogganing, bobsleigh, and ice yachting are also winter sports. The first two are adaptations of the great winter pastime of sledging.

Tobogganing

Anyone riding a sledge over snow is tobogganing, but as a sport it is divided into two types, called lugeing and Cresta tobogganing. Both involve sliding down ice-covered tracks on small sleds.

Luge sleds are made of wood with steel runners and a fibreglass seat. Riders lie almost flat on their backs. Mechanical braking and steering is not allowed; steering is by leg pressure on the front runners and a hand rope. There are events for one- and two-person teams, and winners are decided by taking the lowest total time for a certain number of runs down the course. Speeds can reach 120 kilometres per hour.

Cresta tobogganing takes place on the Cresta Run, a winding, steeply banked channel of ice built by the St Moritz Tobogganing Club, Switzerland. The single rider lies chest down. Speeds can reach 135 kilometres per hour.

Bobsleigh

Bobsleighs also began as sledges, but they are now streamlined machines made of steel and aluminium with mechanical brakes and steering. They are guided down specially prepared tracks of ice with banked bends. Four-person bobs are slightly faster than twos, and speeds exceed 135 kilometres per hour.

Ice yachting

This is travelling across ice in craft with runners and sails. The techniques are like those of ordinary sailing. ◆

In the middle of the 19th century, British tourists started sled-racing on snowbound mountain roads in the Alps. Three racing sports emerged – lugeing, Cresta tobogganing and bobsleigh.

▼ **Find out more**
Ice hockey
Ice skating
Olympic Games
Skiing

Wire

In southern Africa, dies were being used to make wire over 1600 years ago.

Wire is made by passing a metal rod through a series of moulds, called dies, with tiny, funnel-shaped holes. The rod is squeezed into a thinner and thinner shape, so forming wire. Steel wire can be stiff and springy, or pliable and bendy, depending on its thickness and the type of steel.

Wire can be chopped up to make pins, needles and nails, bent into springs, and woven into netting for fencing. Wire for fences is usually galvanized (coated in zinc) to stop it rusting. Twisted or plaited wires make wire rope or cables, used in cranes and lifts. Bicycle brakes use thin wire cables, and in suspension bridges the roadways are hung from wire cables.

Electric power cables in houses are made of copper wire, coated in plastic for insulation. Wire is also used for carrying signals between telephones, though this job can now be done more efficiently by optical fibres. ◆

▼ Find out more
Aircraft
Cables
Copper
Fibre optics
Springs

Witches

A female witch is called a witch or a sorceress. A male witch is called a wizard, sorcerer or warlock.

A coven is the name given to a group of witches, usually 12 in number.

▼ **Three witches being burned at the stake. A German woodcut of 1555.**

Witches in stories have pointed hats and black cats, and ride broomsticks through the sky. They chant magic spells. They are wicked women, unless their spells go wrong, and then they are people to laugh at.

If you had lived 400 years ago, you would not have thought witches were a joke. Almost everyone believed that some women were the servants of the Devil. If they cursed you, you were in trouble; you might even die.

It was usually poor, old women who were accused of being witches. Because they were poor they often begged from their neighbours. Sometimes the neighbour refused to give them anything. The old woman might go away mumbling to herself. The neighbour would feel guilty because it was everyone's duty to help the poor. Perhaps then one of the animals became ill, or one of the children. Why did it happen to them? Had they been cursed? What had the old woman mumbled? The woman might be taken to court and accused of being a witch.

One way of testing a witch was to tie her up and throw her in a river or pond. Only the guilty would float, because water rejected evil (so people thought). So the innocent drowned and those who floated were then killed. In most of Europe witches were burnt; in England they were hanged.

During the 17th century, witch-hunting became a mania. In parts of Germany there were a hundred burnings a year. In England over 200 women were hanged in just two years. Matthew Hopkins, the 'Witch-Finder General', was partly responsible. Parliament paid him £1 for every town he visited looking for witches.

As scientific knowledge grew, belief in witchcraft faded, and there were few trials after 1700. In Salem, in Massachusetts in the USA, 30 people were executed for witchcraft in 1692. Only five years later, the judge and jury publicly admitted their mistake and they begged forgiveness.

Many people in Europe used to believe in a 'witches' sabbath'. This was a night-time gathering of witches, often in a bleak or mountainous place. It was believed to take place on a special date, such as the night before May Day or Hallowe'en (31 October). ◆

A witch who does good, like healing sick people, is often called a *white witch*.

The last English witch to be executed was Alice Molland, in Exeter, England, in 1684.

Jane Wenham of Walkern, in Hertfordshire, England, was sentenced to death in 1712 but was given a royal pardon.

Witch laws were abolished by Act of Parliament in 1736.

Women who practised traditional and folk medicine were sometimes accused of being witches. Nowadays traditional medicine, for example herbal medicine, is valued more highly. The World Health Organization of the United Nations said in 1978 that traditional healers in Africa should become part of official local health teams.

▼ Find out more
Hallowe'en

Wolves

Usually only one
male in a pack
produces cubs. All the
members of the pack
help to feed and rear
them, bringing them
meat from kills made
many kilometres away.

Number of young
4–7 suckled for about 5
weeks and then fed and
cared for by all members
of the pack
Lifespan About
10 years in the wild,
16 years in captivity
Subphylum
Vertebrata
Class Mammalia
Order Carnivora
Family Canidae
(dog family)
Number of species 2

▼ **Find out more**
Dogs
Foxes
Mammals

Wolves live in family groups called packs whose size depends on food availability. The pack centres around the breeding pair (which mate for life) and can contain up to 20 members.

Because they hunt as a group, wolves are able to kill animals larger than themselves, and feed mostly on deer, usually preying on the weaker ones. After making a kill, a wolf can eat about 9 kilograms of meat. The pack will finish the carcass completely. All domestic breeds of dog are descended from the wolf. ◆

Wombats

Distribution Mainly in
New South Wales,
Tasmania and Victoria
Size Head-and-body
length up to 115 cm
Weight Up to 39 kg
Number of young 1,
pouch life about 6 months,
remains with mother for
about 11 months or more
Lifespan 5 years in
the wild; up to 20 years
in captivity
Subphylum Vertebrata
Class Mammalia
Order Marsupialia
Family Vombatidae
Number of species 3

▶ A common wombat.
When attacked, it turns
its back on its attacker
and kicks out with its
hind legs.

▼ **Find out more**
Australia
Kangaroos
Koalas
Mammals
Marsupials

Wombats are pouched mammals whose closest relative is the koala. Unlike koalas they live on the ground and burrow. Each common wombat has several burrows which it may share with other wombats, but each wombat has its own separate feeding area. Wombats are active at night, when they emerge to feed on grasses, or sometimes the roots of trees and shrubs. They sometimes have to travel several kilometres in search of food. ◆

Women's movement

For many centuries there have been people who want women to have the same rights as men. From about 1850 there were campaigns in both the USA and Britain for married women to be able to own their own property, instead of everything belonging to the husband when they married. Women also took part in the anti-slavery movement and other public activities. They were refusing to stay at home as they were expected to do.

The US state of Wyoming granted women the right to vote in 1869, and in 1893 New Zealand became the first country to do so. Women elsewhere then demanded this right. In Britain, many women joined the Suffragette movement to force Parliament to agree to their demands. By the end of the 1920s, the right to vote had been won by women in Australia, Canada, Finland, Germany, Britain, Sweden, the USA and other countries.

After this, women's organizations campaigned for such things as help with child care. Then in the 1960s, the women's movement grew even stronger when the women's liberation movement started in the USA. Feminists, who believe in equal rights for women, began to work for equal pay, equal education and equal opportunities for women.

In the 1990s, the women's movement has changed emphasis and women's groups are now an accepted part of society. In business, sport, music, in the trade unions and in many other areas, there are women's organizations which meet regularly and give positive advice and support to each other.

Many women believe that they will only become completely equal when there are many more facilities for child care and when men do their fair share of work in the home. Then women will be free to work away from the home and will have more power over their own lives. ◆

Two-thirds of the world's work is done by women; they earn less than 70% of male earnings and they own less than 7% of the world's wealth.

International Women's Day is celebrated on 8 March.

Writing for women's equality
A Vindication of the Rights of Women, Mary Wollstonecraft (1792)
The Second Sex, Simone de Beauvoir (1949)
The Feminine Mystique, Betty Friedan (1963)
Sexual Politics, Kate Millet (1969)
The Female Eunuch, Germaine Greer (1970)

▼ **Find out more**
Peace movement
Suffragettes

BIOGRAPHY
Pankhurst family

Wood

Wood is the material that makes up the trunks of trees. When we use it for crafts or building we call it *timber*. It is strong and hard-wearing, but can be cut and carved easily. Each year, as a tree grows, it produces more wood in its trunk, and this yearly growth shows as 'annual rings' on the cut log. These bands add an attractive pattern ('grain') to the timber. Perhaps the greatest advantage of wood over other building materials is that trees continue

▲ **Timber being cut into regular lengths at a sawmill in British Columbia, Canada.**

1171 million tonnes of logs were grown around the world in 1990 and 32 million tonnes of plywood were made. In the same year, 239 million tonnes of paper were produced, mostly from trees.

▶ **The three main types of manufactured wood: plywood, blockboard, and chipboard.**

One way to reduce the need for new forests to be planted is to recycle paper. However, the tough fibres that form the paper get broken if it is recycled too often, so new wood pulp is often added to recycled paper to restore its strength.

producing more of it. Wood is therefore a renewable resource – a material which, with care, we can go on using for ever, without supplies running out.

Preparing timber

Foresters use power saws or chain-saws to fell (cut down) trees, and large machines to trim the branches off the tree trunk in seconds. At the sawmill, large saws slice the logs into planks. Before the wood can be used it must be seasoned (dried), otherwise it will twist shrink. Sometimes the planks are seasoned the air. More often this is done in a speci building called a *kiln*, where warm air is blow over the planks to dry them quickly.

Manufactured wood

Not all logs are cut into planks. Some a turned against a sharp blade so that thin sheet called *veneers*, are peeled off. Three or mor veneers may then be glued and presse together to make *plywood*, which is stronge and cheaper to produce than solid woods of th same thickness.

Any spare wood left over at the sawmill is cu into chips, mixed with sawdust, sprayed wit glue and pressed into sheets to make *chipboar* This is often covered with veneers or plastic and used for many purposes, including kitchen fittings and furniture.

Carpentry

Cabinet makers and carpenters select the typ of wood to use depending on what they wan to make. Hardwoods from broadleaved trees such as oak, walnut and mahogany, have beautiful grains and polish up well, so they are used in good quality furniture. Some of the most expensive hardwoods come from trees in the tropical rainforests, but so many of these have been felled that the trees are becoming very rare. Softwoods, from coniferous trees such as pine or cedar, are used mainly in building. They are easy to saw, drill, chisel and plane.

Paper manufacture

Vast quantities of softwoods are pulped to make paper. Even trees with poor trunks can be used in this way, so in some countries forests are planted where trees will never grow well, just for the paper industry. This can provide valuable work in remote areas, but some people say the forests spoil the landscape and destroy wild habitats. ◆

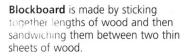

Plywood is made by sticking together thin sheets of wood.

Blockboard is made by sticking together lengths of wood and then sandwiching them between two thin sheets of wood.

Chipboard is made from tiny pieces of wood mixed with glue, then pressed into large boards.

Woodlands

Woodland is the name often given to small patches of forest. Usually these are in areas where human beings have cut down most of the trees, as in Britain or much of north-west Europe. Woodlands in such places are oases in which the natural wildlife of the region can survive.

Within a wood, trees are the dominant plants. In cool parts of the world there may be several species in the same wood, but in the forests of the tropics there may be more than 100 species in a small region, while in the cold forests of the north there may be only one species. Beneath the canopy of the branches few other plants can thrive. Even so, in deciduous woodlands, where the trees drop their leaves in winter, there may be a shrub layer, formed of small, bushy trees, such as hawthorn, holly or dogwood. At ground level there are plants that flower in the spring. These grow and bloom before the trees have put on their leaves, while there is still enough light reaching the ground.

The trees give shelter and food to many kinds of animals. Deer are the largest creatures in woodlands in cooler countries. They browse on the leaves and eat the bark of many kinds of trees. Many of the inhabitants of woodlands, such as squirrels, can climb and many can glide or fly. Yet others, such as shrews, scuttle and tunnel among the fallen leaves, while some, such as badgers, dig deep safe burrows underground.

The trees themselves are the home for a host of tiny animals. Insects feed and take shelter among the leaves, and their grubs often burrow deep into the wood. Most woodland insects are marvellously camouflaged so that they are very difficult for us, or the birds that prey on them, to see. In spite of this, they are eaten by many woodland birds. Woodpeckers winkle wood-boring grubs from their tunnels, while warblers pick aphids and similar tiny insects from leaves. Small birds and some small mammals are food for predators such as owls and foxes. The fruits of the trees are eaten by squirrels and mice, while in autumn some bigger creatures, such as wild boars, become fat on a diet of acorns. Over 300 species of animal probably depend on the European oak. These include deer, many kinds of birds, and insects such as the purple hairstreak butterfly.

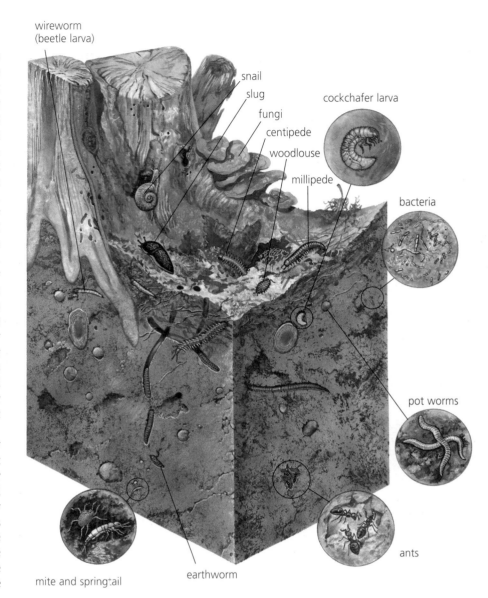

▲ The rich brown earth of deciduous woodland is formed by the nutrients from dead plant and animal material released into the soil by the many decomposers at work on the woodland floor. Leaves, plants and dead trees are fed on and broken up by the tiny animals, insects and bacteria on and in the soil. As dead animals and droppings rot, yet more nutrients are released.

When a tree dies, its remains decay and are returned to the soil by insects which eat the wood, helped by fungi and a host of bacteria. The space and light given by the tree's fall make it possible for there to be new growth of the many plants and animals for which the woodlands are home.

If people's activities were to stop this afternoon, today's woods would spread and in 200 years great forests would stretch throughout Britain, and across most of Europe and North America. ◆

Woodlice

Distribution
Worldwide, in suitable damp places
Size
Between 5 and 15 mm
Phylum
Arthropoda
Class
Crustacea
Order
Isopoda
Number of species
About 4000 isopods, mostly water-living or parasitic forms

▼ **Find out more**
Crustaceans
Invertebrates

Woodlice have armoured bodies and seven pairs of walking legs. They are not insects, but crustaceans. Woodlice live in damp places, because they breathe through gills which can only work if they are moist.

Woodlice feed mainly on rotting plants. They protect themselves from enemies, such as spiders and centipedes, by producing a nasty-tasting fluid or rolling themselves into a tight ball. Female woodlice lay up to 200 eggs, which they carry with them. The baby woodlice also often stay with their mother for some weeks after hatching. They take about two years to become fully mature. ◆

Woodworms

► A woodworm beetle.

Size of beetle
About 4.5 mm long
(full-grown grub is about 7 mm long)
Number of eggs laid
Up to 80, usually less
Lifespan
About 3 years as a grub (dry wood is not very nutritious). The adult survives for only a few weeks.
Phylum
Arthropoda
Class
Insecta
Order
Coleoptera
Species
Anobium punctatum

▼ **Find out more**
Beetles
Insects
Larvae

Woodworms are not true worms, but the larvae of certain small wood-boring beetles. They usually eat dry wood, which has been dead for years. In the wild, they act as recyclers, breaking down the remains of dead trees and returning them to the soil. The adults, called furniture beetles, sometimes fly into houses and lay their eggs on furniture, or any other wood. The larvae, or grubs, that hatch out, tunnel into the wood, and eventually destroy it.

Many kinds of insect larvae feed on timber, but they generally prefer damp wood, so they are not as common in our homes as the woodworm. ◆

Wool

Wool comes from sheep, goats, llamas and some other animals. It grows from follicles in the animal's skin just like the hair which grows from our skin. It has some unusual qualities which make it a very useful fibre. Its cells still carry on trying to stay in balance with the surrounding moisture even when the wool is no longer alive and growing. This is why wool is said to breathe. It absorbs and evaporates moisture. It is also soft but strong and resists dirt, static and tearing.

Raising and shearing sheep

Many countries have sheep and produce wool, but four countries dominate the world trade in wool. They are Australia, New Zealand, South Africa and Argentina. These countries export more than half their wool to countries in the northern hemisphere.

The fleece is removed from the animal with special clippers. This is called shearing. The shearer aims to remove the fleece in one piece. This usually takes about 5 minutes. After the fleece has been shorn it is examined for quality and then graded. The sheep will grow a new coat for the following winter and can be shorn again.

Prehistoric people clothed themselves with sheepskins, but soon learned to make yarn and fabric from the fleece.

▲ The woolmark is the International Wool Secretariat's symbol for products made from pure new wool. It is one of the world's best-known trade marks. Four hundred million labels are applied every year.

▼ To make woollen yarn the fibres in a sheep's fleece have to be combed by a carding machine. They are then twisted so that they form a strong, continuous strand.

shearing the sheep   fleeces baled for   washing the fleece
                            transport to mill   to remove dirt

Woollens and worsteds

Two kinds of yarn are made from wool for weaving and knitting. Woollens are spun from fibres which vary in length and are jumbled up together. Worsteds are spun from combed wool. Combing removes the shorter fibres and leaves the longer ones lying parallel to make a smoother and more even yarn.

FLASHBACK

From ancient to medieval times the spare moments of the women of the house were often spent spinning. Weaving was considered to be more difficult and was left to men who specialized in the art.

In Britain in the Middle Ages the wool trade was concentrated in southern England, the Cotswolds, Devon and East Anglia. Trade in wool and cloth with Flanders and France made huge fortunes for the wool merchants. Powerful Weavers' Guilds were set up in many towns. By the 15th century, sheep-farming had spread in Yorkshire, and wool was made in Derbyshire and Yorkshire as well as in the south. Three hundred years later, in the Industrial Revolution, these counties began to take over as the centres of cloth manufacture. This came about because they had plenty of fast-running water which could be used to power some of the new machines. ◆

The Lord Chancellor in Britain's House of Lords sits on a seat called the Woolsack. It is made of wool covered with red cloth, and is said to have been introduced in the 14th century to remind people of the importance to England of the wool trade.

▼ **Find out more**
Farming
Goats
Industrial Revolution
Knitting
Llamas
Sheep
Spinning
Textiles
Weaving

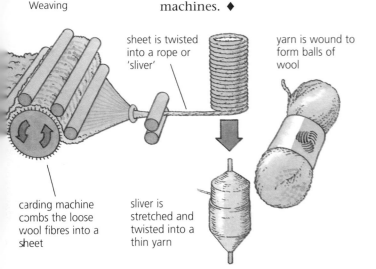

carding machine combs the loose wool fibres into a sheet

sliver is stretched and twisted into a thin yarn

sheet is twisted into a rope or 'sliver'

yarn is wound to form balls of wool

Word processors

A word processor is a computer which can be used as a typewriter. You type at the keyboard and the words appear not on paper, but on a screen. By using special keys, you can change the words and move them about. You can even store or save the words on cassette or computer disc and get them back again whenever you like. When your work is finished and there are no more changes to make, an electronic printer prints out the words on paper.

In offices throughout the world, reports and letters are prepared using word processors. Most of the articles in this encyclopedia were prepared in this way. The authors wrote their articles on word processors and altered them until they were happy with the results.

Some word processors can handle pictures as well as words. Journalists use these to design and prepare whole pages for magazines and newspapers. This is sometimes called desk-top publishing. At the printer's, signals from a word processor can be sent straight to the machine which makes the printing plates.

Mail order companies and many other organizations use word processors for sending out 'personal' letters. Everyone gets the same basic letter, but the word processor changes the name and address each time so that every letter looks as though it has been typed specially for that person.

Many word processors are just ordinary desk-top computers with a special program in them for word processing. Some have special spelling and grammar checkers. Some even 'learn' words you use a lot and complete them as soon as you have begun to type them. Most word processors plug into the mains electricity. But some run on batteries and are small enough to be used on trains and planes. These small portable computers are often called lap-tops. ◆

WYSIWYG (pronounced 'wizzy-wig') is short for 'What You See Is What You Get'. This is a word processor that shows on the screen exactly what will appear when printed.

Word processors sometimes use a mouse, a small device that does the same job as a joystick or a keyboard. Its full name is WIMP (Window Icon Mouse Pointer). When you move the mouse about on your desk, a pointer moves about on the screen. You use the pointer to make changes to the words.

Words and numbers on a word processor screen are called *text*. Pictures on a screen are called *graphics*.

▼ **Find out more**
Computers
Information technology
Printing

World War I

Military loss of life

Germany	2,000,000
Russia	1,700,000
France	1,358,000
Austria-Hungary	1,200,000
UK	761,213
Italy	460,000
USA	114,095

World War I was also called the 'Great War'. It started in August 1914 and ended in November 1918. For four years it was the biggest and most terrible conflict between nations that the world had ever seen. Millions of soldiers, sailors and airmen were killed or wounded. Large numbers of civilians were killed, injured or made homeless. Even though later wars were in some ways more terrible, and even though we now have the fear of nuclear war, we still remember the Great War as a particularly terrible and tragic happening.

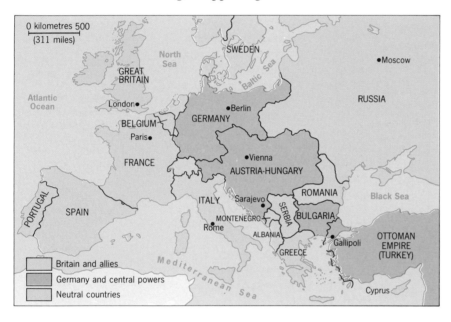

▲ Germany and the central powers fought against Britain, France, Russia, and their allies.

Britain and allies
British empire
Russia
France and empire
Romania
Belgium
Italy
Serbia
Japan
Portugal
USA (from 1917)

Germany and central powers
Austria-Hungary
Bulgaria
Ottoman (Turkish) empire

Assassination!

No war has just one simple cause. World War I came after many events which showed that countries were jealous of each other's power. Germany and Britain each wanted an empire and a big navy: Austria and Russia wanted to take over weak countries in the Balkan region of Europe. France wanted to win back land lost in a war against Prussia in 1870. Sooner or later there was bound to be conflict. The spark which set it all off came on 28 June 1914 when the Archduke Franz Ferdinand, heir to the throne of Austria, was killed by a Serb in Sarajevo, the capital of the Balkan province of Bosnia. Austria threatened her small neighbour Serbia, which Russia supported. Germany sided with Austria. France backed Russia, and Britain was friendly with France. By 4 August much of Europe was at war.

The war starts

For many years the Germans had known what they would do if war broke out. They would first attack France by passing through Belgium. In this way they would bypass the defences along the French border. Belgium was 'neutral', which means that it said it did not want to be involved in any war. Germany intended to ignore this and gain the advantage of surprise. The plan was to knock France out quickly and then turn to deal with Russia. The plan only partly worked. The German armies swept through Belgium into France, but they were held by the British and French. The armies dug in, facing each other in positions which were to stay the same for almost four years.

The Western Front

Where the German armies met the British and French, a 'front' developed which stretched from the Channel to the Swiss border. Each side dug trenches which were difficult to capture. To make progress, soldiers had to leave their trenches and run across open ground ('no man's land') towards men firing rifles and machine-guns. Neither side was able to break through into the countryside beyond. Huge numbers of men and guns were used to fight the long battles on the Western Front, and there were millions of casualties.

The Eastern Front

There were other fronts. Most important was the Eastern Front, where the Austrian and German armies faced the Russians. This front too eventually became bogged down. Many millions of Russian soldiers were killed or wounded, and even though the Russians began to be successful in 1916, the war had been too much for a country already in crisis. The casualties and the great hardship caused to the Russian people added to their discontent. In 1917 the Russians rebelled against the tsar and set up a republic. After the Bolshevik revolution in October, the government abandoned the fight.

A world at war

In the southern Alps the Germans and Austrians faced the Italian army, while in the south Balkans (Gallipoli), British troops, with others from Australia and New Zealand (Anzacs), fought the Turks (the Ottoman empire was allied with Germany and Austria). Other troops came from Canada, India and other countries of the British and French empires to fight on the Western Front. In Africa, British, French and African troops occupied the German colonies.

In the Far East, Japan declared war on Germany and occupied the Qingdao peninsula, which Germany held. At the same time, the powerful Japanese fleet occupied German island colonies in the Pacific. Japan later expanded its territory from these islands.

In the Middle East, Britain encouraged the Arabs to revolt against their Turkish rulers. An Anglo-Indian army advanced into Mesopotamia from Basra. At first it suffered humiliating defeat at Kut-al-Amara, but in 1917 it entered Baghdad. At the same time troops from Egypt, with Arab partisans (led by T. E. Lawrence), advanced into Palestine and occupied Jerusalem.

In April 1917 the USA declared war on Germany. Much-needed American weapons then came to Europe, and eventually key troop reinforcements for the Western Front also arrived from the USA. This was now a world war.

The war at sea

Before the war Britain and Germany had each tried to build a huge fleet of warships. When war started, each side was reluctant to risk its fleet in a big battle for fear of losing it. There were lots of skirmishes, but only one real sea battle with battleships slugging it out. This was between the British Grand Fleet and the German High Seas Fleet, at Jutland in the North Sea in May 1916. Even then, there was caution on both sides and the result was not decisive.

The most effective sea warfare was the German submarine, or 'U-boat', campaign against cargo and passenger ships. Britain depended on importing food and goods, and the U-boats had a very serious effect on British shipping all through the war.

▼ Ships of the British Grand Fleet. Battleships blockaded German ports to prevent food and other supplies from getting through. The Germans were desperately short of food by 1918.

The war in the air

All the main countries had aeroplanes. They were used at first for spotting and scouting. Then the 'scouts' started to shoot at each other, and air 'dogfighting' began. Both sides dropped bombs on each other's armies, and also on cities. The Germans used big hydrogen-filled airships called Zeppelins to attack British and French cities. They also bombed London with Gotha bombers. By the end of the war it was clear that air power would be vital in the years to come.

The end

When war started in August 1914, people said, 'It will all be over by Christmas'. In the end the war was won by a long, hard and expensive trial of strength. The British and French and their allies gained the victory simply by wearing down the enemy. The entry of fresh troops from America in 1917 was crucial in the final victory.

The end came in November 1918. An 'armistice' (end to the fighting) with Germany was called for at 11 a.m. on 11 November, the eleventh hour of the eleventh day of the eleventh month. The guns stopped and all went quiet.

In the peace settlement that followed, the Russian empire collapsed. The Austro-Hungarian empire was divided into numerous small countries. Modern Turkey emerged from the Ottoman empire, whose Middle Eastern provinces were divided between France and Britain. Germany was financially humiliated, which later helped the Nazi Party to grow and to start a new war. ◆

▲ A trench scene on the Somme river by André Devambez. The purpose of digging a trench was for protection from enemy gunfire. The muddy trenches on both sides stretched from the English Channel to the frontiers of Switzerland. Soldiers ate, slept and stood guard in mud. To attack they had to go over the top and face the lethal power of machine-guns.

Zeppelins were used by the Germans to bomb British and French towns, and both sides used aeroplanes for bombing raids. Over 1000 British civilians were killed in air raids.

World War II

▼ German troops
marched into Prague
in March 1939. The
year before, Hitler
had annexed the
Sudetenland, an area
of north-western
Czechoslovakia
inhabited mainly by
German people. Britain
and France accepted the
German takeover of the
Sudetenland at Munich
in September 1938.

After defeat in World War I, Germany lost lands which had belonged to her in 1914. The countries which had defeated Germany were determined to keep her weak, without powerful armed forces. Many Germans resented this. So when Hitler and the Nazis came to power in the 1930s, they gained popularity by saying that Germany should get back the lands it had lost, and take over other neighbouring lands where there were German-speaking people. The Nazis also set about rearming Germany. German expansion into neighbouring countries eventually led to war.

A step too far

Germany began its expansion in 1936 by reoccupying the Rhineland. Then in 1938 German soldiers marched into Austria, which was made part of Germany. This was called the *Anschluss*. The next country to be taken over, in 1939, was Czechoslovakia, where there were many German-speaking people. Throughout the 1930s, too, Hitler had been building up the German armed forces.

Britain and France allowed each of these things to happen without much protest. People called this policy 'appeasement'. It was hoped that when Germany regained her 1918 position, she would stop threatening other countries. In 1939, Germany threatened to occupy parts of Poland. This was a step too far for Britain and France, who warned that there would be war if Poland was invaded.

War breaks out

In August 1939, the German Nazi government made an agreement with the Soviet Union. This took Britain and France by surprise, because Nazis and communists had seemed natural enemies. The agreement meant that if war came, the Germans would not have to fight Russia on the eastern front. In September 1939, German troops marched into Poland, as did others from the Soviet Union. The Germans used the tactic called 'Blitzkrieg', or 'lightning war'. Troops and tanks moved quickly, backed up by very effective dive-bombing. Hitler probably thought that the British and the French would once more allow Germany to have her way. But they responded by declaring war.

Britain and France could do little to help the Poles, who were quickly defeated. The British army went to France and waited for months for the Germans to attack. In spring 1940 the German army invaded Norway, Denmark, France, Belgium and the Netherlands, and the British army had to retreat in ships and small boats from the French port of Dunkirk. Germany was soon in control of most of Europe, and Britain stood alone, in danger of invasion.

USSR: the Great Patriotic War

In June 1941, with western Europe under Nazi rule, the Germans invaded the Soviet Union, breaking the agreement made in 1939. German troops drove deep into Russia and besieged Leningrad and Stalingrad. Russian losses were enormous, and civilians endured great hardships.

The Germans had expected a quick victory, but the Russians resisted with determination, and the Russian winter killed many German soldiers, unprepared for such cold weather. In January 1943 the Germans were defeated at Stalingrad and over 90,000 German soldiers became prisoners. This was the beginning of the end for the Nazis, though two years of war were still to come.

The Soviet Union suffered terribly in World War II. There were millions of civilian casualties, and Russians were badly treated by German troops. Only by knowing this can we

...understand some of the actions of the Soviet Union after the war.

Global war

Even more than World War I, World War II was a truly global war. Japan allied itself with Germany and eventually overran several British and French colonies in the Far East. In December 1941 a surprise Japanese air raid destroyed American ships at Pearl Harbor Naval Base in Hawaii, in the Pacific Ocean. After this attack, the USA entered the war on the side of Britain and the USSR.

Fighting went on across the Far East, the Pacific, the Atlantic Ocean, the Middle East and North Africa. American, Soviet, British and Commonwealth forces, together with 'Free' forces of people from France and other countries in German hands, fought against Germany, Italy and Japan in a terrible and costly conflict.

Armaments on land

The main land weapon was the tank. Commanders tried to get their armies into positions where the tanks could be given freedom to travel across the countryside against the enemy. Great tank battles were fought, especially in Russia and the deserts of North Africa. There were also heavy guns, but at the heart of the army there was still the infantryman marching with rifle and bayonet.

In the air

Commanders tried to get air supremacy – a situation in which their aircraft could roam the skies attacking targets at will. The 'Battle of Britain' was a battle for the skies over southern Britain in 1940. Had the RAF lost, a German invasion would have been possible. Small fighter aircraft battled each other, and big bombers penetrated deep into enemy territory.

At sea

By 1939 the big battleship was already becoming old-fashioned, because it was too easily attacked from the air. Aircraft carriers and submarines became the most important fighting ships. Submarines ranged far from home, attacking cargo ships and battleships. The Germans had a large and very effective fleet of submarines or 'U-boats'.

Victory

Once the Soviet Union and the USA were in the war, the defeat of Germany, Italy and Japan was only a matter of time. From early 1943, the

War dead

USSR	27,000,000
Poland	4,300,000
Germany	4,200,000
China	2,200,000
Japan	1,200,000
France	600,000
USA	406,000
UK	388,000

German defeats

Battle of Britain
August–September 1940
El Alamein, North Africa
October–November 1942
Stalingrad, Russia
November 1942–January 1943
Kursk, Russia
July 1943

▼ The Japanese conquests were greatest by August 1942. The Germans were still advancing up to November 1942. By the end of that year the Allied reconquest had begun in the Pacific and the West.

☐	The Allies and neutral countries
▨	German conquests and allies
▨	Japanese conquests and allies

▲ The British and American air forces throughout the war flew more and more bombing missions against Germany, attacking factories and also civilian areas so as to sap German morale. In February 1945, Dresden was almost obliterated, with many thousands of deaths.

▲ As the great armies battled to and fro, millions of people were forced from their homes and took to the roads with their possessions. Many never succeeded in returning home, and children lost contact with their families.

▶ The banner of victory hoisted over Stalingrad (now Volgograd) in January 1943. The city had been besieged for over 6 months and street fighting had reduced it to rubble before the German army surrendered. This was the turning-point of the war.

Japanese defeats in the Pacific

Coral Sea
May 1942
Midway Island
June 1942
Guadalcanal
Winter 1942–Spring 1943
Leyte Gulf
October 1944
Okinawa
April–June 1945

Soviet Red Army rolled the Germans back towards their border and then pressed on to Berlin. In 1942 the US navy won important battles in the Pacific, and American forces began to recapture the Pacific islands taken by the Japanese. In November 1942 the British defeated the Germans and Italians at El Alamein in North Africa, and in 1943 allied troops crossed the Mediterranean to invade Italy itself. Then in June 1944 came the long-awaited 'Second Front': the invasion of northern France by British and American troops on 'D-Day'.

Now Germany was under pressure from east, west and south. Gradually her troops were pushed back as far as Berlin, and Germany surrendered in May 1945. The Japanese surrendered in August after American planes dropped atomic bombs on the cities of Hiroshima and Nagasaki. The first atomic bomb destroyed over 13 square kilometres of the city of Hiroshima and killed nearly 80,000 people instantly. The scale of destruction shocked people on both sides of the war.

After the war

In the autumn of 1945, the world was in a desperate condition. European cities lay in ruins. Millions were homeless. Japan was laid waste by firebombs and two atomic bombs. Germany was occupied by British, French, American and Russian troops ('the Allies'). Everyone was grateful for peace, of course, and countries began to pick themselves up, though for some it was a long process.

Many of the effects of World War II have lasted for nearly half a century. Until the autumn of 1990 Germany was divided into two separate states and Berlin was a divided city. The war resulted in the end of the European colonial empires of Britain, France, the Netherlands, Belgium and Portugal. In Asia, India, Burma, and Sri Lanka won immediate independence, while Indonesia, Malaysia and Indo-China followed. African troops from British and French colonies had fought away from home, many in the Far East. On their return to both East and West Africa, their demands for independence could not be resisted. Thus, in many ways, we cannot understand the history of the world since 1945 without knowing something about World War II. ◆

▲ Commandos landing on 6 June 1944 (D-Day) on a beach in Normandy, northern France. British and Canadian troops landed on the eastern beaches and Americans landed to the west.

Worms

Number of species
Segmented worms 15,000
Bootlace worms about
800
Flatworms about 10,000
Roundworms about
12,000 already known;
perhaps a million kinds
still to be discovered

Earthworms are segmented worms and belong to the phylum Annelida.

To most people the word 'worm' means an earthworm, but there are many other kinds of creatures, also called worms, which are very different indeed. Most are unfamiliar because they live in remote places or in the sea. Bootlace (or ribbon) worms, which may be more than 30 metres long yet no thicker than a pencil, can sometimes be found on a rocky beach. They are soft-bodied hunters, but harmless to us.

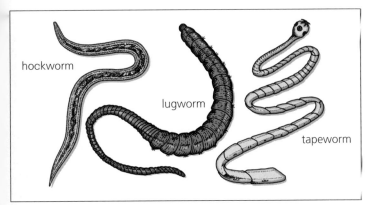

▲ Three different types of worm.

hockworm
lugworm
tapeworm

Flatworms

Flatworms, which are sometimes called *flukes*, usually live in water. Many of them are brightly coloured, so although they are in general less than 1 centimetre long, you can see them gliding over stones or weeds. Some kinds of fluke are parasites on other animals, and may cause serious diseases. At first sight tapeworms may look different from other flatworms, but they are like a series of flukes, one behind the other. As adults they are parasites, living in the guts of their host.

Roundworms

Roundworms are almost all tiny – most of them are less than 2 millimetres long. Huge numbers of roundworms live in the soil, in the sea and in fresh water. Some, known as eelworms, cause diseases of plants. Others, called threadworms or pinworms, may be parasites of animals, including humans, and often cause diseases. ◆

▼ **Find out more**
Animals
Earthworms
Leeches
Parasites
Tapeworms

Wrestling

Wrestling is an unarmed combat sport in which two people struggle to throw one another to the ground. Wrestling dates back to at least 4000 BC, and played a prominent part in the ancient Greek Olympics.

There are two main wrestling styles, Greco-Roman and freestyle. These are on the Olympic programme and have their own world championships. In Greco-Roman, the wrestlers are not allowed to hold the body below the waist or use their legs to hold or trip an opponent. Freestyle wrestling does not have these restrictions. In both styles a competitor fights an opponent of similar weight. There are 10 weight categories, ranging from light flyweight (48 kilograms) to super-heavyweight (130 kilograms).

Bouts are scheduled to last five minutes. Certain throws and moves earn technical points, and these count when a bout goes the full distance. But a wrestler may win outright by a 'fall', pinning his opponent's shoulders to the ground for one second, or by gaining a lead of 15 or more points.

Sumo wrestling

In Japanese sumo wrestling, two contestants weighing at least 130 kilograms grab hold of each other's belts and try to push, pull or throw their opponent to the floor or out of the ring. Each bout is preceded by much ritual, but the fighting rarely last more than a few seconds. ◆

Traditional styles of wrestling include the Swiss *schwingen* and the Icelandic *glima*, in which the wrestlers must hold onto their opponent's trousers or a special harness. In 'Cumberland and Westmorland' wrestling, practised in the north of England, the combatants lock their hands behind their opponent's back and rest their chin on his right shoulder. In the Turkish *yagli*, wrestlers oil the upper half of their body.

Professional wrestling has a strong following and is popular on television. But, although the wrestlers might possess considerable skill, it is not regarded as a sport, more as a staged entertainment.

▼ **Find out more**
Martial arts
Sport

▼ Sumo wrestlers face each other inside the ring before the referee (right) gives the signal to begin. This confrontation, often broken as one of the contestants stands up and moves away, might last several minutes. When they are both ready, the clash is like two mountains colliding. But sumo is more than just a battle of strength. It calls for quick thinking and movement, practised skills and split-second timing.

Writers

A writer is, quite simply, anyone who writes. Yet we use the word in a special way for those people who use words to entertain us. They usually write stories, but may also write about facts and ideas. Popular writers are read by a great many people. Great writers are those who write works of great value even to later generations.

Ancient tales

Much writing in ancient cultures takes the form of myths (stories about gods), legends (stories about heroes or heroines who were half-god and half-human) and epics (stories about brave individuals that were thought to be true). These were often written in rhythm or metre, which we call poetry.

The earliest of these is called *Gilgamesh*, written in the Babylonian empire, and the longest is the *Mahabharata* verse epic from India. The earliest epic in Anglo-Saxon or early English is *Beowulf*. The most famous ancient epics in the West are the *Iliad* and the *Odyssey*, traditionally credited to Homer in ancient Greece.

The Greeks

The ancient Greeks developed other sorts of writing, too. They wrote words for songs to be sung in public, and from these performances came their poetry (rhythmic writing) and drama (stories with speech and actions). Other writings reflected their interest in the lives of their own people – history, essays, speeches and biography. Some of the writing was personal, such as autobiography, diaries and letters.

Drama

Some of the greatest writers have written stories to be acted on the stage. Ancient Greek drama reached its height in the poetic tragedies of Aeschylus, Sophocles and Euripides, and in the comedies of Aristophanes. Their dramas tell a story that takes place in one day in one place, though the physical action takes place offstage.

Perhaps the most celebrated playwright of all time is William Shakespeare. He was one of a number of playwrights writing in England around the time of Queen Elizabeth I. Shakespeare wrote histories, comedies and tragedies. Elizabethan drama is full of exciting events, lively characters and rich language.

In the 17th century, French playwrights included the tragedy writers Racine and Corneille and the comedy writer Molière. In more recent times, writing for the theatre has continued to thrive with the work of Anton Chekhov, Bernard Shaw, Henrik Ibsen, Arthur Miller and Tennessee Williams, among others.

Novels

The novel, a long story in prose, is sometimes said to have started in the 17th century, with the Spanish writer Cervantes and his novel *Don Quixote*. It developed out of early tales and romances, such as Boccaccio's *Decameron* and Chaucer's *Canterbury Tales*.

Many of the best early stories seem to have started with some political or social purpose. *Robinson Crusoe* was written by Daniel Defoe to feed the public's fascination with the great sea voyages and their dangers. Other writers took as their theme the great religious questions of the day. For example, John Milton wrote about the fall of Adam and Eve in his epic poem *Paradise Lost*, while in *Pilgrim's Progress*, John Bunyan wrote a story about the travels of the main character, Christian, and his spiritual struggle for salvation.

Many writers today deal with problems of race and gender, in the same way that 19th-century writers wrote about the social classes. Some of the most famous of these are Margaret Atwood (Canada), Nadine Gordimer (South Africa), Gabriel García Márquez (Colombia), Salman Rushdie (India/Britain), Ben Okri (Nigeria), Toni Morrison (USA).

The Thematic directory at the back of the Biography volume lists all the writers who have entries in the Encyclopedia.

▼ Shakespeare was the greatest of the Elizabethan playwrights. Of the many others, Christopher Marlowe and Ben Jonson are perhaps the best known.

1605 (Part 1)

1719

181

▼ A page from *A Christmas Carol* by Charles Dickens, with one of the original illustrations by John Leech. Dickens, one of the greatest 19th-century writers, made people in Victorian Britain aware of social injustices.

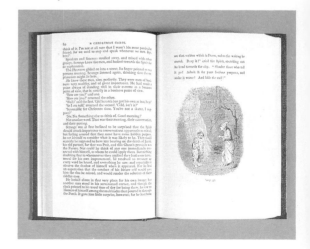

◄ A few of the great novels written between the 17th and the 19th centuries.

1847   1851   1868   1880

In the 18th and 19th centuries, educated readers wanted to understand the ways of their own society. Many of these readers and writers were women. The novel is perhaps the one major art form in which the achievement of women has at least matched that of men.

Today the novel is an international form, and a number of specialized genres have developed, such as detective, horror, romance, fantasy and children's stories. Some of these genres trace their roots back to earlier centuries.

Detective stories

Two of the first detective stories were written by Wilkie Collins in the mid-19th century – *The Woman in White* and *The Moonstone*. Not long afterwards, Arthur Conan Doyle created the most famous of all detectives, Sherlock Holmes, in a series of popular stories. American detectives tend to take on a more dangerous role, as in the novels of Raymond Chandler, which feature the tough and weary private eye Philip Marlow.

Thrillers

The thriller is a modern development of the kind of adventure story that Robert Louis Stevenson developed in stories like *Treasure Island* and *Kidnapped*. Increasingly in the modern world, the thriller overlaps with the novel of crime or political intrigue. Graham Greene wrote some political thrillers, which have a wry comic touch. Ian Fleming wrote a series of novels featuring the suave super-spy James Bond.

Horror and science fiction

The horror story is about the dark side of human imagination. It began in the 18th century when there was a fashion for novels full of ruined churches and dungeons, and was developed by Bram Stoker in his novel *Dracula* and by Robert Louis Stevenson in *Dr Jekyll and Mr Hyde*. Mary Shelley added a new twist when she introduced a scientist, Dr Frankenstein, who creates a monster. In doing so, she created another genre which today we call science fiction.

▲ Ghost stories, detective stories, science fiction and Westerns are four types of story, or *genres*, that are very popular in the 20th century.

Fantasy

Both horror and science fiction are really parts of a larger genre – fantasy. The fantasy novel featured magic, and includes stories as diverse as *Sinbad the Sailor*, *Gulliver's Travels* and *Alice in Wonderland*.

Romance

An ever-popular branch of fiction is the love story. The most famous love stories are often tragic, as with *Romeo and Juliet* by Shakespeare or *Wuthering Heights* by Emily Brontë. Many popular love stories have a happy ending and are given a historical setting.

Writing for other media

In the 20th century, the art of story-telling has been affected by new inventions, including radio, film and television. Many writers now write for these media, often adapting novels and other written materials. Even though the audience may never read a word, a film's success often depends on the skill of its scriptwriters.

Other writers today are reporters or journalists. They write vivid accounts of the events and concerns of the day, for radio and television as well as in newspapers and magazines. ◆

Famous novelists writing in English
(asterisked names have entries in the Biography volume)
* Alcott, Louisa May
* Austen, Jane
  Baldwin, James
* Brontë, Charlotte, Emily and Anne
  Cooper, James Fenimore
* Defoe, Daniel
* Dickens, Charles
* Eliot, George
  Faulkner, William
  Fielding, Henry
  Fitzgerald, F. Scott
  Forster, E. M.
  Greene, Graham
* Hardy, Thomas
  Hawthorne, Nathaniel
  Heller, Joseph
  Hemingway, Ernest
  James, Henry
  Joyce, James
  London, Jack
  Melville, Herman
* Poe, Edgar Allan
* Scott, Walter
  Steinbeck, John
* Stevenson, Robert Louis
* Twain, Mark
  Wharton, Edith
  Woolf, Virginia

Some famous writers in other languages
French
Balzac, Honoré
Flaubert, Gustave
Proust, Marcel
Stendhal (Henri Beyle)
Zola, Emile
Russian
Chekhov, Anton
Dostoevsky, Fyodor
Pasternak, Boris
* Tolstoy, Leo
  Turgenev, Ivan
German
Kafka, Franz
Mann, Thomas

▼ **Find out more**
Arabian Nights
Books
Drama
Fables
Fairy tales
Folk tales
Legends
Myths
Poems and poetry

Writing systems

We send language messages in two quite different ways – we say them or we write them. We write ideas or words down when we want either to keep them and remember them later, or to let someone else read them at a later time or in a different place. Writing is a way of recording and storing words and ideas. Famous books, the country's laws, scientific discoveries, letters to friends are all written down, to be read or remembered for various purposes later.

Before writing

Many early peoples kept an 'oral' record of the great events of their history or beliefs. This means that some people learnt the record by heart (perhaps in a long poem) and recited it to others in their society. The poem about the great war between the Greeks and Trojans called the *Iliad* is an example of this. It was recited for a long time before it was finally written down.

Pictograms and ideograms

Pictograms are an early form of written communication. Pictures of objects, such as a circle for the Sun, represented the object itself. In ideograms the whole idea of the word is explained in a shape rather like a picture. The Chinese and Japanese use ideograms instead of using an alphabet.

▶ The Sumerians wrote their signs on blocks of wet clay and then let the clay dry in the sun. The clay blocks became very hard and were stored. Some have survived over 4000 years.

We use signs for mathematical ideas such as $+ - = \div \times$, and for money: £ and $. These are similar to ideograms.

▶ Chinese ideograms. The earliest forms were simple but recognizable drawings. Over the centuries they changed into stylized shapes that are easy to write.

Early writing systems

The earliest true writing was developed by the Sumerians in the land of Mesopotamia (now Iraq). The earliest examples found come from Tell Brak and are dated to about 3250 BC. The language was discovered on a very large number (over 250,000) of clay tablets. They used wedge-shaped signs on the tablets to develop a type of writing known as cuneiform. Cuneiform was used for about 3000 years.

From about 3100 BC the ancient Egyptians developed a different form of writing called hieroglyphics. Their writing system used pictures at first, but the pictures did not enable them to explain complicated ideas. They developed a system which used picture-signs to represent sounds. The Egyptians carved and painted these hieroglyphs on stone, but they also wrote with rush pens on papyrus, a sort of paper made from crushed reeds.

The first proper alphabet to be used was probably developed in Syria in the 15th century BC. ◆

X-rays

X-rays are a kind of energy which can be both useful and dangerous. They are waves like radio waves and light but they have much more energy. They travel at the same speed as light, but can go right through some solid things which light cannot penetrate. The Sun and stars produce X-rays, but our atmosphere protects us from these. The X-rays used in our hospitals, factories and laboratories are produced using X-ray tubes.

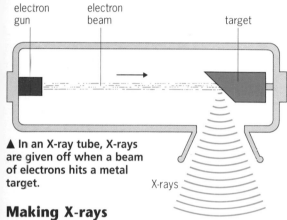

▲ In an X-ray tube, X-rays are given off when a beam of electrons hits a metal target.

Making X-rays

Electricity is lots of tiny particles called electrons. In an X-ray tube, a beam of electrons is shot out from an electron gun at one end. The electrons travel down the tube, gaining speed all the time as they are pulled towards a metal target by a very high voltage. When the electrons smash into the target, some of their energy is changed into the penetrating radiation called X-rays. The tube has no air in it because this would disturb the beam. The target gets very hot under the electron bombardment. It is often cooled by passing oil through it.

Using X-rays

Doctors and dentists use X-rays to take pictures of growing teeth and broken bones inside your body. X-rays make shadow pictures because they go through soft parts of your body, like skin, but are stopped by the hard bones or teeth. Doctors also use much stronger X-rays to treat cancers. These are carefully measured and aimed to kill the cancer without damaging the rest of the body. X-rays can also check inside machinery for cracks or faults. At airports, they are used by security staff to check luggage for weapons and bombs. Scientists use X-rays to study how atoms are arranged inside solid materials like crystals. Astronomers can learn more about the stars by studying the X-rays that come from them.

Dangerous X-rays

X-rays with high energies can damage the cells in our bodies, so they must be used carefully, especially by people who work with them all the time. A screen, often made of lead, protects nurses and dentists while an X-ray picture is taken. Lead is also used to shield your body when your teeth are X-rayed.

FLASHBACK

Wilhelm Röntgen discovered X-rays in 1895. He was experimenting with a beam of electrons in a glass tube when he noticed that invisible rays were escaping from the tube. He found that these X-rays, as he called them, would go right through some solid materials. Very soon doctors were using them to look at broken bones. Now doctors use computers to build up very detailed X-ray pictures of the inside of a patient's body. ◆

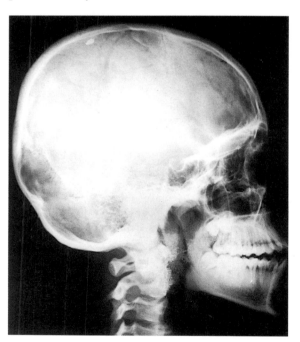

Some X-rays come from the clouds of dust and gas left when a star explodes. Other X-rays can show astronomers where black holes might be.

TV screens and computer VDU screens give off X-rays because they have electron beams striking them. However, the amount of radiation is far too small to be dangerous.

▼ **Find out more**
Lead
Radiation
Scanners
Waves

BIOGRAPHY
Röntgen, Wilhelm

◀ **X-ray of a normal human skull.**

▼ **X-ray machines are used at airports to check the contents of bags to prevent passengers taking weapons or bombs onto an aircraft.**

Yachts

The word yacht comes from the old Dutch word *jaghtschip* meaning 'ship for chasing'.

Yachts are boats or small ships used for racing or leisure. There are sailing yachts which have sails and motor yachts which have an engine, but sailing yachts are much the more popular of the two types. The smallest yachts are also called sailing dinghies. Most have a crew of one or two. The biggest ocean-racing yachts may have a crew of more than 20. The person who steers the yacht is called the helmsman and those who help to adjust the sails are the crew.

Cruising yachts

The early yacht was used by Dutch royalty in the 17th century as a pleasure craft. Cruising yachts today are slower and usually larger and much more comfortable than the racing yachts. They often have a small outboard or inboard motor which makes it easier to enter and leave harbour and can be used if the wind drops.

▶ A sailing dinghy is a small yacht, normally sailed by a crew of one or two.

Racing yachts

These have hulls and sails which are designed to make the yacht go fast. The hulls are shaped so that they will move through the water with least effort. And there is a keel or a centreboard to stop the yacht being blown sideways when sailing across the wind. The sails are made of strong lightweight synthetic materials, like nylon and Terylene,

of as large an area as possible. A big yacht will go faster than a small one, so yachts are grouped in classes such as Firefly, Enterprise, Mirror, or Lark. All the yachts in one class are the same size, so they can race against each other with an equal chance of winning. When yachts of different classes race each other, each one is given a handicap. The yacht with the lowest handicap starts first and the one with the highest handicap last. If the handicaps have been worked out correctly then all the yachts have an equal chance of winning.

Other types of yacht

A catamaran is a yacht with two hulls joined by a platform which carries the mast. A similar yacht with three hulls is known as a trimaran. This type of yacht can get up quite a speed because its wave-piercing design cuts down water resistance while maintaining excellent balance on the water surface. Catamaran car ferries are used in parts of Europe and North America. ◆

Find out more
Boats
Sailing
Sailing ships
Water sports

Yeasts

Brewer's yeast is a rich source of Vitamin B and some people take it in tablet form to supplement their diet.

Yeasts are single-celled fungi, related to mushrooms and moulds. They are found growing wild in the soil, on the skins of fruit and in dust. Wild yeasts have been cultivated and their properties used in baking, brewing beer and wine-making.

The enzymes in yeast work on starchy materials to produce sugars on which the yeast can feed. As it does so fermentation starts and produces alcohol and carbon dioxide. This activity is used in bread-making to make the dough rise. The carbon dioxide is trapped in the mixture and forms minute holes. The alcohol evaporates in the heat of the oven. Both fresh and dried yeast can be used in bread-making. Yeast needs a warm place to make the bread rise well.

In beer-making and wine-making it is the carbon dioxide which is lost to the air and the alcohol that is retained. In wine-making some wild yeasts from the skins of the fruit are used to start off the fermentation. These are usually killed off before cultured yeasts are added later. ◆

Find out more
Beer
Bread
Enzymes
Fungi
Wine

Yemen

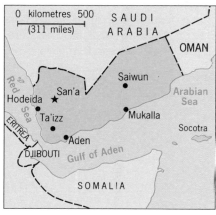

Area
528,000 sq km
Capital
Sana a
Population
12,050,000
Language
Arabic, English
Religion
Muslim
Government
Republic
Currency
1 Yemeni dinar = 1000 fils

The Republic of Yemen is an Arab country on the southern tip of the Arabian peninsula. It was formed in 1990 from two separate countries – the Yemen Arab Republic (YAR) which bordered the Red Sea and the People's Democratic Republic of Yemen (PDRY) on the southern tip of Arabia.

From a fertile plain adjacent to the Red Sea in the west, the land rises sharply to reveal spectacular scenery. There are high volcanic plateaux and villages perched on the sides of mountains. Life in these villages has not changed for hundreds of years. To the east beyond the mountains the land is mostly barren and rocky desert, although there are some fertile valleys. Here the temperatures remain high throughout the year. To the north lie the deserts of Saudi Arabia.

The Yemen has only recently been opened up to modern development. It is very poor, but oil has been discovered, raising hopes for the future. The other main industries are agriculture and fishing. Yemen society is based on tribal loyalties and the people have a reputation for being fierce fighters.

Its strategic position at the entrance to the Red Sea and its fine port of Aden made the former PDRY an important possession for Britain for 130 years. The country became independent in 1967 and was until 1990 allied to communist countries of Eastern Europe and to the former Soviet Union. The PDRY suffered civil war in 1986. The revolution in Eastern Europe in 1989–1990 removed the country's communist support. An uneasy union with the YAR took place in May 1990, but troubles between Sana'a and Aden escalated into civil war, ending with the occupation of Aden by northern forces in 1994. ◆

The PDRY was called the Protectorate of Aden when under British rule.

It is hoped that Aden, the country's economic capital, will be redeveloped as a free port and regional centre for trade.

▼ Find out more
Arabs
Middle East
Muslims

Yoga

The eight 'limbs' or stages of yoga practice
1 Avoiding doing wrong (*yama*)
2 Acting rightly (*niyama*)
3 Physical exercises (*asana*)
4 Control of breathing (*pranayama*)
5 Control of the senses (*pratyahara*)
6 Concentration (*dharana*)
7 Meditation (*dhyana*)
8 Contemplation (*samadhi*)

What most people in Western countries mean when they say that they practise yoga is that they regularly perform special exercises, which are often easier for children than for adults, such as balancing on one leg, putting their limbs into unusual positions or standing on their heads. But there is more to yoga than this.

The exercises are good not just for the muscles, but also for the whole body, and you perform them slowly, holding the positions for some time. Also, you breathe very carefully. The exercises and the breathing together help you to relax, and for some people are the first stage of meditation.

Yoga is not a religion. It is practised by Hindus and Buddhists, but also by many other people. For those who take it seriously, it becomes a way of life. It keeps people fit and relaxed and helps them to cope with stress and develop their natural abilities. Yogis believe that control of the body will lead to a calm mind and to a better understanding of oneself and the world around.

Yoga comes from India, and is at least 5000 years old. It used to be passed on by a *guru* (teacher) to chosen pupils. Now anyone can be taught it by an expert. ◆

▼ Find out more
Fitness

Area
102,350 sq km
Capital
Belgrade
Population
10,500,000
Language
Serbo-Croat
Religion
Christian, Muslim
Government
Parliamentary republic
Currency
1 new Yugoslav dinar =
100 paras

Yugoslavia

The federal republic of Yugoslavia
is in southern Europe and has two
regions, Serbia and Montenegro.
On the Adriatic coast the climate of
Montenegro is very warm, but that
of the inland mountain range can
be bitter in winter. The capital
Belgrade lies on the River Danube,
along which, in normal times, sail
fleets of barges. Heavy industry and
coal-mining are centred around
Belgrade, and there are large
deposits of copper in eastern
Serbia. The river valleys of Serbia
are very fertile, growing many
different cereals and fruits, and the
area is known as the 'bread-basket'
of Yugoslavia.

Two-thirds of the population are
Serbian and Montenegrin, most of
whom are orthodox Christians,
who use the Cyrillic script. There
are also minorities of Albanians
and Muslims.

The harsh terrain of Montenegro
enabled it to be the sole area of the
Balkans never conquered by the
Ottoman Turks. Likewise, during
World War II it became the centre of
resistance to German occupation.
Its capital became known as
Titograd, but has now reverted to its
former name of Podgorica.

History until World War II

After World War I Slovenia,
Croatia, Bosnia and Herzegovina
(formerly all part of the Austro-
Hungarian empire) joined with
Serbia and Montenegro to form the
kingdom of the Serbs, Croats and
Slovenes. The king of Serbia was to
be monarch of the whole country,
which in 1929 adopted the name
Yugoslavia (the kingdom of the
South Slavs).

During World War II the country
was invaded by Italian, German
and Bulgarian troops. The king fled
and Yugoslavia disintegrated.
Slovenia was divided between
Germany, Hungary and Italy.
Croatia sided with the Germans,
and its Serbian minority suffered
many atrocities. Bulgaria occupied

Macedonia, while communists in
Serbia and Montenegro operated
successfully against the invaders.
Their leader Josip Broz, known as
Tito, proclaimed a new federal
republic of Yugoslavia in 1945.

Post-war changes

As president, Tito brought Croatia
and Serbia closer together. His
communist government expanded
industry and encouraged the use of
modern machinery in farming. Its
policies encouraged people to
become more involved in decisions
which affected their lives. Some
power was transferred from central
to local government.

Unfortunately, after Tito's death
in 1980 old quarrels re-emerged. By
1990 people in Slovenia and Croatia
were demanding more freedom and
independence from what they
considered Serbian domination.
War broke out in 1991, and by 1992
Croatia, Slovenia, Bosnia and
Herzegovina, and Macedonia had
all declared independence. Because
of Serbian aggression, other
countries refused to trade with
Yugoslavia and the UN would not
grant it recognition. In 1995 its
president and the president of
Serbia (who had been accused of
supporting the Serbs in Bosnia and
Herzegovina) reached an agreement
in Dayton, USA, which brought
about an uneasy peace. ◆

'Tito' was the undercover
name of Josip Broz
during the resistance.
He continued to use the
name after the war.

▼ **Find out more**
Alphabets
Bosnia and Herzegovina
Croatia
Europe
Macedonia
Ottoman empire
Serbia
Slovenia

BIOGRAPHY
Tito, Josip Broz

Zambia

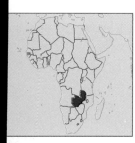

Zambia, in south-central Africa, has high grassy plains, with some woodland and swamps. It is a warm country, with a rainy season between November and April. The River Zambezi flows through Zambia and in the south forms the border with Zimbabwe. On this border are the beautiful Victoria Falls and Lake Kariba, which has been created behind a large dam.

About 70 languages are spoken in Zambia, although English is used for official business. The majority of people are farmers and live in villages made up of groups of thatched houses similar to those found all over Africa. Zambians grow and eat a lot of maize, which is finely ground and cooked to make a thick porridge. Tobacco and cotton are also grown and sold as cash crops. Zambia's most valuable product, copper, is mined in the north in a region called the 'copperbelt'.

FLASHBACK

In 1889, the British South Africa Company, which was searching for valuable metals, took over the area that is now Zambia. A railway was built, and soon many Britons arrived and began to farm the land near the railway. The area became a British colony named Northern Rhodesia in 1924. It was renamed the Republic of Zambia when it gained its independence during 1964 under President Kenneth Kaunda. ◆

Area
752,620 sq km
Capital
Lusaka
Population
9,000,000
Language
English, Bemba, Tonga, Nyanja, others
Religion
Christian, traditional
Government
Parliamentary republic
Currency
1 kwacha = 100 ngwee

Even though the population is growing fast there is no shortage of agricultural land. Indeed the government try to encourage people to remain in villages rather than drifting into towns.

▲ In this Zambian village, a family prepares the maize they have harvested. The maize is sifted and pounded into a fine powder before it is cooked into a thick porridge.

A traditional market in ▶ Zambia's capital, Lusaka. Skyscrapers in the background show how modern the city has become.

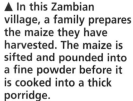

Find out more
Africa
African history

Zebras

▶ Large numbers of plains zebras still survive in some parts of Africa. A herd consists of many family groups and the adults in each group stay together for the rest of their lives.

Distribution
Savannah and dry scrub areas from Ethiopia to South Africa
Size
Head-and-body length 200–240 cm; shoulder height 120–140 cm
Weight
About 350 kg. Grevy's zebra is the largest species.
Number of young
1 suckled for about 7 months
Lifespan
Up to 25 years
Subphylum
Vertebrata
Class
Mammalia
Order
Perissodactyla
Family
Equidae (horse family)
Number of species
3

▼ **Find out more**
Extinct animals
Horses

Zebras have been called 'ponies in pyjamas', for these African wild horses are covered with black and white stripes. No two zebras have the same arrangement of stripes. A herd of plains zebras consists of many families, and they recognize members of their own family and their neighbours by their different patterns.

Family life

As a family moves, it keeps a strict order. A mare (adult female) leads. She is the dominant female and is followed by her foals. Behind her comes the next most dominant mare, and so on. In a big family, there may be as many as six mares. Right at the back comes the stallion, who is the father of all of the foals. If there is a weak or injured member of the family, it will be protected by the whole group, who go slowly so that it is not left behind. The stallion fights off predators, such as lions, and sometimes loses his life so that his family can escape.

When a foal is being born, the stallion stands near by to protect the mare. The foal is able to walk within an hour of birth and can keep up with the family within a few days. A female plains zebra will leave her family at about the age of 2. She may join and leave several groups before she finally settles down in the group where she will spend the rest of her life. She will probably have her first foal when she is 4 years old and then may have a foal each year.

Young males leave their family and join a bachelor group when they are about 4 years old. They will take over a family of their own by the age of about 6.

Social life

When they are not grazing, zebra stallions visit their neighbours. A stallion may know 30 family groups that keep station near his family within the herd. He will visit most of them each day, as if to make sure that everything is in its right order. Zebras also spend a lot of time nibbling each other's fur. This not only keeps them clean, but is part of their social life.

The mountain zebra and Grevy's zebra are both much rarer and live in drier and more remote country. Mountain zebras also live in family groups, but Grevy's zebras have a far less complex social life.

FLASHBACK

The quagga was a zebra-like animal that was once common in South Africa. Huge numbers were killed for food and hides, and the last wild one was killed in 1878. The species became extinct when the last one, kept in captivity, died in 1883. ◆

Zimbabwe

Zimbabwe contains large areas of high grassland, called the high veld. On the River Zambezi, in the north, are the Victoria Falls and Lake Kariba, which Zimbabwe shares with Zambia. Most of Zimbabwe has a warm, moist climate. In the south is a hot region called the low veld.

Zimbabwe is mostly savannah (tropical grassland) with lots of trees which flourish in the wet summers. The country has a rich animal life which includes lions and other cats, elephants, hippos, gorillas, hyenas, crocodiles and antelopes.

The largest groups of people in Zimbabwe are the Shona and the Ndebele. Some whites (people of European origin), Asians and coloureds (people of mixed origin) also live in Zimbabwe. About 70 per cent of Zimbabweans work on farms. Other people work in towns, and some work in asbestos, chrome and gold mines. The chief food is maize. Farmers also grow tobacco as a cash crop. (A cash crop is one grown solely for sale rather than for the farmer's own use.) Most children go to primary schools, but Zimbabwe does not yet have enough secondary schools for all of its older children.

FLASHBACK

About 1000 years ago, the ancestors of the Shona people founded a prosperous civilization. The word Zimbabwe means 'house of stone'. These stone buildings are unusual, because most old houses in southern Africa had clay walls. The ruins of some of these towns still stand. The largest is called Great Zimbabwe. The people who lived there traded gold, copper and ivory on the coast for goods from China and India, and their land was later known as Mashonaland. To the west was Matabeleland, peopled by the Ndebele, who settled in the 1830s, refugees from Shaka the Zulu.

British people began to settle in the area from 1888. In 1923 Mashonaland and Matabeleland became a single British colony called Southern Rhodesia. It was named after Cecil Rhodes who formed the British South Africa Company in 1889 to colonize and promote trade in the region. In the 1960s, the black Africans demanded independence from Britain. Fourteen years of unrest and warfare followed, when thousands died and almost a million people lost their homes. The ruling white minority finally agreed to multiracial elections and Robert Mugabe won a landslide victory. The country was renamed Zimbabwe. ◆

◀ The Zambezi River at the mile-wide Victoria Falls.

Area
390,580 sq km
Capital
Harare
Population
10,700,000
Language
English, Shona, Ndebele
Religion
Christian, Traditional
Government
Parliamentary republic
Currency
1 Zimbabwe dollar = 100 cents

▼ **Find out more**
Africa
African history
British empire

BIOGRAPHY
Mugabe, Robert
Rhodes, Cecil John
Shaka, the Zulu

Zinc

Zinc is a bluish-white, brittle metal. Its main use is to protect iron and steel from rusting. Buckets, dustbins, wire netting, corrugated iron for roofing, and some parts of cars are dipped into molten zinc. This is left to harden. Then, even if the zinc is scratched, the iron or steel underneath does not rust. Coating iron with zinc in this way is called galvanizing.

Zinc also forms many useful alloys, including brass and solder. Like other animals, we need minute quantities of zinc salts in our food if we are to grow properly. Zinc is made from ores such as zinc blende, smithsonite and hemimorphite. Most of these ores are found in the USA, Canada, Mexico and New South Wales in Australia. ◆

The chemical formula for zinc is Zn.

▼ **Find out more**
Alloys
Metals

Zips

The idea of the zip was thought up in 1893 by an American engineer called Whitcombe Judson.

A zip makes a temporary join between the edges of two pieces of material. Zips are widely used in clothes, bags and other items made from textiles. The first modern-style zip was patented in 1913. Originally, all zips had metal teeth. Most modern zips have tough plastic teeth.

A zip has two rows of small teeth, one row on each of the two edges that are to be joined. A sliding mechanism makes the teeth interlock with each other as it slides one way, and split open as it slides the other way. ◆

▶ How a zip works.

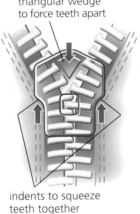

triangular wedge to force teeth apart

indents to squeeze teeth together

▼ **Find out more**
Sewing

Zodiac

We cannot see the stars during the day because the Sun is too bright, but if we could we would notice the Sun slowly moving through the star patterns and making a trip right round the sky once a year. The band of constellations through which the Sun's path goes is called the zodiac.

The ancient Greeks divided the zodiac into 12 equal parts, called the signs of the zodiac. Each sign corresponds roughly to one of the zodiac constellations, though the official constellations astronomers use are not all equal in size.

Astrologers use the signs of the zodiac to make predictions about people's lives and characters. This depends upon a person's Sun sign – the sign that the Sun was in on the date of their birth. ◆

Aries 21 March–19 April	**Leo** 23 July–22 August	**Sagittarius** 22 November–21 December
Taurus 20 April–20 May	**Virgo** 23 August–22 September	**Capricorn** 22 December–19 January
Gemini 21 May–21 June	**Libra** 23 September–23 October	**Aquarius** 20 January–18 February
Cancer 22 June–22 July	**Scorpio** 24 October–21 November	**Pisces** 19 February–20 March

▼ **Find out more**
Constellations
Horoscopes
Sky

For drawings of the signs of the zodiac see the article on Horoscopes.

Zonation

Zonation can occur on a small scale. As you walk into a wood, look at the way the pattern of plant growth changes from the sunlit areas outside to the shaded places under the trees.

Zonation is also found on seashores, because of the movement of the tides.

Zonation is the way in which plants and small animals gather in zones, each zone having environmental conditions suited to particular animals and plants.

If, for example, if you climb a high mountain, you pass through several different zones. At the lowest levels, the slopes are covered with forests. As you climb higher, the temperature drops and there is more wind. The tall trees are replaced with much shorter shrubs. Higher still, there is a zone of grasses and low-growing plants. Above this only mosses and lichens cover the bare rocks. Highest of all there is nothing but snow and ice. ◆

▼ **Find out more**
Mountains
Seashore

Zoologists

Zoologists are scientists who study animals. Professional zoologists generally work in universities or large museums, or sometimes for industrial firms. They do research to find out about animals and how they live. They also meet to discuss their work, and publish accounts of it in books and journals. Usually zoologists have a degree in zoology.

If you are interested in animals and want to become a zoologist, remember that the training is long and that jobs are few. You might consider instead becoming an amateur zoologist, someone who studies animals just because they enjoy doing so. ◆

Zoology comes from the Greek words *zoion* meaning 'animal' and *logia* meaning 'study'.

▼ **Find out more**
Animal behaviour
Animals
Biologists
Ecology

BIOGRAPHY
Darwin, Charles

Zoos

'Zoo' is short for zoological gardens. It comes from the Greek word *zoion*, meaning 'animal'.

The earliest known animal collection was owned by Shulgi, a ruler in what is now Iraq, around 2000 BC.

Zoos are extremely costly places to run. The animals have to be securely housed and kept warm. Their food may also be expensive. Some zoos used to allow visitors to feed the animals, but often people gave them the wrong things. Nowadays, many zoos have a scheme that allows you to adopt an animal and pay for its upkeep.

Keeping a zoo elephant for a year costs £5000; a lion costs £1500.

Zoos are places where wild animals are kept in captivity. In recent years many zoos have realized the importance of putting the interests of the animals first, so they now have reasonable-sized enclosures and are given adequate amounts of the correct food. In good zoos most animals live far longer than they would in the wild. There are still some bad zoos but fewer than there used to be.

Today many zoos specialize in particular sorts of animals. Perhaps the most popular are the oceanaria, which keep dolphins and other sea creatures. Another new type of zoo is the safari park, in which it is the visitors who are caged in their cars, and the animals have large areas in which to roam.

Apart from keeping animals, modern zoos have three main functions: to study the animals and find out as much as possible about their habits; to educate visitors; and to breed from the captives. Often a zoo will send a single animal to another zoo where it may mate. Many wild animals are on the brink of extinction, so producing young in zoos may be the only way to save such species. This has already been done with Père David's deer, while nene (Hawaiian geese) and Arabian oryxes have been returned to their native lands where they had become extinct.

FLASHBACK

The first zoos were collections of animals made by kings and noblemen in ancient Egypt and China. Wild animals were often taken as tribute from conquered countries. The Roman emperor Nero is said to have had a tame tigress called Phoebe, while the favourite of Charlemagne, who kept many animals, was an elephant called Abul Aba.

In the past, zoo animals generally had a short life, for the right food and conditions were seldom available. The first elephant was brought to Britain in 1254; it was housed in a special building 6 by 12 metres, which was certainly not big enough by modern standards. Over many centuries most zoos were miserable prisons for many animals, which were kept on their own. Such solitary confinement is the height of cruelty for social animals such as monkeys and apes. ◆

◀ A panda in the Bronx Zoo, New York City, USA.

▼ **Find out more**
Biodiversity
Conservation
Ecosystems
Endangered species

Zoroastrians

Although Zoroaster was inspired by visions at the age of 30, it took him 10 years to persuade anyone to follow his teachings.

Zoroastrians belong to one of the oldest religions in the world. They follow the teachings of the prophet Zoroaster (Zarathustra), who lived in Persia (modern Iran). Scholars argue about his dates, which may be about the 6th century BC or earlier. Some scholars think that Zoroaster may have lived as long ago as 1500 BC. Zoroastrian ideas were known over a wide area for a thousand years after Cyrus the Great established his empire in the 6th century BC. They probably influenced Jewish, Christian, Buddhist and Muslim ideas.

A small group of Zoroastrians moved from Persia to India in the 10th century and were called Parsis (Persians). Their descendants live mostly round Mumbai (Bombay) and they are the largest surviving Zoroastrian community. There are also small groups still in Iran and in Australia, Hong Kong, North America and Britain.

Beliefs

The evil force which opposes *Ahura Mazda* is called *Angra Mainyu*.

Zoroastrians call God *Ahura Mazda* (*Ohrmazd*), the Lord of Wisdom who created the world. He is constantly opposed by an evil force. God is symbolized by a sacred fire looked after by hereditary priests in a temple.

Men and women join equally in the struggle for good over evil in their lives through truth, compassion and active service for fellow human beings. After death, human souls will stay in heaven or hell until God finally triumphs over evil.

The sacred scriptures are called the *Avesta* and are in a language of their own called Avestan. They contain a variety of material, including 17 hymns which were revealed to Zoroaster. Here is a prayer used daily by Zoroastrians.

'Blessed is he who leads the righteous life for its own sake and not in the hope of earthly gains or heavenly rewards.' ◆

The 17 hymns are known as the *Gathas*.

▼ **Find out more**
Persians
Religions

Zulus

The Zulus are the largest of the 10 main groups of black Africans in South Africa. Of the 5,680,000 Zulus, nearly two-thirds live in KwaZulu, which was once called Zululand. This was set up as a 'homeland' – an area in Natal province set aside for the Zulus by the South African government. KwaZulu is not an independent nation, although it has an elected government to handle local matters.

In KwaZulu the men herd cattle, while the women grow crops such as maize. Many men cannot support their families, so they work in other areas of South Africa and send money home. Many of these migrant workers support Inkatha, a political movement for Zulus.

◀ Like many black Africans, the Zulus have a tradition of being superb musicians and dancers. Here young girls are stamping out the rhythm of the drums with their feet.

FLASHBACK

The Zulu nation was created by a great warrior called Shaka. The Zulus clashed with white settlers until they were defeated by the British in 1879. During the apartheid years, the Zulus suffered with other black people, but they kept apart from the African National Congress (ANC) because they feared they would be badly treated by an ANC government. When elections were held in 1994, the Inkatha Freedom Party won many votes, and Chief Buthelezi became a minister in Nelson Mandela's government. ◆

When KwaZulu, the Zulu homeland, was set up in 1970, Chief Gatsha Buthelezi became Chief Executive Officer or Prime Minister. Buthelezi is the great-grandson of the Zulu chief Cetewayo who was defeated by the British in 1879.

▼ **Find out more**
Africa
African history
South Africa

BIOGRAPHY
Luthuli, Albert
Shaka the Zulu